TV DETECTIVES

TV DETECTIVES

RICHARD MEYERS

San Diego
A. S. Barnes & Company, Inc.
In London:
The Tantivy Press

First Edition
Manufactured in the United States of
America

For information write to:

A.S. Barnes & Company, Inc.
P.O. Box 3051
La Jolla, California 92038

The Tantivy Press
Magdalen House
136–148 Tooley Street
London, SE1 2TT, England

**Library of Congress Cataloging in Pub-
lication Data**

Meyers, Richard.
    The T.V. detectives.

    Includes index.
    1. Detective and mystery television
programs—History and
criticism.   I. Title.
PN1992.8.D48M47   791.45′09′0916   81-3576
ISBN 0-498-02576-4 (Hardcover)   AACR2
ISBN 0-498-02236-6 (Papercover)

1 2 3 4 5 6 7 8 9   84   83   82   81

To Stanley Meyers, my father,
who would suggest I liven up
the dedication a bit.

Contents

Acknowledgments

Ms. Gerry Duclow of The Free Library, Philadelphia
Mr. Art Bourgeau of The Whodunit Bookstore, Philadelphia
Mr. Chris Steinbrunner of the Mystery Writers of America
Mr. Otto Penzler of The Mysterious Book Shop, New York City
Mr. James Sirmans of CBS
Ms. Natalie Terano of NBC
Mr. Vic Ghidalia of ABC
Mr. Rob Mandel of ITC Entertainment
Mr. Phil DeGuere of Universal Studios
Mr. Robert Short of Industrial Light and Magic
Mr. Jack Nolan
Mr. Anthony F. Slez, Jr.
Mr. Adam Francis Slez
Mr. Robert Randisi
Mr. Christopher Browne
Mr. Steve Hartov
Mr. Tom O'Neil
Mr. James O'Neill
Mr. John Koffend
Ms. Cindy Tillinghast
Mr. Julien Yoseloff
Mr. Jeff Rovin
Mr. Kerry O'Quinn
Mr. Ed Naha
Melissa

Preface

Everyone on television, at one time or another, has been involved in a mystery. From *The Addams Family* to *Zorro*, someone has played detective if only to find a lost dog or to track down Aunt Bea's prize cherry pie. Mystery abounds on all the stations.

Within the following pages, however, I will deal only with series featuring private eyes, cops, secret agents, mercenaries, lawyers, and reporters—those people for whom mystery and/or detection is part of their jobs. The one-shot specials, movies, and anthology shows will not be included. Nor will most made-for-TV movies.

At times, how I determined who was and was not a television detective became a problem.

Take Westerns, for example. Many of them dealt with aimless drifters whose answer to every problem was a six-shooter. No difficulty there. But on many of the shows the principal character was a lawman. Should I include Marshal Dillon, Wyatt Earp, and all the other rustic rangers? The answer came from watching a dozen or more of the series they figured in. For the most part, these guys solved their mysteries by shooting them. And the shows were never called anything but Westerns—not "crime drama," "thriller," "action adventure," or "mystery." So they are not included.

As you read on, you will find exceptions to almost everything just said. You'll find *The Wild, Wild West* but no *Lawman*. You'll find *The Fugitive* but no *Route 66*. You'll find *The Blue Knight* but no *The Dain Curse*. The shows were seen, considered, then accepted or rejected on the basis of whether or not investigation was inherent in the concept. And what the title of the principal character was. If the sign on his office door said "detective," then the show was in, no matter if every solution was delivered on a silver platter . . . as in *Charlie's Angels*.

Finally, a word about dates. The dates mentioned throughout this book are the dates of a show's American premiere. If a series started December 31 at 11:59 P.M., 1959, it will be considered a 1959 series. A series that began January 1, 1960, at 12:01 A.M. is a 1960 show. The same principle applies to imported shows. It makes no difference whether the series was made in London during the Blitz. If it was shown on American television during 1973, it is a 1973 program. I have researched very hard to make sure that the syndicated series' dates—those programs produced independently and then sold to local stations—are those of the first syndicated year. I will acknowledge, however, that since syndicated shows premiere at different times all over the country, a date may seem inaccurate. But what may be wrong for Albany, New York, may be right for Akron, Ohio, and vice versa.

So much for the fine points. Inside there are hundreds of hard-boiled detectives, lousy coppers, suave spies, noble knights-errant, detecting attorneys, and infernal journalists. Turn off the television, turn on a light, and read. Better yet, leave the TV on.

The First Few Years

Television's first star was Felix the Cat. In a 1928 experiment, a three-dimensional model of the famous cartoon character was placed on a turntable and its image was transmitted from New York to Kansas by the National Broadcasting Company. The fuzzy, heavily lined picture hardly seemed to place the new invention in the category of the electric light bulb or the telephone, but in just two decades television was well on its way toward matching both in its effect on the world.

1947–1948

The actual network beginnings were inauspicious. In truth, the first few years were a miasma. There were four networks vying for time during the short evening schedules. While the three most famous, ABC, NBC, and CBS, were churning out various newscasts, sporting events—like the roller derby and wrestling—and game shows, the fourth, the DuMont television network, was investigating the possibilities inherent in the mystery genre.

Among these early entertainment efforts were *Public Prosecuter* and *Rackets Are My Racket*. The former was a half-hour series hosted by John Howard in which three contestants were shown a filmed whodunit and then had to guess the guilty party. The latter, though a 15-minute show, established a format which was to be used constantly during the next three years.

In this case, Sergeant Audley Walsh, a real-life New Jersey police officer, exposed confidence games through lectures and, more importantly, through dramatizations.

DuMont's contribution to detective fiction in 1948 was *They Stand Accused,* which combined two formats: the game show and the drama. Each week a different fictional court case was plotted by Illinois' Assistant Attorney General William Wines. A group of actors would ad-lib their roles as suspects for the benefit of some real-life lawyers and judges as

Here's a look inside RCA's Studio 86 in New York—then the newest and largest one they had—where Barney Blake: Police Reporter *was filmed. On the left is Judy Parrish, who played Jennifer Allen, the reporter's girlfriend. Leaning on the camera is Gene O'Donnell, who played Barney, and to the right of him is Joan Arliss, an actress who played varying roles on the live show. (courtesy Theater Collection, Free Library of Philadelphia)*

well as the studio audience who served as the jury.

The unscripted spontaneity added realism and freshness that would be missing from many future legal series. Its novelty lasted until 1954 when the networks were filled with mysteries of a more dramatic flair.

The first of these out-and-out fictional dramas was created for NBC and premiered in April 1948. Sadly, the producers decided to ignore years of great mystery literature, great mystery movies, and hugely successful radio heroes to give life to *Barney Blake: Police Reporter.*

The half-hour, live series, sponsored by the American Tobacco Company, starred Gene O'Donnell as an intrepid investigator who, with the help of his trusty secretary Jennifer (Judy Parrish), interviewed various suspects about a multiplicity of crimes. This staid format excited neither viewers nor the sponsor,

who canceled the show after 13 weeks.

1949

NBC learned its lesson quickly, however. For the new season they mounted *Martin Kane, Private Eye.* Several things combined to spell Kane's success. First of all, the concept came from an already-popular radio series on the Mutual network. Second, the TV industry's writers, directors, and actors had a little time to perfect their craft on such programs as *The Philco Playhouse* and *Studio One.* Finally, Kane's sponsor, U.S. Tobacco Company, had a much stronger hand in the production.

By 1949 television had ceased to be a gimmick or a curiosity and had become an industry. An industry based on commercial advertising. And during these days of live broadcasts, it was not unusual for the show's leading character to not only use the sponsor's product, but to actively hawk it on the air.

William Gargan was the first Martin Kane, a New York detective who solved his cases through determination, cooperation with the police, and just a little bit of roughhousing. Gargan worked the Big Apple beat until 1951, utilizing Happy McMann's (Walter Kinsella) tobacco shop as headquarters and reporting to N.Y.P.D.'s Lieutenant Bender (Fred Hillebrand), all while nonchalantly smoking Sano cigarettes, one of the sponsor's best-sellers. Astonishingly, newsman Walter Cronkite served as the series' announcer. He went on to far greater fame in the real world.

The next Kane was Lloyd Nolan, no stranger to the hard-boiled detective role, having been a movie tough guy since 1934. He amply filled Kane's shoes and smoked Sano cigarettes for one season (1951–1952) until Lee Tracy took over on May 29, 1952.

Tracy had also made his mark in movies, playing fast-talking characters, so he was a natural for the Kane brand of hard-hitting detection. Kane's manner and method stayed basically the same, but his smoking habits changed. Even back then the sponsor's voice was a strong one.

U.S. Tobacco's cigarettes were selling well, but they wanted to push their Old Briar pipe tobacco. So for his two seasons, Lee Tracy ran the bad guys to earth while contentedly puffing on a pipe.

In 1953 the producers decided to give the series a shot in the arm. They retitled it *The New Adventures of Martin Kane* and recast the lead. The new private eye was the much younger, classically handsome Mark Stevens. In fact, once the young actor secured the role, *TV Guide* proclaimed Kane to be "the most improved show on the air today."

Naturally U.S. Tobacco wanted to push a product as fashionable as their new star, so Stevens fought crime with a king-sized Sano between his lips. He did not have to sell them as well, however, since commercials had been integrated into the show by that time. At first, Walter Kinsella as Happy McMann interrupted the show to deliver a selling spiel, but when that character was dropped, Don Morrow, playing himself, did the ads.

Martin Kane was fortunate in that the production quality, the writing staff, and the authenticity got better as time went on. Usually the opposite is true. And live television had its own built-in charm and wonder. The delight of seeing actors performing murder and mayhem live before one's eyes was a treat that has not diminished over the years. Just imagine a series like *The Rockford Files* performed like *Saturday Night Live*.

This first television private eye was a worthy predecessor to those who followed him. First, he was from the Dashiell Hammett/Raymond Chandler school of dogged, noble detectives. Second, each actor who portrayed Kane embodied a different facet of the detective personality. Gargan was the weary man of the world who still knew how to be smooth. Nolan was the casual wiseacre. Tracy was the hound dog master of determination. And Stevens was the sophisticated matinee-idol type.

One month after the *Martin Kane* 1949 premiere CBS's answer appeared—*Man Against Crime*. This 30-minute, harder-hitting series starred Ralph Bellamy as Mike Barnett, a New York private detective who did not carry a gun. He used his fists instead. Originally broadcast live, the program switched to film earlier than its action brethren, so the fights and chases were a bit more realistic. This made the series so popular that in its third year it won a national popularity poll as "best mystery."

Reviews of the era cited "intricate plotting, suspenseful scripts, exciting adventure plus superb acting" to explain its success. Unfortunately these ingredients were not reborn when *Man Against Crime* was reactivated in 1956 with Frank Lovejoy as the new Mike Barnett. Although he was just as hard-boiled and did not seem to mind packing a gat, the series' sharpness and snap was gone.

The same was true when Martin Kane was brought back in 1957. William Gargan, having been the voice of Kane on radio as well as in the first TV version, starred as Kane again. He was eight years older and definitely too tired for this sort of thing. Also undercutting the series' original concept was producer Harry Allen Towers' decision to set the new adventures in England and incorporate a different beautiful girl in each episode. It was probably best that *The New Adventures of Martin Kane* died shortly after it began.

Not all of the mysteries in 1949 were well-conceived or well-received. Into every season, it seems, a little *Mysteries of Chinatown* must fall. This was ABC's first contribution to the genre and it gives a good idea of what programmers were going through. One might assume that the producers were trying to attract the audience that made Dr. Fu Manchu and other "Oriental" pulp characters so successful. In the television creation Marvin Miller—soon to be the agent of the legendary John Beresford Tipton on *The Millionaire* (1955)—starred as Dr. Yat Su, a San Francisco Chinatown shop owner and amateur detective. His kinescoped adventures lasted less than a year.

1950

The first real decade of network television began in the fifties. The DuMont system could not get enough affiliates and was doomed to failure by 1955. ABC was also having a tough time, but was preparing to enter into a merger with United Paramount Theaters that was worth $25 million. CBS was set to do battle with NBC's parent company, RCA, over the development of color. Meanwhile, the daily business of creating shows that people would watch went on.

And in 1950, the producers and creators discovered genres and characters as yet untapped by the new medium. The first of these new programs was based on the man who has been called "America's Master Crime Solver": Ellery Queen.

The honor of playing America's greatest fictional amateur sleuth on television went to, not one, but seven men. When Richard Hart, a young Hollywood actor with four films to his credit, made his Queenly debut in the first series, *The Adventures of Ellery Queen* (1950), Ellery already had a career as a writer, editor, literary force, and radio star spanning more than two decades. The real Ellery Queen turned out to be two cousins—Frederic Dannay and Manfred Lee—who produced the first novel, *The Roman Hat Mystery*, in 1929. Queen became a radio fixture in 1939 on the CBS network, but it was the DuMont network who worked up the first TV program with Hart in the lead.

Tragically, Hart died of a heart attack less than four months after the series

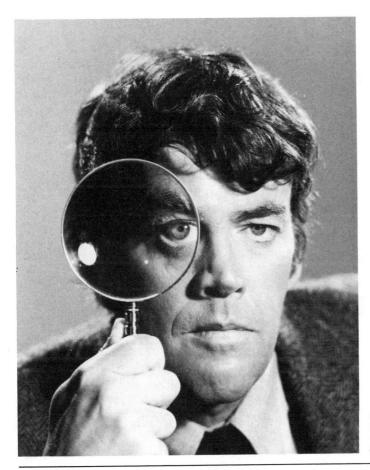

Jim Hutton, the seventh actor to portray America's master crime solver, the great Ellery Queen. (NBC)

premiered. The distinguished actor, Lee Bowman, replaced him for a year before the program moved over to ABC in 1951. Bowman sleuthed through another year of cases like "The File of Death" and "One Week to Live" before the initial cancellation.

It was not long before a new Ellery Queen series was launched with Hugh Marlowe—one of the actors who portrayed Queen on radio—in the lead. Marlowe was of a type with Bowman, Hart and, indeed, Ralph Bellamy, who played a movie Queen. All were essentially smooth-talking hunks of men who played Queen like a mellow-toned mannequin.

The basic plots of the books, the radio plays, and the TV shows were the same: Queen was a mystery writer who would solve crime for, with, and sometimes in spite of his father, N.Y.P.D. homicide Inspector Richard Queen. The movies introduced Queen's flighty secretary, Nikki, who was integrated into the books and the television series.

The only difference between the award-winning books and the many short-lived series was the manner in which Queen was presented. In literature Queen was as psychologically complex as Sherlock Holmes, but on TV, that complexity was not apparent. The many fans of the literary Queen may have found this disappointing. The Marlowe *Adventures of Ellery Queen* went off the air in 1954—the same year it started.

Although these series failed to generate large viewer interest, Albert McCleery decided to revive the character, having been given the promise of a higher budget to insure higher quality. Titling the new effort *The Further Adventures of Ellery Queen*, he hired handsome George Nader to play the lead and secured an hourly slot on NBC starting in September 1958.

But by October, production shifted from California to New York and Nader was replaced by Lee Philips. Even so, the quality McCleery had promised was not showing up in the scripts. By August 1959, Ellery Queen was off the air again. But like before, he would not stay down. The wait was a lot longer this time, however. It would be 12 years before Queen would be seen on television

again. And this reincarnation was to be the most controversial version of the Queen character ever.

Universal Studios took *Cat of Many Tails*, published in 1949, and turned it into a television movie called *Ellery Queen: Don't Look Behind You*, keeping the complex, double-barreled mystery intact. The book created a sensation among mystery readers because it dealt with Queen's guilt as much as a madman's murder spree. Rarely had a legendary detective suffered such angst over what he saw as his own amateur meddling. They hired Barry Shear as director and he handled the proceedings with style. Their only mistake was in hiring Peter Lawford, a middle-aged British light leading man, to play the all-American Queen. The reaction in mystery circles could not have been stronger if they had hired Robert Wagner to play Sherlock Holmes.

A miscast Peter Lawford as an urbane Ellery Queen in an otherwise credible TV movie based on the Cat of Many Tails *book,* **Don't Look Behind You.** *(Universal Studios)*

David Wayne, the fine character actor who succeeded Harry Morgan in the role of Inspector Richard Queen—Ellery's uncle in the TV movie and Ellery's father in the books and 1975 series. (NBC)

It was probably the woeful casting error that hamstrung this effort and kept the ratings low. Although the film was made as a series pilot, the Lawford Queen was never heard of again. But Ellery was. Three years later the Holmes and Watson of TV mystery writers— Richard Levinson and William Link— wrote "Too Many Suspects" based on the 1965 Queen novel *The Fourth Side of the Triangle*. The show was played as a period piece, set in the forties when the Queen books were all the rage.

In addition they revitalized the feature of challenging the audience to solve the murder before Queen does. In fact, in the early books the final chapters were separated by a page detailing the challenge. In radio the actors would interrupt the play to quiz the studio visitors. But in the television version, Queen would openly address the camera, recapping and asking the audience if it knew the killer.

This time, the detective was played by the late Jim Hutton, a perennial youth who was the closest physical equivalent that TV had given mystery readers yet. The supporting players were also well chosen. David Wayne, famous for his portrayal of a leprechaun in Broadway's *Brigadoon*, enacted the crusty, diminutive Inspector Queen, while Tom Reese played the inspector's trusty, hulking Sergeant Velie.

In 1974 the effect was charming and the charm was effecting. By 1975 Ellery Queen was back on the air. Levinson and Link stayed on as producers, showering their expertise all over the show. The first few episodes, including the David

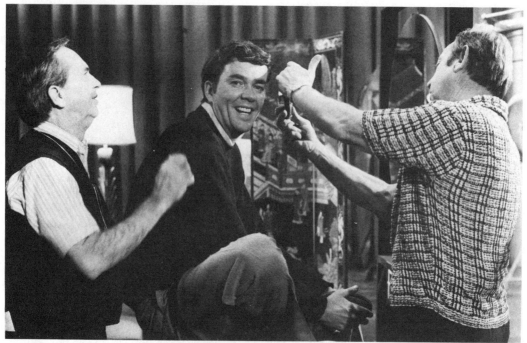

Jim Hutton off screen seems far more lively than Hutton-as-Ellery Queen while
the film was running. Here he shares a laugh with the crew between set-ups.
(NBC)

A lifeless, apathetic Hutton on camera with guest stars Monte Markham (left) —
later to be cast as the "new" Perry Mason — and Ray Milland (on Hutton's right),
among others. (NBC)

Greene-directed pilot, "The Adventure of Auld Lang Syne," were wonderful—chock-full of terrific guest stars and boasting a full-scale murder mystery every week.

All too quickly the thrill disappeared. Even though the new Ellery Queen series had all the complexity it would ever need, it had almost no compassion. For a fictional character who spent most of the sixties and seventies agonizing, the Hutton portrayal was annoyingly lifeless. He just did not seem to care about the victim or the guilty party. Hutton approached each murder as the most boring of mental exercises. Playing Queen as an even-tempered, absentminded bookworm, his apathy soon spread to the audience. After a season, this series was canceled.

Still, Ellery Queen proved to be one of the most beloved, durable detective characters ever to appear on television. It is even money that there will be new actors joining the ranks of Hart, Bowman, Marlowe, Nader, Philips, Lawford, and Hutton behind the magnifying glass in Ellery Queen.

In 1950, the same year as the first Ellery Queen series, another detective character was created exclusively for television. Success came to *Rocky King, Inside Detective* because of its good writing and because of Roscoe Karns, the Hollywood character actor who made the police officer believable and humorous.

While Barney Blake could be considered part of the force, Rocky King was really the first important cop-hero. Even though the show was produced by the smaller—and slowly failing—DuMont network, *Rocky King* was probably the best-loved mystery of its time.

Its very eccentricity worked in its favor. Rather than being a young, handsome cop who dazzled the ladies while effortlessly tracking the criminal, Rocky King was a middle-aged bulldog of a policeman, happily married and generally unconcerned with the flashier aspects of his trade. King was a dependable veteran of the 24th Precinct in New York City.

This crime series was produced in a curious fashion in comparison with today's standards. Filmed live, using tacky-looking interior sets, Rocky might start his half-hour show by sitting down to breakfast with his never-seen wife, Mabel. And while this started out as a money-saving device—an unseen wife needed no costume or makeup—the audience weaned on radio liked using its imagination when it came to King's wife and family.

Once he was called to duty, King's phone conversations with Mabel would serve as the show's framework. If the plot ever got too muddled, a quick call to Mabel would serve to give a rundown on what had transpired. Then, if a summation was ever needed, another call to Mabel would provide a conclusion.

Actually the cases King came up against were never very complicated. Through episodes called things like "Take a Card," "The Bearded Lady," and "Dark Room Murder," Rocky followed rather simple clues around three sets, then engaged in a minor fistfight or shoot-out to apprehend the culprit. Given the show's low budget, there were no fancy fight efforts. Rocky either swung his arm to knock the bad guy down silently or he pulled his gun out and pushed. Occasionally a small explosion would ring out. Occasionally not. But the criminal fell down anyway.

If the man on the left looks like a younger version of the man on the right, it's no coincidence. Roscoe Karns played Inspector **Rocky King** *(seated) while his son, Todd, played Sergeant Hart (standing) in the series' final years. (courtesy Theater Collection, Free Library of Philadelphia)*

Although not as good-looking or energetic as Martin Kane, Rocky matched him in popularity and far outdid him in longevity. While Kane was played by four men during the five years he was on, King was always played by Roscoe Karns, best known for his more than one hundred film appearances.

Karns was respected as a perfectionist who worked to make *Rocky King* as entertaining as it was. The actor had a great love for the cop character, fueled by the fact that Rocky saved him from a forced retirement. Just a short time before, he had been reduced to hosting a kid's TV show with the embarrassing title of *Roscoe Karns and Inky Poo*. Becoming the *Inside Detective* put him back on the right track.

Television gradually got its mystery act together. It took three years of trial and error to see what audiences liked before the networks started grinding out new TV series. Since one of the more practical ways of creating product is to recycle movie material, it was not long before Roy Rogers, The Lone Ranger, Hopalong Cassidy, and other Western stars found a new home on TV. And it was not long before some enterprising producers mined the detective film lode.

In 1950, Dick Moore and Keith Kalmer came up with *Dick Tracy*, the most popular of all comic strip cops and one of the most popular serial heroes as played by strong-chinned Ralph Byrd. The two producers brought Byrd, along with Joe Devlin as Tracy's assistant Sam Catchem and Dick Elliott as Police Chief Murphy, to ABC for a little over six months.

It was a short but wild network run. In addition to the strong, moralistic Tracy, the series also featured the villains that Chester Gould's Edgar-winning strip made famous. The Mole and Pruneface were just two of the criminals TV brought to surprisingly effective life.

In 1961 United Productions of America, the famous animation company that produced *Mr. Magoo*, distributed a cartoon series, *The Dick Tracy Show*. In this version, unfortunately,

Tracy was rarely more than a host doling out comedy cases to the likes of "Joe Jitsu," a diminutive karate expert, and "Heap O'Calorie," an Irish cop lampoon.

Although both the writing and animation were mediocre, the opening of the show, incorporating high-angle views of a city, a wailing police car, and lettering made from machine gun bullet holes, created the proper mood.

Mood contributed to the success of another long-running 1950 series: *The Plainclothesman*. It was another in the short line of inventive DuMont cop shows. Here the "eye" of the television camera was used as never before or since. Borrowing a technique director Robert Montgomery used in the famous Philip Marlowe movie *The Lady in the Lake* (1946), they made the camera eye into the hero's eye. That is, if a gun was pointed at the camera, it would "duck." If a question was asked by a character, the camera might "nod" for yes or shake from side to side for no.

Ken Lynch was given the thankless job of starring as the unnamed, as well as unseen, lieutenant—a New York City cop. The camera-eye gimmick proved successful for the pioneering series, which ran until 1954 with episodes like "The Missing Coat," "A Matter of Honor," and "Machine Gun Dottie."

Although Lynch's face was seen on one show involving flashbacks and whenever he had to look into a mirror— the anonymous role requiring little more than a voice might have ended the career of many another aspiring actor—he endured to costar in many films.

The year 1950 introduced newspaper dramas to television. Energetic investigative reporters were a staple of radio for

many years, but it was not until the *Big Town* series that they prowled the TV airwaves for their scoops.

Like the private-eye program *Martin Kane*, *Big Town* started on radio. There, the part of the crusading *Illustrated Press* editor was once played by Edward G. Robinson. Also like *Martin Kane*, *Big Town* went through several stars and a few formats. First, middle-aged Patrick McVey played editor Steve Wilson to fine effect. He lasted through four years, the change from New York live production to Hollywood filming, a change of networks, and a liberal number of co-stars in the Lorelei Kilbourne role. For some reason, the actresses who played this reporter just could not hold the job down for long. First there was Margaret Hayes, then Mary K. Wells, then Jane Nigh followed by Beverly Tyler, Trudy Wroe and Julie Stevens. None lasted more than a season or so and most were never heard of in the genre again.

A final change came in 1954 with the transfer of *Big Town* from CBS to NBC. And in this instance the comparison to *Martin Kane* is more than skin deep. *Big Town's* new Steve Wilson was none other than Mark Stevens, the second-to-last Kane, who had just finished his single-season tenure as the famous detective.

For him the program's format was altered even further by dropping the role of Lorelei for that of Diane Walker (as played by Doe Averdon) and adding city editor Charlie Anderson (Barry Kelly) as Wilson's inner-office foil. These moves were enough to keep the series going until the end of the 1956 season.

In addition to the newspaper detectives, 1950 also introduced the government agent series to television. These Washington-based adventures shed little light on what our public officials were really doing. There was no red tape, incompetence, or corruption—only stern, moral men who never failed.

Getting everything off on the right— the far Right—foot was *Treasury Men in Action,* also fondly remembered as *T-Men in Action.* Here was a good example of propaganda that worked as both series and title. For five years the Treasury agents proudly caught the likes of counterfeiters, smugglers, and tax evaders to the joy of the actual public agencies. The program garnered many civic awards during its run on both ABC and NBC.

Viewers saw actor Walter Greaza playing an officious-looking leader known only as "The Chief." Every week he would be heading up a different Treasury division and from behind his desk would introduce a wide variety of stories that were based on "actual Treasury files."

There was good reason for programs utilizing files from law enforcement agencies. Primarily it saved time and money. Plots from true cases gave writers a storehouse of material to draw on. Since writers had to produce an original script every seven days, these agency files seemed to be gifts from heaven.

Even when a series had files to fall back on, the staff still needed a little vacation time. But the networks had to have material to fill their ever-growing number of schedule hours. The "Summer Replacement Series" solved this problem. These substitute shows were produced in the hope they would outlive their original runs. Unfortunately, the first mystery sub disappeared immediately after its 11 episodes aired.

Donald Curtis played Adam Conway and Lynn Bari portrayed Connie Conway in *Detective's Wife.* The program, drawing on the popularity of Rocky and Mabel King, replaced *Man Against Crime* for the summer of 1950. It was about a private eye, Adam, who tried to get through a case without the interference of his well-meaning wife, Connie. It was a theme that would appear often.

1951

Among the many shows introduced in 1951 were some popular favorites, some crazy concepts, a new genre, and a flat-out classic.

The weirdest first: *Fearless Fosdick Puppet Show.* The great and glorious Fosdick, as all readers of the comics knows, is the satirical cop character created by Al Capp for his "L'il Abner" strip. Essentially a lampoon of Dick Tracy, Fosdick also represented the harried real-life cop, underpayed, overworked, and unrespected.

Although a bit ahead of its time, the Mary Chase Marionette troupe brought Fosdick's eccentric adventures to life for ABC, with John Grigg supplying the hapless hero's voice. Not surprisingly, the series could not find an audience. It was too sophisticated for children when aired in the afternoon and too childish for adults when switched to an evening hour. It died in a few months.

Now, scraping the bottom of the barrel, one finds *Crime with Father,* an abysmal concept which seemed to prove that the family which solved murders together stayed together. Rusty Lane starred as New York Police Chief James Riland, whose investigations were constantly confused, interrupted, and ultimately solved by his teen-age daughter Chris, played by Peggy Lobbin. The show was good for 16 bad weeks.

Besides these two borderlines comedy capers, 1951 had its share of proven themes. It also had the benefit of some very active ad writers who sought to excite the viewers before the shows got on screen. And for the year's private eye and legal series, the copy writers were really working overtime.

"He's hard-boiled," went one commercial, "and dedicated to the proposition that crime does not pay. He's a man's man . . . but the ladies, too, go for Charlie Wild, Private Eye. Follow him into adventure!" To be honest, good old Charlie, known officially as *Charlie Wild: Private Detective*, was somewhat hard to find. His two-year run included stints on CBS, ABC, and the DuMont network.

Kevin O'Morrison was the first Wild, with John McQuade taking over during the last season. Both men had Cloris Leachman, of all people, as their secretary Effie Perrine. And although Charlie was pretty wild with his fists and gats, not enough people followed him into adventure.

"It's the thrilling inside story of our courts in action!" cried another advertisement. "Watch Mr. District Attorney expose the schemes of the dishonest to ensnare the unsuspecting. Join him behind the scenes of our law enforcement agencies as he fights vice and corruption wherever he finds it!"

It is fair to assume that the brassier the ad, the worse the show. In the case of *Mr. District Attorney*, viewers hardly had a chance to find out. Not only did it go off after a year, it was only on every other week. But what the program lacked in visibility, it made up for in pretension. The opening announcement of each episode set the tone:

"Mr. District Attorney, champion of the people, defender of truth, guardian of our fundamental rights to life, liberty and the pursuit of happiness!"

Jay Jostyn played Paul Garrett, D.A., a role he originated on the radio show of the same name. The same court thrills that held listeners did not work with viewers, so the series was canceled.

Going with it was a companion court series, and, like *Mr. District Attorney*, *The Amazing Mr. Malone* started on radio. And like *Big Town*, it shared its star with *Martin Kane*. Lee Tracy played John J. Malone for the one year it was on ABC before filling his Kane pipe. And finally, like *Ellery Queen*, the man known on TV as the amazing Mr. Malone derived his fame first from books (a series of 14 books written by Craig Rice, the pseudonym of the late Georgiana Ann Randolph).

In the novels Malone was a heavy-drinking, seemingly irresponsible Chicago lawyer who just managed to keep his head above water. If nothing else, the novels were enjoyable combinations of homicide and humor. In films, Malone was portrayed as a heavy-set wise guy. Pat O'Brien played him in *Having A Wonderful Crime* (1945), Brian Donlevy handled the part in *The Lucky Stiff* (1949), and James Whitmore took over for *Mrs. O'Malley and Mr. Malone* (1950). Lee Tracy cut a more svelte figure for the TV version, where the no-longer indigent lawyer was more likely to eye the ladies than guzzle the gin.

Much the same sort of homogenized character was enacted by Edmund Lowe,

One of the Treasury Men In Action
(ABC), gives the lowdown to a lowlife.
(courtesy of the Jeff Rovin Collection)

only his detective was a reporter, not a lawyer. Coming from a long and successful film career which began in 1917—he played Sergeant Quirt in *What Price Glory* (1926) and Philo Vance in *The Garden Murder Case* (1936)—Lowe starred as David Chase, the *Front Page Detective*, a newspaperman with an "eye for the ladies, a nose for the news, and a sixth sense for danger!"

The two-season DuMont series was based on the pulp magazine of the same name. "Presenting an unusual story of love and mystery," intoned an announcer at the beginning of every episode. "And now for another thrilling adventure as we accompany David Chase and watch him match wits with those who would take the law into their own hands."

What *Front Page Detective* did not give audiences, they could find on *Crime Photographer*. George Harmon Coxe created the tough newshound Jack "Flashgun" Casey in 1934, then detailed his escapades in dozens of stories and in six books. It was not long before Hollywood found him. Stuart Erwin played Casey in *Women Are Trouble* (1936), and Eric Linden handled the part in *Here's Flash Casey* (1937).

CBS Radio discovered Casey's charm and showcased it as a long-running favorite starting in 1946. Five years into its decade-long run, CBS adapted the character for television. The basic framework was the same. Flashgun Casey (né Jack Casey) worked for *The Morning Express*, a New York newspaper, but his regular hangout was The Blue Note Cafe, where Ethelbert the bartender lent an interested ear A supporting hand was also contrib-

He's got a nose for murder! At least that's what the original caption for this scene from Front Page Detective *(ABC) said. Star Edmund Lowe (left) puts actor John Davidson on the spot during the episode which aired March 17, 1952. (courtesy Theater Collection, Free Library of Philadelphia)*

uted by fellow reporter and girfriend Ann Williams.

While Staats Cotsworth was supplying Casey's voice on radio, Richard Carlyle was the initial *Crime Photographer* on TV. His face did not do the trick, so two months after the premiere, Darren McGavin was brought in as Casey. Backing him up was Cliff Hall as the bartender and Jan Miner—now famous as "Madge the manicurist" on dishwashing liquid commercials—as the girl reporter. McGavin's acting efforts only managed to keep the series on for one more year. Casey left television in 1952, but stayed on radio for another four years.

Teetering on the edge of the newspaper genre was NBC's *Foreign Intrigue*, which started as the story of a bunch of globe-trotting reporters but ended up as something else again. At first, it featured Robert Cannon, a foreign correspondent for *Consolidated News* played by Jerome Thor, who spent his time infiltrating spy rings. That exercise was good for two years until Associated News correspondent Michael Powers took over the beat. He was played by James Daly, who gave spy rings equal time with the other stories a reporter is prone to.

Powers' adventures lasted a year, then the entire format was shaken up and aired out so that actor Gerald Mohr could star as Christopher Storm, a Viennese hotel owner who fought overseas organized crime for kicks. The entire series checked out in 1955.

A slightly more successful show was

an out-and-out spy adventure, just about the first of its type on television. _Doorway to Danger_ began as a summer replacement series and was used by both NBC and ABC for three years running.

Given its history, perhaps a better title for the series would be _Revolving Doorway to Danger_ because every time it showed up on the schedule it had a new cast. Mel Ruick was first, playing John Randolph as the head of a super-secret undercover agency. It was his job to send intrepid agents on awful missions. His top man in the field was Doug Carter, played by Grant Richards.

The next time the series appeared, Roland Winters—who was in the midst of six Charlie Chan movies at the time—was Randolph, and the Carter character was nowhere to be seen. The following summer Carter was back and being played by Stacy Harris while his boss, Randolph, had become Raymond Bramley.

Far more consistent was a crime show closer to reality. Screen smoothie Tom Conway starred as New York City homicide detective Mark Saber in _Mystery Theater._ _TV Guide_ called it "one of the better series. Little in the way of new ideas, but credible stories and a competent cast. Conway is probably the most suave of the TV detectives."

Conway came upon his elegance naturally. He was the brother of screen star George Sanders and followed him into movies. In 1942, Conway and his brother were teamed in a movie that hit close to home. Up until then Sanders had starred as both the Saint and the Falcon and the work load was getting to be a bit much. So, with _The Falcon's Brother,_ George handed over the Falcon role to Tom.

Conway worked that part over until 1946, did three more lightweight movies, then tapped the Mark Saber role and played it to the hilt.

It was a fine part for the Englishman. Saber was a lot like Conway in real life, dapper, elegant, erudite. To add to the realism James Burke was cast as Saber's somewhat slow assistant, Sergeant Tim Maloney. Both characters proved so popular that the series title was quickly changed to _Mark Saber Mystery Theater._ From then until 1954, the program wandered around the ABC schedule, changing titles as it went. Soon it was plain _Mark Saber,_ then _Mark Saber— Homicide Squad,_ then finally just _Homicide Squad._

The strangest change came three years after the Conway Saber went off the air. In October 1957, NBC brought out _Saber of London,_ starring Donald Gray. But any anxious lover of sophisticated detection was in for a surprise when tuning in. Mark was no longer a debonair police officer with the N.Y.P.D., but a _onearmed_ detective tracking evildoers in the shadow of Scotland Yard.

The new show, featuring Michael Balfour, with Neil McCallum and Colin Tapley as Saber's assistants, ran for just the summer of 1957 at first, before being revived as a regularly scheduled series which lasted until 1959.

Despite all the lawyers, reporters, and private eyes, 1951's greatest contribution

---

**Suave yet tough Tom Conway went from playing "The Falcon" in the movies to playing Mark Saber on TV. Not one ounce of unctuous charm was lost in the process.**

to the genre were generated by dramatizations. First was *Crime Syndicated*, a
half-hour CBS series hosted by Rudolph
Halley, former chief counsel for the Sen-
ate Crime Investigating Committee and
future president of the New York City
Council. Each week dramatizations of
the government's work in allaying crime
proved successful. The show lasted until
1953 in a biweekly version cut from the
same cloth as *Rackets Are My Racket*.

But the big winner of the 1951 season,
indeed the biggest winner of any season
with regard to the television detective,
was *Dragnet*. In some fashion this program affected every crime show that followed it. *Dragnet* started on radio in
1949 and proved so successful that the
producers decided to transfer it to television. On December 16, 1951, the *Ches-*

terfield Sound Off Time program pre-
viewed *Dragnet*.

"Dum-de-dum-dum." The first four
notes of the theme music by Walter
Schumann was seared into viewers'
memories. Then came a quiet, clipped
monotone voice: "This is the city. Los
Angeles, California. I work here, I carry a
badge." It was the voice of Jack Webb, a
powerhouse of a writer, producer, actor,
and director whose exterior calm belied
an incredible talent and will.

After appearing in *The Men* (1950) and
Sunset Boulevard (1950), Webb played
Sergeant Joe Friday, a noble cop who
was shortly to become a legend. Friday's
morality was as staunch as *Dragnet*'s
format. Every half-hour episode was a
dramatization of an actual police case
with, as the announcer said, "the names

Saber of London *predated the likes of* **Ironside, Longstreet,** *and those other
handicapped detectives by more than a decade. In 1957 Donald Grey played the
one-armed Scotland Yard investigator, shown here during the "Hands Across the
Sea" episode co-starring Neil McCallum and Jan Holden. (courtesy Theater
Collection, Free Library of Philadelphia)*

... changed to protect the innocent." After the theme and Webb's opening line, he would continue to narrate the episode as Friday. One of his most memorable intros was "We were working the day watch out of homicide."

The show emphasized the mundane reality of a cop's life as well as the details that added flavor. Viewers were told the time of each occurrence throughout so they would understand how long police work took. At times police codes were used to heighten the authenticity and mood. And at the close, after the criminal was caught, the announcer revealed what sentence was meted out as the "perpetrator" stared uncomfortably at the camera.

Here were the makings of a phenomenal hit that got off to a tragic start when Barton Yarbourough, the actor who played Friday's Mexican-American partner Detective Sergeant Ben Romero for the first three episodes, died of a heart attack. Webb, in keeping with his penchant for authenticity, had the character die of the same cause and replaced him with Barney Phillips as Sergeant Ed Jacobs.

Jacobs was a cool, "hip" type of cop, a foil for the dour Friday, but actor Phillips decided the grass was greener elsewhere and left the show to try to become a leading man in his own right. Undaunted, Webb replaced him with the man most identified as Friday's sidekick: Ben Alexander as Officer Frank Smith. It was another unusually effective casting coup. Alexander looked like everybody's uncle—chunky and affable—hardly the type of cop one would expect from watching Dick Tracy or Mark Saber. But his presence only served to sharpen the realism.

Together Friday and Smith investigated crime with a solemnity that was alternately thrilling and hilarious. Webb's delivery of "Just the facts, ma'am," passed into the language and Dragnet was lampooned everywhere. The master satirist Stan Freberg made a best-selling record, "St. George and the Dragonet," which began: "The legend you are about to hear is true. Only the needle should be changed to protect the record." TV Guide published a "Dragnet to English Dictionary," which was captioned: "Surprise Your Friends! Understand Jack Webb!"

By 1953 Webb had had it with the ridicule of Dragnet at his expense. He put the series on hold to produce, direct, and star in a movie version of Dragnet (1954), as well as Pete Kelly's Blues (1955), a movie about the life of a 1920s jazz musician. But NBC would not let Dragnet slip out of its schedule; they syndicated the show as Badge 714, which was Friday's badge number.

Webb's films were unsuccessful, so he returned to his most famous role. By 1955 both an original Dragnet and the syndicated Badge 714 were on the air. In 1956, Webb added a new touch in the form of Friday's girlfriend, played by Marjie Miller. The series rolled along until 1959 with Webb taking time off to produce, direct, and star in The D.I. (1957).

As the show was preparing to depart the airwaves, Ben Alexander said of Jack Webb: "He's the closest thing to a genius Hollywood has seen in years."

Webb was certainly the closest thing to an auteur ever to emerge from television. He eventually became a major producer of other crime shows under the banner of his company Mark VII Productions.

Webb produced, directed, and co-starred with Robert Mitchum in one other film, *The Last Time I Saw Charlie* (1962), before picking up badge 714 one more time.

In January 1967, Dragnet was reborn as *Dragnet '67*. This time veteran character actor Harry Morgan played Friday's partner, Officer Bill Gannon, a laconic cop about to retire with a good pension and a bad denture job. Friday's fiancée was also introduced. She was Ann Baker, an attractive woman played by Dorothy Abbott. Otherwise little changed.

Webb, apparently ageless, still played Joe with the same sour intensity, the cases were still dramatizations of actual police files, and the theme and narration gimmicks remained intact. If anything, the mood was even more serious even though there were instances of "light" banter delivered with all the finesse of a roll call.

The only time the new *Dragnet* took off was in another film version. Made in 1969 specifically for television, it put Friday on the trail of a crazed sex kidnapper and killer. The movie's opening let audiences know they were in for some strong stuff. It began with views of Los Angeles and Friday's narration, then cut to a bound-and-gagged blonde piteously mewling for her life as a strangler moved in. Then the camera moved back to reveal the strangler watching a film of the blonde about to die. It seemed the murderer had taken pictures and filmed all four of his captives before he got them to admit they would rather die than be with him. So he killed them.

Jack Webb created a television empire from the police files of 50 states. It all started with **Dragnet** *(NBC) in 1952.*

Such nastiness had not been seen on TV since the fifties.

1952

The producers of the new shows preferred to copy old hits rather than try new ideas of their own. To be fair, the networks and sponsors were really responsible for the "monkey see, monkey do" attitude because they wanted guaranteed successes. And the only way to get guaranteed successes, they figured, was to ride the coattails of already proven works.

The new season provided several such instances. *Police Story* was one, based on the files of police all over the country. Whether the names were changed to protect the innocent is something only Providence knows. The series' host, Norman Rose, never said.

Superior in its attempt to emulate *Dragnet* was *Racket Squad*, a blossoming of the concept started with *Rackets Are My Racket*. Sharp-featured Reed Hadley starred as Captain John Braddock of the San Francisco bunco squad. The similarities to Webb's show were striking.

Hadley, like Webb, narrated every episode and in the same way: "What you are about to see is a real-life story taken from the files of police racket and bunco squads, business protection associations, and similar sources all over the country. It is intended to expose the confidence game. The carefully worked out frauds by which confidence men take more money each year from the American public than all the bank robbers and thugs with their violence."

Hadley was the featured player in such episodes as "The Used-Car Scam," "The Spanish Prisoner," and "The Star

Maker." *Racket Squad* was an extremely popular show that lasted many years in syndication because of audience interest. People wanted to know what confidence games to look out for, especially since real con artists were stinging people in every state and at every monetary and social level. About the only thing *Racket Squad* did not have was the powerful pull of Jack Webb himself. As it was, producers Hal Roach, Jr., and Carroll Chase could not keep the series in production beyond 1953.

Besides the *Dragnet* clones, 1952 also boasted a few detectives made famous in literature. Examining the group in alphabetical order, *Boston Blackie* is first on the list. Jack Boyle first wrote of Blackie, a professional safe cracker, in 1919. To Boyle, the character was a "university graduate, scholar, gentleman . . . an incorrigible criminal made doubly dangerous by intellect."

Hollywood took it from there, making Blackie a long-term movie hero. In seven silent films such actors as Bert Lytell, Lionel Barrymore, David Powell, William Russell, Forrest Stanley, and Raymond Glenn played him the way Boyle originally intended. The change came in 1941 when Columbia released *Meet Boston Blackie*. Chester Morris, an actor who looked like Ralph Byrd, played Blackie in a style reminiscent of Lloyd Nolan and other wisecracking adventurers of the day.

Fourteen films and ten years later, Blackie made it to radio. "Friend to those who have no friends. Enemy to those who make him an enemy," was his motto and the serial's introduction. Chester Morris did the radio voice for awhile, then Richard Kollmar took over. Even so, Blackie was still a con using his talents to catch crooks.

But not on TV. Held over from the films was his police contact, the distrusting Inspector Faraday, played on the tube by Frank Orth. Held over from radio was Blackie's girlfriend and girl Friday, Mary Wesley (Lois Collier). Only Blackie had changed—from a thief to an ex-thief turned New York private eye. He was played by Kent Taylor. His new-fangled adventures were good for nearly 60 syndicated episodes shown on NBC.

Second of the literary adaptations was *Craig Kennedy, Criminologist*. Kennedy began life in 1912 in the Arthur B. Reeve book *The Silent Bullet*. He proved popular enough to be labeled the "American Sherlock Holmes" by the time the final book, *The Stars Scream Murder*, was published in 1936. The character also appeared in six movies between 1915 and 1936.

Donald Woods played the detective in 26 syndicated episodes produced by Adrian Weiss. By the early fifties, interest had all but waned in the character, so Craig Kennedy was a minor figure in TV history.

Taking a much larger part were Mr. and Mrs. North, an extremely popular pair of amateur sleuths created by Richard and Frances Lockridge in a 1940 novel. By 1941 they were on Broadway, being played by Peggy Conklin and Albert Hackett. The movie version of the stage comedy premiered the same year with Gracie Allen as Mrs. North and William Post, Jr., as Mr. North.

In 1942 the Norths found their way to radio and were given voice by Alice Frost and Joseph Curtin. It took TV ten years to catch up, but both CBS and NBC finally did, sharing the couple until 1954. Barbara Britton, who appeared in *Till We Meet Again* (1944) and *Champagne for Caesar* (1950), played Pamela North and

Richard Denning was her ever-patient husband Jerry.

The format remained unchanged: Jerry was still an ex-private eye turned publisher while Pamela was still a vivacious, attractive, somewhat addlebrained woman whose main occupation was stumbling over corpses. She was so good at finding murder, in fact, she probably inspired the producers of the earlier *Detective's Wife* and *Crime With Father*. Sadly, those two inferior shows did much to undercut the Norths' effectiveness. And the decade between their radio and TV premiere did much to cool their attraction. The series lasted 57 episodes.

Closing out the 1952 season were a pair of adventurers. Doing his thing in syndication was *China Smith*, an easygoing soldier of fortune who fought injustice in the East. Dan Duryea played the character for a year before returning to his film career.

The TV spy of 1952 was *The Hunter*, another elaborately conceived summer replacement series for *Man Against Crime*. Edward J. Montague produced the adventures of Bart Adams, a wealthy playboy turned Commie killer for the United States government. Barry Nelson—who was to become TV's only James Bond/Agent 007 just two years

This composite special effects photo was created to celebrate the double-duty of Richard Denning and Barbara Britton, who were playing the roles of Mr. and Mrs. North on both radio and television (CBS). (courtesy Theater Collection, Free Library of Philadelphia)

later—took pleasure in playing the world-hopping master of disguise during its initial run on CBS.

Montague kept the production going even after *Man Against Crime*'s return in September, replacing the busy Nelson with Keith Larsen so that NBC could pick up the show for a short 1954 run. The audience's interest did not continue along with the production, however, so *The Hunter* hunted no more after that.

1953

The United States government sent out a lot of agents over the years, but few were as suave as Steve Mitchell, a world-wise mercenary forever out on a *Dangerous Assignment*. Mitchell's style was provided by the syndicated show's star, Brian Donlevy, a fine actor capable of playing both heroes and villains with equal ability. Shortly after embodying Steve Mitchell for one season, Donlevy played the brilliant English scientist Quatermass in the cult science fiction classics *The Quatermass Experiment* (1955) and *Quatermass II* (1956).

Another 1953 TV star who also came from a film career was Richard Carlson. While fighting *The Magnetic Monster* (1953), seeing that *It Came from Outer Space* (1953), and defeating *The Creature from the Black Lagoon* (1954), it must have been a pleasure for Carlson to perform his relatively staid television duties as a man who infiltrated the Communist party for the FBI.

For nine years Herb Philbrick worked as an undercover agent and then wrote a bestseller based on his experiences, *I Led Three Lives*. TV created a series of the same name, filming Philbrick's work on location, and otherwise claiming to

be 100 percent accurate. At least that is what the producers attempted in the beginning. As the program became a hit, the writers ran out of real-life material.

The less realistic the show became, the less liked it became. Reviewers noted that "When it stuck to facts, it was a good taut thriller. But once the writers took over, the quality went down. Now it is a fairly common cops and robbers actioner." Even so, the series kept Carlson busy for more than 110 episodes.

The closest the spy/mystery genre came to science fiction in 1953 was the wildly conceived and cleverly titled *Cowboy G-Men*. Some smart cookie decided to combine the best of all those westerns with secret agent shenanigans and came up with a short-lived, 26-episode series starring Russell Hayden and Jackie Coogan as government good guys Pat Gallagher and Stoney Crockett.

Modern day government workings were not being ignored in the meantime. CBS gleefully attacked the Army investigations files to produce *Pentagon Confidential*. Addison Richards, Larry Fletcher, and Edward Binns played the Army investigators who carried on the fight against the nation's enemies any way they could. Their efforts were not enough to keep the series going beyond a summer run.

There were some unusual series concepts that season. One was called *Postal Inspector*. It was the stirring saga of a man who reads *your* mail. Only slightly more pedestrian was *Hollywood Off Beat*, which was also know as *Steve Randall* during its short run on the DuMont network. Randall was the dapper character played by Melvyn Douglas,

Brian Donlevy (left) takes in some high life during his TV tenure with the Dangerous
Assignment *series. Seated beside him is Arthur Brown, owner of The Harwyn Club,
the New York bistro where this photo was taken. (courtesy of The Harwyn Club)*

and Hollywood was where disbarred
lawyer Randall did some private detective work in an effort to get his shingle
back.

Hollywood Off Beat went on to obliv-
ion. Happily, however, Steve Randall got
his law license back on the last episode.

Jimmie Hughes, Rookie Cop was a
frightfully short-lived (eight weeks) series, but interesting in its attempt to be
slightly different. First of all, instead of
casting some young hunk to play the
leading role, as any producer would do
today, they got William Redfield—then
known as "Billy" Redfield—to star as a
Korean War veteran who returns home to
find his father, a cop, has been killed in
the line of duty.

Jimmie joins the New York Police Department to find his dad's killers and
exact vengeance, but finds instead the
comradery of his fellows and the morality of the cop's code is a cure for his
bloodlust. Rusty Lane, late of *Crime With
Father*, played the crusty, lovable Inspector Ferguson while Wendy Drew played
Jimmie's sister. Both helped Jimmie get
through as a rookie.

Two other cop series lasted longer
than *Jimmie Hughes*, though neither
could be considered different or original.
Man Behind the Badge, a warmed-over
Dragnet, lasted a year. Charles Bickford
served as host for weekly dramatizations
of more "official law enforcement records." The gimmick here was that cops

were not the only ones to wear a silver star. Park rangers, MPs, and parole officers also got fictional treatments. If the show had lasted, even the Men Behind the Big Bright Texaco Star might have made it it onto the program.

City Detective, 56 syndicated episodes of rough-and-tumble action, starred manly Rod Cameron as New York police lieutenant Bart Grant. Cameron, a lead in many B films and a Fred MacMurray stand-in, ably solved a variety of barely memorable big-city crimes until 1955.

The final new show of the year was given credence by the presence of one of filmdom's toughest tough guys, George Raft. Before starting his Hollywood career in 1929, Raft had been a professional athlete, a nightclub dancer, a gambler, and a friend of well-known gangsters.

In the early fifties his career had slowed somewhat, so he was willing to star as Lieutenant George Kirby, N.Y.P.D., a man dedicated to infiltrating and eliminating organized crime in the Big Apple. The title of the fairly successful syndicated series was *I'm the Law*; a fitting declaration to come from the lips of the iron-hard Raft.

1954

If for nothing else 1954 will be remembered as the season the greatest detective—living or dead, fact or fiction—was brought to the television screen. For 39 episodes audiences thrilled to the one and only *Sherlock Holmes*, the "scientific consulting detective."

The wise producer of the series, Sheldon Reynolds, filmed the programs in Paris, which added to the mood of the tense dramas. He then cast in the leading

role the vulnerable, sensitive, delicate-looking Ronald Howard. He juxtaposed the youthful hero with the robust, active H. Marion Crawford as his Baker Street roommate Dr. John Watson. The episodes gave the critics reason to rejoice. "Low-key writing, acting, directing, even lighting mark each episode," *TV Guide* proclaimed. "H. Marion Crawford plays Watson as a skillful aide and Ronald Howard does a fine job. The supporting players are top notch." The main supporting player was Archie Duncan as the detective duo's famous foil Inspector Lestrade.

All in all, it was a surprisingly pleasing show to mystery lovers and Holmes fanatics. It is a shame it did not last longer.

Years later Holmes returned to television in the person of white-haired Stewart Granger in the 1972 version of *Hound of the Baskervilles* on ABC's *Movie of the Week*. Granger, who had many swashbuckling roles in movies, was the closest thing to Peter Lawford the producers could find, so he got the part at about the same time Lawford was mishandling Ellery Queen. Granger was not wildly miscast, but he cut a stockier figure than most of the rapier-thin actors who played Holmes in films. Bernard Fox was Watson and Alan Calliou was Lestrade in the 90-minute effort, which also featured William Shatner and Anthony Zerbe.

Three years later NBC tried its luck with the well-intentioned *Sherlock Holmes in New York*. It was an original tale that theorized that a much hand-

---

This is the example that all the TV detectives aspired to. The inimitable Basil Rathbone as the classic Sherlock Holmes. He makes the pipe, the deerstalker cap and tweed cape look natural.

Roger Moore made a somewhat naive, uncomfortable Holmes for Sherlock Holmes in New York. *On him, the cap and pipe look to be mere affectations. (NBC)*

somer Holmes had an affair with "the woman," as the detective called actress Irene Adler, which produced a son. Well, when the evil Professor Moriarty got wind of it, he kidnapped the boy, who lived with his mother in New York. This brought Holmes to the scene. The casting was clever; two of England's best-known portrayers of two much revered fictional secret agents—Roger Moore and Patrick Macnee—played the two famous sleuths. To top it off, the great John Huston played Holmes' arch-enemy.

Unfortunately, the writing was beneath the actors' abilities. In order to keep the plot moving, the creators made Holmes fairly stupid—the stupidity being disguised as vulnerability. The scriptwriters undermined Holmes' heroic

stature to make him more "accessible." In *Sherlock Holmes in New York*, the effect simply made him seem stolid.

This vulnerability was given an interesting about-face when *They Might Be Giants* premièred in 1971 and starred George C. Scott as an addled eccentric who escaped from reality by thinking he was Sherlock Holmes. The film was an affectionate, remarkably effective one. In 1975, TV remade it as *Alias Sherlock Holmes* with Larry Hagman in the Scott role. And as good as Hagman has proven himself to be on *Dallas*, he was no George C. Scott. The TV movie hardly made it, either critically or popularly.

Sherlock Holmes was not the only literary detective to appear on television in 1954. That was the year *The Lone*

Wolf, originally a gentleman thief in the tradition of *Boston Blackie*, showed up. Louis Joseph Vance first created the character in a 1914 novel. Six more books were written before *The Lone Wolf's Last Howl* in 1934, but the delightful cat burglar was held in good stead by the movies. Twenty adventures of the charming jewel thief were made between 1926 and 1949, mostly by Columbia.

In the books, Michael Lanyard, soon to be known as the Lone Wolf, started his career as a desperately poor man who was taught the three cardinal rules of safecracking by a veteran known only as Bourke: "Know your ground, strike like a hawk, and be friendless." In the theatrical versions Lanyard—played by either Francis Lederer, Bert Lytell, Jack Holt, Warren William, Gerald Mohr, or Ron Randall—was almost always a reformed thief who used his talents for the good of humanity.

On television Louis Hayward played the French gentleman by day and the Lone Wolf by night in what was called "a strictly one-dimensional manner." The reviews also mentioned a change from civilized crime to "blood-and-guts melodrama." Audiences did not seem to mind since the series, which opened with a shot of the Lanyard family crest, a wolf's head, ran for several years in syndication under the title *Streets of Danger*.

A slightly less successful syndicated show appearing that season was *Captured*, based on the very successful radio

An even wilder TV movie conceit cast Larry Hagman as a loony who thought himself Sherlock Holmes in Alias Sherlock Holmes. *Here, even the crew has trouble sizing him up.*

program *Gangbusters*. Just like its radio predecessor, the television incarnation took the form of an anthology. One copywriter described the series as "an explosive series as factual as today's headlines! Each story, taken from police files, is sparked by narrator Chester Morris." Morris had achieved success earlier with *Boston Blackie*.

Another earlier television favorite returned this year. *Racket Squad*'s Captain John Braddock himself, Reed Hadley, leaped from a bunco squad to the courtrooms of California for *Public Defender*. Here he played hard-bitten attorney Bart Matthews, a lawyer sure to set the poor or just plain cheap defendant's heart aflutter. For a little more than a year Hadley portrayed the lawyer employed by the court to defend the poor accused of crimes.

The most popular new show of the season proved to be *The Line-up*, basically a warmed-over *Dragnet* featuring Warner Anderson as Detective Lieutenant Ben Guthrie and Tom Tully as Inspector Matt Grebb. Based on the files of the San Francisco police, it was made in cooperation with the S.F.P.D. and had a brutal realism that was missing from the other Sergeant Friday spinoffs. Contributing to this realism was the production crews filming on the San Francisco streets.

The Line-up remained on CBS Friday nights in a half-hour format until 1959. When it moved to Wednesday night, it was an hour long and had a new cast. The part of Grebb was dropped and replaced by four other characters. Marshall Reed was Inspector Fred Asher, Tod Burton was Inspector Charlie Summers, and William Leslie was Inspector Dan De-

laney. For added color Rachel Ames co-starred as policewoman Sandy McAllister. These changes did nothing to improve the quality of the series, however. Eighteen episodes later, in the winter of 1960, the last *Line-Up* was put together.

The low point of 1954 came with a summer substitute called *The Telltale Clue*. Anthony Ross as Captain Richard Hale of New York City tried to solve mysteries with the help of one vital clue . . . one seemingly innocuous item that would throw the case wide open. *TV Guide*'s critic, however, only needed the evidence of the first episode to deliver his own verdict.

"Uninspired stuff," he declared, "filling one of those half hours that might be better served reading a good book." The show did not last beyond September.

1955

Reading a good book has its hazards. Good mysteries often take place in exotic locales. And while series about government spies and worldly adventures had exploited these places in the past, television never concentrated on foreign police departments the way literature did.

All that changed this season. Producers suddenly discovered what content readers had enjoyed for years: international police departments. But rather than borrow already-established literary fellows like Georges Simenon's Maigret, TV came up with two of its own. First, there was *Paris Precinct*, a television oddity if ever there was one. Not only was the syndicated show about the exploits of two detectives of the Paris Sûreté, but the ABC network show actually had two Frenchmen playing the parts!

Usually television and movie casting agents went for whoever was popular and easiest to sign at the time—which often meant that if the role needed a foreigner, a noted character actor would be hired to put on the proper accent. Here, real Frenchmen Claude Dauphin and Louis Jourdan played Inspectors Bolbec and Beaumont. Jourdan co-starred in *Madame Bovary* (1949) and *Letters from an Unknown Woman* (1947), but he is better known in this country for his performances in *Gigi* (1958), PBS's *Dracula* (1979), and TV commercials. Dauphin, an eminent actor, has appeared in European and American films since the late 1930s.

While the *Paris Precinct* program was interestingly conceived—indeed, daringly conceived for its time—it was not impressively presented.

"The factor most required," said one reviewer, "is missing: excitement. Don't count on this one." No one seemed to. Within six months the France-based series was off the air.

But it was enough to set a precedent. It seemed to convince other producers that a mystery show set abroad might interest the networks. That very year, programs concentrating on faraway cops started cropping up. The series' creators tried to avoid the same fate as *Paris Precinct* by either loading their shows with action and intrigue or adapting tried-and-true American themes to an international framework.

The latter method was employed for *Scotland Yard*, which appeared in syndication during this season, but was not shown on the ABC network until 1957. The half-hour program, hosted and narrated by Edgar Lustgarten, could have been called "Dragnet in English Dress" since it dramatized actual cases from the Yard. Interestingly, Lustgarten was a respected real-life criminologist who left the acting to professionals like Australian-born Russell Napier, who played Inspector Duggan, a recurring character. The program was active in various berths on the ABC schedule until 1958.

Far more florid, thereby making it far more entertaining, was a syndicated companion series—also with a Scotland Yard background—*Colonel March of Scotland Yard*. The character of March was derived from the stories of master puzzle-maker John Dickson Carr. Writing under the pseudonym Carter Dickson, Carr, famous for his locked-room mysteries, created the Scotland Yard D-3 department, otherwise known as the Department of Queer Complaints.

Colonel March, described in the stories as looking like a caricature of a retired British officer, was delightfully embodied by Boris Karloff, veteran star of stage and screen, who was then 68. Sporting an eye patch for some additional color, the colonel rarely had anything as simple as a locked-room mystery to solve. In the one season of 20-odd episodes (telecast at different times over several years), March faced such adversaries as an abominable snowman and the missing link.

TV Guide called it a series that "concentrates on bizarre and eerie themes," although it "looks tightly budgeted." Their highest praise, not surprisingly, went to Karloff, who they said played March as a "soft-spoken and amiable crime-solver." The experienced actor brought style and class to the inexpensive proceedings, making the shows watchable no matter how outlandish the subject matter.

Another famous literary creation, however, did not fare so well during the transition to the TV version. *The Falcon*, created by Michael Arlen in 1940, had as its hero a man who described himself as hard-boiled, taciturn, mercenary, and a gambler. In the movies this personality was warped to fit the persona of actor George Sanders. Starting in 1941, Sanders performed in four films about the debonair adventurer before he got tired of the role.

But RKO Pictures had a successful film series they did not want to die and Sanders had a handsome, personable brother he wanted to promote, so the studio and the bored thespian worked out an interesting as well as successful ploy to maintain the Falcon's good cinematic graces. In that fourth film, *The Falcon's Brother* (1942), Gay Lawrence is killed but his brother, Tom Lawrence, vows to carry on his fight for truth, justice, and a lot of pretty girls.

That sibling switch was good for nine more RKO movies, all starring Tom Conway as a suave do-gooder before he took up the TV reins as *Mark Saber* in 1951. But The Falcon's gauntlet was not let down for good. Radio had picked up the character in 1945, reincarnated as Mike Waring, hard-boiled insurance investigator on the Mutual Network.

The success of this third version led to another short film series produced by Film Classics. John Calvert, an unknown actor, was signed to portray the Mike Waring Falcon for three movies in 1948 and 1949. It was this Falcon of the Waring name that television decided to present in 1955. But the tradition of changing the approach did not end with radio and film. To give him a broader base of operations, the Falcon's TV producers gave him a new job.

"There's international intrigue," the ads promised, "as Mike Waring, famous undercover agent, operates around the world on his hazardous missions." It must have been pretty tough to do things on the sly when you're a "famous undercover" spy, but Charles McGraw managed to bash his way through almost 40 syndicated episodes as the new Falcon. By the time the Falcon got to television the character had come full circle. The Mike Waring the gravel-voiced McGraw played was basically the same rough-hewn adventurer Arlen had presented to his readers in 1940.

A Diamond, A Gunn, and
The Untouchables

The middle of the fifties would come to be known as the "Golden Age" of television: the era of great comedy, terrific variety shows, and compelling drama. There was some great work done in the mystery field, but mostly within the framework of one-shot specials.

In 1954 the dramatic series *Climax!* presented two telling detective efforts a fortnight apart. On October 7, Dick Powell starred as Philip Marlowe—a role he made famous in *Murder My Sweet* (1944)—in the TV production of Raymond Chandler's *The Long Goodbye*, co-starring Teresa Wright and Cesar Romero. On October 21, the program presented Ian Fleming's *Casino Royale*, the first of the novels featuring James Bond, agent 007. American Barry Nelson played Bond in this first and only TV rendering of Fleming's famous character. Peter Lorre co-starred as Le Chiffre, a thief, cheat, and villain who fought Bond over the gaming tables of the Casino Royale, and Linda Christian was featured

as Valerie, the beautiful double agent who betrays Bond.

These two notable mysteries were dropped into the television ocean without causing so much as a ripple. In fact, Albert Broccoli, producer of the wildly successful James Bond movies, had not even heard of the TV hour special until informed of it during the summer of 1979. That encapsulates the sadness of the television effort. As hard as the many writers, technicians, producers, directors, and actors work on any one TV project, their effort is mostly seen and then quickly forgotten.

1956

Programmers did their best in 1956, coming up with a couple of successful originals as well as the usual assortment of retreads. In the latter category was *Fabian of Scotland Yard*, a tired attempt to cash in on the interest aroused by the two prior Scotland Yard series. Bruce Seton, the British star of *Sweeney Todd* (1936), played a civilized English inspector with clipped reserve. The series, also known as *Fabian of the Yard*, was not known by either title for very long. The singer of the same name was more successful and a lot more exciting.

Coming hot on the heels of *The Falcon* were three new programs which counted on international intrigue and action to bolster the ratings. "Now it can be told!" said one advertisement, "Dramatic stories of secret agents from every country in the world . . . taken from the secret government files and unfolded in electrifying reality!"

After *I Spy* went on the air in syndication in 1956, the secret files about secret agents were splashed all over the screens of America. What the ad did not say, however, was that these secrets were hardly important anymore. This program should not be confused with its famous namesake of a decade later. The 1956 *I Spy* dramatized espionage events that took place over the centuries. Raymond Massey, playing the host/narrator role of Anton, a gregarious spy-master, might tell a story about a little American boy who unknowingly fed information to the Japanese during World War II or the story of a little girl who worked for Stonewall Jackson during the Civil War. Or Anton would delineate events of the Revolutionary War or even ancient Rome. It was a fairly interesting series, maintaining the same sort of fascination that *You Are There* (1953) had in its heyday.

More common fiction was offered by *The Man Called X*. The man called X—Ken Thurston—was played by Barry Sullivan who came to television from a successful stage and film career.

"It's for those who like their TV adventure filled with intrigue and unsullied by romance," said *TV Guide*. Many viewers liked the formula, because *The Man Called X* stayed in syndication for its full run of 39 episodes. It was no great hit, certainly, but fondly remembered, especially the episode when Thurston took on a ring of woman spies.

That same year, Cesar Romero followed in the footsteps of his film colleagues by starring in a TV adventure series. His syndicated series borrowed from most genre efforts before it and in addition had some originality of its own. *Passport to Danger* concerned the assignments of one Steve McQuinn, a United States diplomatic courier. While most real-life couriers were plain and affable men, McQuinn, as embodied by Romero, was not above getting involved beyond his messenger-boy status, effectively utilizing his fast fists and smooth style.

"Romero doesn't take his acting chores too seriously," said one review. "He has fun and so will most viewers. If you like intrigue, pretty girls, and Cesar Romero, not necessarily in that order, you'll probably go for it." Romero played around for 39 episodes, entertaining himself and the audience, then went back to his film and business careers.

Reporters made their way onto the international scene this year. Up until 1956, the newspaper dramas were basically contained in a regional framework with one intrepid news hound sniffing out the dirt in Anytown, U.S.A. But for *Wire Service*, the reporter's beat was the world. Producers Don Sharpe and Warren Lewis brought in consultants from International News Service to lend authenticity and credibility to their one-hour ABC series about the exploits of seasoned press people.

Once the show hit the air, however, the creators seemed more intent on pushing up the action content rather than the intelligence factor. Dane Clark starred as Dan Miller, Mercedes McCambridge was Katherine Wells, and veteran thespian George Brent appeared as Dean Evans; each was a country-hopping investigative reporter for Trans-Globe News, the "wire service" of the title.

Each week, one of these three would star in a story about international affairs. And each week the starring actor would preface the adventure with the words: "Nothing travels faster than news. An electronic impulse splinters distance at 186,000 miles per second. From Tokyo, from London, from Rio, from New York! An age of speed and curiosity, the news probes and the probe is truth."

So much for scientific accuracy. In terms of its authenticity, a *TV Guide* critique had other things to say. "It's a generally entertaining hour. Clark is the most believable, McCambridge the most intense, and Brent the most likeable. It's solid but needs some realism and missing humor." *Wire Service* remained on the air for three years.

Producers were still trying to find a new wrinkle in the *Dragnet* scheme of things. To their credit, they were trying to infuse the cop genre with new life. To their chagrin, many were probably doing it because all the *Dragnet* clones were failing. One production company's an-

swer to the problem was to set the police action in a rather unusual location. For 39 weeks, viewers witnessed the exploits of Senior Detective Beaujac and Detective Conroy, two cops attached to the New Orleans Police Department.

The show used the initials of that august organization for its title *N.O.P.D.*, and Stacy Harris starred as the senior partner with Lou Sirgo as his underling. These two tramped around the bayous of Cajun country for awhile with hardly anyone noticing, so the series peacefully left the air after one full season.

The locale utilized by the most famous of the year's TV detectives was more familiar to most viewers: the beat of *Highway Patrol* was wherever there was happy motoring. The series has passed into the television book of classics not so much for its content, but because of its star, Broderick Crawford. The star of such films as *All the King's Men*—for which he won an Oscar—and *Born Yesterday* played Dan Matthews and turned two simple sign-off numbers, "ten-four," into a national craze.

There are other reasons the show is noteworthy. It was one of the highest rated non-network shows in the medium's history. Filmed by Ziv Television Programs, which lasted as long as the show did (four years and 156 episodes) it turned out to be one of the most respected, most copied formulas on TV. The reviews were full of praise for star and stories alike.

At the beginning of each episode, over the theme music by Richard Llewelyn, the announcer intoned: "Whenever the laws of any state are broken, a duly authorized organization swings into action. It may be called the state police, state troopers, militia, the Rangers, or the highway patrol. These are the stories of the men whose training, skill, and courage have enforced and preserved our state laws."

So, for this year, ten-four.

1957

Initially, 1957 was not a very good year. As soon as the producers saw *Highway Patrol* making money, they sent their own crews out to get a piece of the action any way they could. A well-financed but obvious attempt to emulate Broderick Crawford's successful format could be found in the syndicated *State Trooper*. Believing the weak point of *Highway Patrol* to be the lack of a handsome leading man, Rod Cameron was signed to play Rod Blake, chief of the Nevada State Troopers.

The producers' reasoning was sound. Combining a higher-than-average budget with solid production values added up to a crackerjack show in its own right. Cameron, as solid as the show's production planning, came to the series fresh from *City Detective* and kept up his acting end, so *State Trooper* kept scouring Nevada's highways for speeders and even worse types for three years.

Other producers refused to copy *Highway Patrol*'s success so precisely. Instead they went diving for the concept of their shows and came up with two wet series. The first, and most ludicrous, was *Harbor Command*, which was billed as "true-to-life stories of America's Harbor Police."

Figuring that a stern-looking lead would not hurt their chances to emulate *Highway Patrol*'s popularity, dependable, experienced Wendell Corey was

picked to play Captain Ralph Baxter of the United States Harbor Police Command. Corey, having just finished six action movies in a row, seemed willing to take on his first starring role in a TV series. *Harbor Command* sank after only one year.

Wendell Corey came back to TV occasionally as a guest star and then in 1962 hosted *The Eleventh Hour*, a borderline detective series in which he played Dr. Theodore Bassett, a psychiatrist police advisor. The program's only other connection to the mystery realm was that its producers, Sam Rolfe and Norman Felton, teamed up a few years later to create *The Man from U.N.C.L.E.* Another borderline effort, *Harbourmaster*, bobbed to the surface of the networks' schedules and managed to brave it until the middle of 1958. Here, Barry Sullivan played Captain David Scott, the one-man police force of Scott Island, off Cape Ann, Massachusetts. Most of Scott's problems were noncriminal since Mother Nature seemed to take a disliking to him at least once an episode, pelting the place with storms and fires and the like.

Buffering him from the worst of it were characters like young Jeff Kitredge, his boatyard assistant (Paul Burke), Professor Wheeler (Murray Matheson), a retired navy man named Captain Dan (Mike Keene), and attractive Anna Morrison, operator of the Dolphin Restaurant (Nina Wilcox). Other than that, the major difference between the two shows was the way in which they spelled harbor. Either way, it didn't matter. Viewers evidently spelled it "harbore," since both series died before a 40th episode could be ordered.

The same fate befell other shows that year as well. Two shows about foreign intrigue were both well thought out, interestingly produced, and came by their authenticity the hard way: they were both produced overseas. *Four Just Men* was a British import featuring four very different but very famous actors. American Dan Dailey, known for his song-and-dance roles in movies like *Mother Wore Tights* (1947) played newspaperman Tim Collier. Englishman Jack Hawkins, known for such films as *The Cruel Sea* (1952) and *Bridge on the River Kwai* (1957), played private eye Ben Manfred. Italian-American Richard Conte, often typecast as a gangster, played a French lawyer named Jeff Ryder. And Vittorio De Sica, the award-winning Italian film director and actor, starred as Italian hotel owner Ricco Poccari.

This quartet of high-powered talent starred in a story about four World War II veterans from the same unit who were reunited by their former commander on his death bed. This noble, farseeing commander asked that they band together once more to fight peacetime evil wherever it might be found.

The four men interacted just a little bit before heading off in different directions, allowing each weekly story to feature one of the four as its lead. The series in syndication in America did not match its popularity in England and consequently lasted only one season.

The ABC television network had its own formula for spy success, but its international intrigue offering fared even worse than *Four Just Men*. Its series, called *O.S.S.*, dealt with the missions of an agent for the United States Intelligence Office of Strategic Services during World War II.

ABC certainly tried with this one.

Robert Siodmak, director of such films as *The Spiral Staircase* (1945), *The Killers* (1946), and *The Crimson Pirate* (1952), was charged with filming the episodes on location in Europe with a cast that combined capable veterans with attractive newcomers. Canadian Lionel Murton played the O.S.S. chief who sent agent Frank Hawthorn on hazardous missions behind enemy lines. Ron Randell, an Australian actor, played Hawthorn with considerable verve until the show was canceled in March 1958.

Also on the international front came *Stryker of Scotland Yard*, which was also known in its syndicated lifetime as *Stryker of the Yard*. Either way, the short-lived, one-season filler starred Welsh actor Clifford Evans as chief inspector Robert Stryker, a very capable, very proper police officer who saved British citizens from master criminals.

On the home front, there were two series that provided interesting contrasts in terms of approach. One used the concept of the detective as a hard-boiled, tough-talking, rough-fighting snooper. The other, a police series, tried to depart from cliché concepts only to become mired in them all the more.

The hard-boiled detective series was *Meet McGraw*, which tried to utilize its star Frank Lovejoy to better effect than did the *Man Against Crime* series the season before. It's hard to tell the two shows apart except for some superficial character changes. Here, Lovejoy was mercenary McGraw, bereft of an investigator's license and a first name. McGraw was not legally allowed to carry a rod, but managed to bash his way out of any trouble he found himself in.

That left only one problem: selling McGraw (who was not a cop or private eye) to the public and press. Lovejoy's credentials helped. Movie audiences had seen him in *I Was a Communist for the FBI* (1951) and *House of Wax* (1953), among others. So the press releases made do by describing McGraw as a "professional busybody who wanders from state to state minding other people's business."

Sounds like just the sort of person we all want living next door. Not surprisingly, *Meet McGraw* did not have a long run: a year and a half on NBC and again in ABC reruns.

The new concept police series was a bit ahead of its time by any standards. Called *Decoy* in the beginning of its one-season syndicated run, it was later retitled *Police Woman Decoy*.

That's right, this was a police show that featured a woman as the lead, star, and hero. Sad to say, there were no cries of *vive la différence* as Beverly Garland, who had roles in *DOA* (1949) and *The Glass Web* (1953), filled out her role as brave policewoman Casey Jones, a specialist in bringing out the worst in men.

Here was a daring police officer doing *her* thing some 20 years before women's lib flourished. Garland did her best, but *Decoy* apparently hit the airwaves a little too early. The series disappeared, but the actress went on to greater success as a regular on *The Bing Crosby Show* (1964) and *My Three Sons* (1966).

On the basis of the 1957 shows reviewed so far, it would not seem to be the best of times for the television detective. Yet the quality and popularity of some programs secured for the mystery genre a firm place in television which it enjoys to this day. For example, *The New Adventures of Charlie Chan*.

In 1925, Detective-Sergeant Charlie Chan of the Honolulu Police Department was introduced in a bestseller called *The House Without a Key* by Earl Derr Biggers. Five more Chan novels followed, all of which were great favorites with the public.

The movies discovered Charlie Chan in 1926, releasing a serial version of *The House Without a Key*. Soon two feature films followed, but it was not until 1931, when Twentieth Century-Fox started its famous series with Warner Oland, that a Chan film enjoyed a real success. Oland started a tradition that has been maintained to this day. No Oriental has ever played Chan.

A weekly radio series started in 1932 with Walter Connolly playing Chan. As time went on, noted character actors Ed Begley and Santos Ortega took over the Chan role, while Sidney Tolar and Roland Winters took over the screen incarnation.

It took TV years to catch up with Chan via English producers Rudolph Flothow and Sidney Marshall, who worked in conjunction with Lew Grade's production company, the Independent Television Corporation (I.T.C.), to produce *The New Adventures of Charlie Chan*. It lasted one season in syndication.

By this time the humble servant had been promoted to full inspectorship, and his connection with the Hawaiian police force was all but forgotten. Essentially, executive producer Leon Fromkess had his heart in the right place when mounting the short-lived series. He got a string of commendable British directors to handle each half-hour episode, including

For comparison's sake, here is Swedish actor Warner Oland playing his most famous role—that of humble Oriental sleuth Charlie Chan.

Alvin Rakoff, Leslie Goodwins, and Don Chaffey. He cast noted English character actors Rupert Davies and Hugh Williams as Inspectors Duff and Marlowe in homage obviously to American actor Howard Duff, who portrayed Sam Spade, and Raymond Chandler's famous creation, Philip Marlowe. He even cast an oriental, James Hong, as Barry Chan, the latest in a long line of Number One Sons.

J. Carrol Naish was woefully miscast as Charlie himself. Naish, a character actor in many films and famous for his portrayal of Italians, proved an ineffective Chan.

After ladling on huge amounts of makeup to make him look somewhat Oriental, it hardly mattered what the producers, directors, and writers did to make the show as entertaining as possible. To American viewers, it was still Naish the "Italian" in a Far Eastern disguise.

Other than that, the series was basically enjoyable. The Biggers character is nearly unshakable, no matter who is warped to fit the role. Still courteous and cunning, Chan always seemed to be a cure for an overdose of hard-boiled detectives with their sarcasm and flame-spitting gats. Even after the disappearance of the I.T.C. Chan series after its one-year run, TV people occasionally revived the character in a number of ways.

First Hanna-Barbera Productions—which is to quality cartoons what fast-food places are to haute cuisine—made a series of half-hour limited animation

And here is TV's Chan—once over the mass media heavily. J. Carrol Naish suffered much makeup to portray the detective for **The Adventures of Charlie Chan.** *(ITC Entertainment, Inc.)*

cartoons called *The Amazing Chan and the Chan Clan* in 1972. Keye Luke, an Oriental actor known for playing Charlie's Number One Son opposite Warner Oland, graduated to supplying the master's voice. Even so, the cartoons were basically about the Chan children, here numbering ten (down one from the 11 of the original novels). To make up for the missing child, the cartoonists supplied Chu Chu, a pet dog, given voice by Don Messick.

The company was pretty good about hiring Orientals to supply the rest of the Chan family voices; a moot point given that these actors were heard and not seen. The gesture was a reputable counterpoint to the badly written, boringly designed, and dully animated show.

In the seventies, Gene R. Kearney, a talented writer, was given the assignment to work up a new two-hour Charlie Chan mystery to be used as a television movie and pilot for a subsequent series. *Happiness Is a Warm Clue*, filmed at Universal Studios, had Ross Martin, a Polish-American character actor, in the lead. Martin, who had been in films since 1955, played Artemus Gordon, the inventive master of disguise in TV's *The Wild, Wild West* (1965).

The made-for-TV movie was shown without fanfare once in 1975 and once in 1979. Granted, *Happiness Is a Warm Clue* was no *Charlie Chan at the Opera* (1936), but it was mounted with a certain warm affection for the great sleuth, especially at the film's beginning. Charlie is shown quite happily resting within the bosom of his large Hawaii-based family. The symbol of his years as a detective is Chan's round-crowned, flat-rimmed black hat, which rests in Charlie's office like a cherished award.

This TV movie did not sound Chan's death knell, however. Neil Simon's *Murder by Death* (1976) had the late Peter Sellers doing a Chan caricature along with other fine actors who parodied the great detectives of film and fiction.

Peter Ustinov, the versatile English actor, starred as the man himself for *Charlie Chan and the Curse of the Dragon Queen* (1981). The producers of this flick did not even try to appease the Oriental actors of the world, since they cast not only Ustinov, but all-American boy Richard Hatch as the Number One Son and Angie Dickinson as the Dragon Queen. It seems that this weird casting was part of their plan; that is, they wanted the obviously Occidental actors to be part of the campy joke.

There were other great characters and shows within the 1957 TV season. Sharing the spotlight with Charlie Chan were Nick and Nora Charles. So famous were they, in fact, that David Niven and Maggie Smith satirized them in Columbia's *Murder by Death*.

Dashiell Hammett, the famous mystery writer and creator of Sam Spade, wrote only one book about Nick and Nora Charles, but it was enough. *The Thin Man* came out in 1934 and the Metro-Goldwyn-Mayer movie based on the novel appeared the same year. It was a double entertainment whammy the public could not resist. People did not so much identify the pair by their names, Nick and Nora, as by the title of the book

and film: *The Thin Man*. The "thin man" was the scientist/inventer who gets murdered at the outset of the adventure.

Nick was an ex-operative of the Trans-American Detective Agency whose real name is Nicholas Charalambides. He is lucky enough to marry money in the form of Nora, a character based on Hammett's real-life love, Lillian Hellman. Although officially retired from the sleuthing racket and quite content to live the life of a well-heeled Riley, Nick is unavoidably pulled into murder investigations by the vivacious Nora. With the help of their dog, a terrier named Asta, they solve case after case—but only on screen and on radio. Except for a few scripts, Hammett went on to write books about The Continental Op, Spade, and others, leaving the Charleses to make money for him in other media.

NBC radio brought Nick and Nora to radio in the early forties with Les Damon and Claudia Morgan. It was not until 1957 that *The Thin Man* made it to TV. It began on NBC September 20 and stayed there for three years and over 70 half-hour episodes. Taking the role of Nora, ably enacted by Myrna Loy in the movies, was the attractive actress Phyllis Kirk. Peter Lawford, who was certainly no William Powell—the movies' Nick did exhibit some panache in the role.

If the TV series had had to live up to the 1934 movie, it would have been hard. But thankfully, the original *Thin Man* had already been followed by five sequels, each entertaining, and each a little worse than its predecessor. By the time Lawford and Kirk assumed the roles, they did not have that much to live up to. Still, the show was fast, easy on the mind, and enjoyable to watch. Not much mystery could be worked up in 30 minutes, but within the rudimentary plots, the two stars interacted well enough to sustain the show for three years.

M Squad provided a different kind of fun. It could be found on NBC just one half hour earlier than *The Thin Man*. It, too, started on September 20, 1957, and lasted a year longer. It provided the kind of fun viewers could have watching a rip-snorting, action-packed police melodrama of the meanest kind.

The show was about an elite group of Chicago police officers who roamed the city as avengers, righting wrongs where they found them—about as subtly as napalm. The series spotlighted Lieutenant Frank Ballinger, played by Lee Marvin. Although he was considered a good if not especially versatile movie actor, *M Squad* showed millions of new fans just how dangerously effective Lee Marvin could be.

The "M" in *M Squad* stood for "Murder," but it also could have stood for "a mixture of mixed-up madmen marauding in mayhem" the way the program concentrated on violence and maniacal killers. Audiences could not feel much sympathy when Ballinger showed up to blast the criminals, for example, a swine who would kidnap a debutante and leave her bound and gagged in the cellar of a building set for demolition.

The program was helped enormously by on-location filming and tight scriptwriting that often combined action with realistic police procedure. It was fun

In the film footsteps of William Powell and Myrna Loy came Peter Lawford and Phyllis Kirk as Nick and Nora Charles (along with their pet, "Asta") in **The Thin Man.** *(NBC)*

to watch Marvin strain at the limits of the rule book while chomping at the bit of heroics. In the same episode in which the debutante is held captive writhing in the basement, the Chicago lab pinpoints her location by analyzing the dirt on the dead kidnapper's shoes. Ballinger arrives just in time to carry the girl out while the place comes down around them.

It was just this sort of breathless adventure that kept *M Squad* eagerly watched in the form of syndicated rebroadcasts beyond the four years it was produced. Marvin had the right idea when he termed the *M Squad* "Chicago's SS," and he played Ballinger like a "noble" storm trooper, gun in hand, and finger tightening on the trigger.

In spite of his hard-hitting performances, Marvin's reputation remained that of a troublemaker. "I change bad scripts," he said in an interview, explaining why he seemed to be giving *M Squad*'s producers a hard time. "Thinking is a cardinal sin," he continued, sarcastically detailing the Hollywood producer's attitude toward actors. He went on to explain the acting method that made him famous: "If you do your cliché well, you'll kill them. They will be dumfounded with its greatness."

Marvin's series was not 1957's only highlight. Mystery fans could also rally around Richard Diamond, a smooth gem in comparison with *M Squad*'s diamond in the rough. The role of Diamond was created especially for Dick Powell, who began his film career as a song-and-dance man and then went on to become a fine dramatic actor and noted TV producer. Powell made one of his greatest impressions as Philip Marlowe, the famous detective creation of Raymond Chandler, in *Murder My Sweet*, a 1944

film adaptation of the 1940 novel *Farewell My Lovely*. As mentioned earlier, Powell played Marlowe in the TV version of *The Long Goodbye*.

Powell had hired writer Blake Edwards to come up with a few creations that would serve Powell's company, Four Star Productions. One of the several commercial projects Edwards devised for him was *Richard Diamond, Private Detective*. The show started on radio in 1949 and was unique in that it was one of the first serials created specifically for that medium.

Powell played Diamond and Ed Begley Lieutenant Levinson, the private eye's inner-police contact. By the mid-fifties Powell was ready to put Diamond on the tube. By then, the producer himself was in his mid-fifties and he wanted a younger man to embody the flip, capable character.

A young man named David Meyer was the 25th actor Powell auditioned. His experience consisted of some very unimpressive films like *Yankee Buccaneer* (1952) and *Toy Tiger* (1956). But Powell liked him. "He has masculinity with a good comic sense," Powell said about him. Meyer then changed his name to something more acceptable to the Hollywood crowd; he became David Janssen.

David Janssen made Richard Diamond and vice versa. Without the actor's stylish ability to look weary and energetic at the same time, it is doubtful that the show would have been as fun to watch. And without Powell's production ability and Edwards' creative spark, it is doubtful that Janssen's career would have taken off so well.

The well-crafted show premiered initially as a summer replacement for *De-*

cember Bride (1954). Richard Diamond was an ex-cop with a good reputation who went to work as a New York private eye. The reaction was favorable enough to put the program on CBS's regular season schedule, taking up the Monday berth previously held by Harbourmaster. From there on, Richard Diamond only improved.

For a season or so, Diamond trekked about New York, having only crusty Lieutenant McGough, played by veteran character actor Regis Toomey, as a helper. Then, to add new spark to the concept, Diamond's offices were moved to Hollywood, California, leaving McGough behind, but adding some telling characters and gimmicks.

On the West Coast, Diamond's police force contact was Lieutenant Kile, played by a less crusty Russ Conway. To accommodate the highway-oriented lifestyle of Los Angeles, Diamond was supplied a snappy convertible, which he occasionally used to give his girlfriend, Karen Wells, a ride. Barbara Bain played Wells with the same cool professionalism she would come to be admired for later in her career. But the Wells character was not the female who captured audiences' imaginations; rather it was the girl who manned Diamond's answering service. Sam, who was never seen, was known for her sultry voice, shapely legs, and—in just a few rare cases—her curvaceous silhouette. Sam was a truly beloved, truly important fixture on the show and contributed to its success as much as the mystery and action pumped into the plots.

While Janssen would perform in episodes like "Short Haul," about the trucking industry, and "Marineland and Mystery," about an undersea box containing

a corpse, audiences would wait for and delight in Sam's "appearances"— whether she was cooing over runs in her stockings or warning Diamond, by car phone, in the nick of time. Surprisingly, for such an important character, the actress who played Sam was given the short end of the stick.

That actress was Mary Tyler Moore, now famous for her comedy and dramatic roles. But at the time, her part as Sam could not even help her make ends meet. Although it was a step up from portraying Happy Hotpoint, a singing advertising character on the Ozzie and Harriet show, she was only paid $80 a Diamond episode. Moore left the show in 1959, making her final appearance on May 17. Roxanne Brooks took over the part for the one year Richard Diamond remained on the air.

The series jumped networks, moving from CBS to NBC. Afterwards the show was syndicated as Call Mr. D., giving it a few more years of screen life. Janssen was off and running without it, however, appearing in higher quality movies than the fodder he had done previously. In 1963, he proved that TV lightning can strike twice by starring in the series that brought him the most fame, The Fugitive (1963).

Undoubtedly the 1957 season will be especially remembered for the longest running, most influential, most entertaining, and most popular judicial series ever made, Perry Mason.

It was the lawyer show to end all lawyer shows. Nearly a quarter century of literary and movie fame had preceded the character's introduction to television. Perry Mason made his debut in 1933 in

The Case of the Velvet Claws, written by athlete, salesman, sportsman, researcher, magazine contributor of fiction and non-fiction, and lawyer Erle Stanley Gardner. Gardner was a hell of a man, as rich in personality and energy as the character he created. In this story, Mason never even showed up in court; he relied on his detective know-how to solve the case even before it came to trial.

Gardner's first-hand knowledge of jurisprudence, combined with his love of a good solid story, made the Mason series of novels a huge success. Even before Mason made it to TV, 51 Gardner novels about the character were released to an ever-growing audience. The first motion picture based on Perry's cases was *The Case of the Howling Dog* (1934), produced by Warner Brothers. In this film, as in five subsequent feature films, the Mason role was played by a slick leading man like Warren William, Ricardo Cortez, and Donald Woods. None of these men seemed to have the depth of character or acting skill necessary to give Mason life and fire.

The same could be said of the Mason radio show, which started in 1943 on CBS. Interestingly, the format was that of a soap-opera serial, presenting five days a week as much melodrama as mystery. Showing considerable business and creative savvy, Gardner separated the melodramatic soap opera from the detective mystery in the mid-fifties. In 1956 he brought the Perry Mason radio cast, the crew, and the soap-opera format to television in a series that can still be seen on TV, *The Edge of Night*.

A year later, Gardner returned the Mason character to the hard-hitting hero he had been in the books and set *Perry Mason* to premiere September 21 on CBS

TV. Although the likes of Art Seid, Sam White, and Ben Brady were the show's producers over the years, Gardner still had script approval and was the series "godfather" for its entire run. Undoubtedly, he had some influence in choosing who would play Mason.

In retrospect, Raymond Burr was the perfect choice, but at the time the various network and studio executives must have been aghast that the Mason role was not to be played by a handsome leading man. In fact, in many of the films Burr appeared in before taking on Perry Mason, he embodied villains beautifully. He was a creepy hood in the last Marx Brothers movie *Love Happy* (1950), a brutish murder victim in *The Blue Gardenia* (1953), and a psychotic murderer in *Rear Window* (1954).

His hulking form and prominent brow made him a fine bad guy, but his famous portrayal of reporter Steve Martin under trying circumstances (both on screen and behind the scenes) in *Godzilla* (1955) and his performance as fiery district attorney in *A Place in the Sun* (1951) may have helped him win the Mason role.

Whatever the reason, Burr got the part and did not let go for the full decade the show was on the air. He made the Mason character and the TV series unswervingly his. It was a showcase for his power as a performer. Gardner and Burr were kindred spirits; both were workaholics. Their combined chemistry took possible lead and turned it into television gold.

Mason is described in the novels as a big man with broad shoulders, piercing eyes, a rugged face, thick hair, and possessing an excellent speaking voice. Given this, the choice of Burr was impeccable. The principal characters remained the same in television. Mason's

The great Raymond Burr as the great Perry Mason, seated in his office listening intently to his solid private investigator, Paul Drake (William Hopper). This same scene, and the subsequent courtroom showdowns, would be replayed many times over a decade. (CBS)

loyal secretary, Della Street, was played by Barbara Hale. The man who did some of Mason's investigative work was private detective Paul Drake, played by William Hopper, the son of famous Hollywood personality Hedda Hopper.

The man who proves to be Mason's biggest courtroom adversary, District Attorney Hamilton Burger, was played by dour looking William Talman, a character actor who looked older than his years. The man who arrested many of the people Burger prosecuted and Mason saved was L.A.P.D. Lieutenant Arthur Tragg, played by Ray Collins, an acting veteran of 54 years.

Throughout the long run of the TV shows, Gardner continued to produce novel after Mason novel, the two enter-

tainment forms sharing an audience. With every episode the books became more popular and with every book the series gained new viewers.

The shows usually involved a murder. We would learn something about the victim, the suspects, and possible motives. An "airtight" case would be established against the innocent party by Tragg and Burger. The poor suspect would run to Mason for help. Then the fun really started. Perry and Paul would investigate, interview, and confront various other characters until the case came to trial.

And that scene in the courtroom was what viewers all over the world waited for: the wildly enjoyable histrionics that occurred week after week. One of the most satisfying scenes played out again and again had Paul Drake come running in at the last moment with new evidence or a surprise witness. If the latter, Mason would call the hapless witness to the stand and he would verbally slap, batter, and bash that person until the truth came out. Invariably, the killer or accomplice would break down and confess. "Yes, yes, I did it . . . but I didn't mean to kill him!" "All right, all right, I admit it!" "What are you sitting there for? Tell them! Tell them the truth!"

It made no difference if the solution did not make sense or was impossible to follow. As long as Mason sounded convincing and the perpetrator admitted his or her culpability, the viewers swallowed anything. As a change of pace, Perry actually *lost* a case during the 1963 season, but it was because the client was covering for someone else and allowed herself to be found guilty. Perry discovered the true villain anyway and got the stubborn victim out of jail.

Although very little seemed to change over the years, things were constantly bubbling behind the scenes. Burr became obsessed with his work and his salary continued to climb until he was the highest-paid actor on TV. Directors and writers came and went, with Gail Patrick Jackson and Arthur Marks handling the executive producers' chores.

Some new characters were introduced. Connie Cezon played Gertie Lade, Mason's receptionist. Paula Courtland played Margo, Paul Drake's secretary. Karl Heid and Wesley Lau played Gideon and Anderson, two of Perry's legal associates. When Ray Collins became too ill to continue his Lieutenant Tragg part (the actor died in 1965 at the age of 75), Richard Anderson was hired to play a much younger Lieutenant Steve Drumm.

William Talman remained as District Attorney Burger during the entire series run, but it was not an easy time for him. Financial obligations as well as disease and death in his family were some of the troubles that plagued him, until he himself was stricken with lung cancer. He died of the disease in 1968 but not before making an incredibly effective anti-cigarette commercial for the American Cancer Society.

Talman's death came two years after the demise of the *Perry Mason* series. After more than 270 individual episodes and 10 seasons on television, the company called it quits with a fitting denouement especially created by Gardner. The final program came on September 4, 1966, and was cleverly called "The Case of the Final Fade Out." In it, Perry had to defend a TV star accused of murdering his producer in order to gain ownership of his own series.

This final show was a family affair in that the line producer had a bit part, the stage hands made up a crowd scene, and the presiding judge of the last courtroom battle was played by none other than Erle Stanley Gardner himself.

Even though the series was canceled, new books about the lawyer continued to appear at least once a year until Gardner's death in 1970. And three stories and two novels were published posthumously. More than 80 novels in all detailed the unbeatable barrister's career.

Gardner's work was not limited to that of creating Perry Mason stories. In 1948 he founded the Court of Last Resort, an organization pledged to free those wrongly imprisoned. Gardner wrote a book about the work of the Court that won the Mystery Writers of America's highest award, the Edgar, for the best nonfiction book published in 1952.

In 1957 Gardner's nonfiction became the weekly fiction of *The Court of Last Resort*, which was televised on NBC. Elliott Lewis and Jules Goldstone produced these half-hour adventures in which lawyers and criminologists, played by actors, attempted to free framed victims of the judicial system.

Paul Birch, a character actor who had co-starred in *War of the Worlds* (1952), played Erle Stanley Gardner with the dependable Charles Meredith and Robert Harris playing Dr. LeMoyne Snyder and Raymond Shindler. Lyle Bettger portrayed the entirely fictional Sam Larsen, the "hero" who worked with the seven-member Court of Last Resort as a special investigator. During more than 35 episodes the group toiled to exonerate the innocent and condemn the guilty. Later these episodes were rerun on the ABC network.

Because Perry Mason's fame was so great and the viewers so consistently watched the syndicated repeats, CBS took a gamble that it was the series' structure that people loved and produced *The New Adventures of Perry Mason* in 1973.

While everything had combined to create a hit in 1957—the burly Raymond Burr; the memorable, oppressive music score by Fred Steiner and Richard Shores; the effective direction of such pros as Ted Post, Richard Donner, and Andrew McLaglen—everything added up to failure in 1973. Monte Markham, a personable, serviceable TV actor who had long been a star in search of a TV series (he had previously failed with *The Second Hundred Years* (1967) and *Mr. Deeds Goes to Town* (1968) was definitely no Raymond Burr.

The same was true of the rest of the cast. Sharon Acker was Della Street,

Harry Guardino was Hamilton Burger, Albert Stratton was Paul Drake, Dane Clark played Lieutenant Tragg, and Brett Somers was given the expanded part of receptionist Gertie Lade. Although these actors had done fine work before, they were being thrown to the wolves in terms of this show. No one had forgotten Burr in a mere seven years, especially when the actor was alive and well doing a popular new series called *Ironside* (1967) and the original *Perry Mason* series was still being rerun in many parts of the country . . . not to mention the world.

The New Adventures . . . was off the air by February 1974, leaving the original to maintain Gardner's reputation. This was a rare case in which television served to enhance a character, not destroy it or rip it off.

1958

As long as you packed a gun— any kind of gun—1958 was your year. This gunplay was not reserved for the TV detective only. The really big winners during the late fifties were western adventures. By 1958 westerns were practically monopolizing the top-ten Nielsen ratings. *Gunsmoke* was America's most watched program, with *Wagon Train* (1957), *Have Gun, Will Travel* (1957), *Bat Masterson* (1957), *Cheyenne* (1957), *Maverick* (1957), *The Rifleman* (1958), and *Rawhide* (1958) not far behind.

Meanwhile, enterprising producers were trying to do what CBS had not done: rip off Erle Stanley Gardner. With the success of *Perry Mason*, it was open season on lawyers. Producers were discovering that the network door for legal series that had been closed before was now wide open.

Law shows that were obviously derivative of both Mason and *Dragnet* proliferated: the "courtroom reenactments" of already-tried criminal cases. It had started, basically, with *Divorce Court* in 1957. Viewers derived plenty of perverse satisfaction by watching once-happy newlyweds go at each other over the objections of noble, well-paid lawyers.

Not long afterwards came ABC's *Traffic Court*, one of the least notable summer replacement series of all time. What pleasure audiences got from seeing speeders, drunken drivers, and double-parkers get hauled in for their just desserts is beyond comprehension. Still, television occasionally gave the format new life. From 1958 to 1965 viewers saw such wonders as *Juvenile Court* (not to be confused with the family-oriented *Juvenile Jury*), *Night Court*, and even *Small Claims Court*.

Thankfully, three other courtroom reenactments of 1958 had loftier motives than these time-fillers.

Accused was a spinoff of the popular daytime *Day in Court*. Here, real judges— most often the Right Honorable Edgar Allan Jones, Jr.— and real lawyers would preside over real actors acting out real cases under the watchful eye of producer Selig J. Seligman, former lawyer and then vice president of ABC-TV. The evening version was taken off the air after one year while the daytime version remained until 1965.

The Grand Jury, a syndicated one-season show, took pretentiousness to new heights. Before each episode an announcer intoned: "The forework of liberty, protecting the inalienable rights of free people, serving unstintingly and without prejudice to maintain the laws of our land . . . the Grand Jury."

And what a grand Grand Jury it was. Lyle Bettger went from working with the *Court of Last Resort* the previous year to star as ex-FBI agent Harry Driscoll here, now teamed up with Harold J. Stone as his partner John Kennedy.

Finally, there was *The Verdict Is Yours*, a gimmick show remarkably similar to *Day in Court*. *The Verdict* . . . was also a successful daytime program as well as a short-lived nighttime effort. Both shows dramatized real court cases utilizing real lawyers and judges. The difference was that the studio audience served as the jury and could declare verdicts that might differ from the actual one. Jim McKay, later to become the most recognized and respected voice of *ABC Sports*, served as court reporter, which in this case meant host/narrator.

One 1958 dramatization took viewers out of the courthouse and into the realm of spies: NBC's half-hour *Behind Closed Doors*. Although noble in intent and execution, the program was pretty much crippled by lack of audience interest. First, it was just one in a long line of shows which dramatized the actual files of something or other. And given that in this case they were the files of Naval Intelligence veteran Rear Admiral Ellis M. Zacharias, not much interest could be garnered.

All Zacharias's files concerned the Cold War, which left it up to the writers to infuse the series with the kind of suspense that would keep people watching. They were all up to the challenge—*TV Guide* called the shows "good strong stuff"—but the watchers were not. The program lasted 26 weeks, with Bruce Gordon playing the fictitious Commander Matson, who hosted, narrated, and sometimes acted in the episodes.

Newspapermen had their moments this season. That special breed of busy-body was transformed by television into noble crime fighters more interested in the truth than a raise. This year they took a photographer—otherwise known as a photojournalist—and turned him into a rough-hewn, crime-busting demon.

Man With a Camera was produced for ABC by Warren Lewis, Don Sharpe, and A. E. Houghton. It told of the exploits of Mike Kovac, an ex-combat photographer in World War II, now a lens-toting mercenary. Most of the cases Kovac dealt with were of a criminal nature, allowing him to click away at dead bodies, shoot at live ones, and have some brittle banter with Lieutenant Donovan of the N.Y.P.D., played by James Flavin.

Kovac was played by the roughest of the rough-looking character actors then around. He originally came to Holly-wood with the name Charles Buchinski and had parts in films like *House of Wax* (1953) and *Machine Gun Kelly* (1957). Later he guest-starred in TV's *Gunsmoke* and *Richard Diamond*, among others. *Man With a Camera* showed he could play more than the coarse, violent heavy and his new name— Charles Bronson— is now well known to movie and TV audiences.

Actors Lonny Chapman and Howard St. John were not so lucky. They had the misfortune to be involved with a defi-nitely minor 1958 summer replacement series called *The Investigator*. The two men portrayed father and son, Chapman playing Jeff Prior a private eye, and St. John his retired newspaperman dad Lloyd Prior. The 13-week series was set in the thirties, with Jeff collecting the clues and Lloyd helping his offspring put them together.

The Priors did a far better job solving crimes than the production staff did put-ting the show together. Surprisingly, *The Investigator* was done live, and hurriedly at that. "The singular mystery," said one review, "is how it got on the air in the first place! Incredibly ill-conceived, it is performed with all the talent of Miss Budgkin's Summer Drama School for Girls. It's a live show with mass line fumbling."

And that review was nice compared to the others. *The Investigator* did its time but was not asked back by NBC—or anyone else, for that matter.

After this, almost any other detective show had to be an improvement. And even though *U.S. Border Patrol* was a rather obvious copy of *Highway Patrol* in all ways, it was more watchable than the Lonny Chapman travesty, though not as funny. Richard Webb starred as Deputy Chief Don Jagger of the U.S. Border Patrol.

Working in conjunction with federal agents to prevent an influx of illegal aliens into this country, Jagger did his thing for one syndicated season of 39 episodes that were billed as "thrilling sagas of the brave and daring work of the men who guard the United States borders by land . . . by sea . . . by air!" The shows had all the interest of those Navy com-mercials which take the most mundane maneuvers and by editing and scoring make them exciting. *U.S. Border Patrol* lacked the disco beat and riveting film work, so the overall effect was far less impressive.

Far more impressive were the rest of the detective shows that premiered in 1958. Of the five new efforts, three turned out to be classics of the genre, while the remaining pair were entertaining. The least memorable, or at least the series many critics would like to forget, *Mike Hammer*, was based on Mickey Spillane's notorious fictional character.

"It could be the worst show on TV," said one aghast reviewer about the half-hour NBC series. "It abounds in murder, torture, sadism, and assorted vice." Now, while this sounds like and was meant to be an outright condemnation of the program, it actually serves to commend the show's producers for a job well done. Given the Mike Hammer novels' subject matter, the translation from the page to the screen was remarkably accurate.

In 1947 Frank Morrison Spillane, a writer for pulp magazines and comic books, had his first book, *I, the Jury*, published under the name Mickey Spillane. It was an instant sensation. Critics were horrified and derisive yet the public bought copies with a fervor rarely experienced in the book business.

Spillane's hero was a tough, brutal, uncompromising private eye, and the finale of *I, the Jury* illustrates this effectively: the murderess, a glorious blonde, rises naked from her bath in an attempt to dissuade Hammer from vengeance. As she puts her arms around him, he puts his gun in her stomach and pulls the trigger.

Stunned, her life blood draining away, she asks, "How could you?"

"It was easy," he answers.

This was the moment all the other Hammer books, movies, and the TV series tried to live up to. And they did not quite make it. Spillane had been careful not to fully describe Mike in any of the novels so the readers could visualize their own hero. Filmmakers managed to cast lackluster actors in the Hammer role until Ralph Meeker was chosen for *Kiss Me Deadly* (1955), which was based on

the 1952 novel. Director/producer Robert Aldrich tried to achieve the cinematic equivalent of the novels and a *film noir* approach was the result.

The television series, *Mike Hammer, Detective*, had Darren McGavin in the role of the quintessential tough. McGavin was experienced and capable while the show was as gritty and nasty as could be. The highlight of the series' two-season run was an episode in which Mike's bride-to-be was murdered. Hammer went on a 20-minute trail of vengeance worthy of his literary counterpart. Before the end credits rolled, accompanied by the soulful theme music of David Kahn, Mike had hung a man out the window of a skyscraper, smashed a man's head between a door and a wall, and literally rammed a mustard container up a guy's nose.

McGavin's fatal flaw was that he was a little too good for the material. No matter how tough he played the part, he could not help being three dimensional, and thereby a bit vulnerable and sympathetic. This was not the Hammer readers had come to know and love/hate. And the series' fatal flaw was in trying to give reality to what was essentially a macho fantasy.

On the other hand, *Naked City* was trying to give reality reality.

"There are eight million stories in the naked city. This is just one of them." That line, though not as famous as Joe Friday's "Just the facts, ma'am," still has its place in the TV detective hall of fame. It was the closing line of producer/writer Mark Hellinger's movie and the opening line of the long-running ABC-TV series. In the film, Barry Fitzgerald starred with Howard Duff as two New York City cops investigating the murder of a young girl only to stumble across a jewel theft ring. But the real star of the movie turned out to be Manhattan, which took on a personality all its own under Jules Dassin's semi-documentary style of direction.

The same was true of the television show, one of the first to feature extensive on-location work. In the beginning it seemed as if the producers were going the regular cops-and-robbers shoot-'em-up-route. Starting as a 30-minute show, *Naked City* had John McIntire as Detective Lieutenant Dan Muldoon, the experienced old police pro, and James Franciscus as Detective Jim Halloran, his young, handsome, blond-haired, and green assistant.

The city added character and grit, but filming in the streets had its own hazards. There were many instances of New Yorkers not cooperating. Their interruptions ranged from staring at the camera and waving to pelting the crew with rotten eggs.

Initially the scripts were not first-rate: the formula was to introduce a cackling killer in the first ten minutes, chase him for the next ten, and kill him during a raucous shoot-out in the last ten. Not surprisingly, most critics reviewed *Naked City* in the negative. "It's disappointing for many reasons," said *TV Guide*. "There are too many close-ups. The supporting players are all dull and lifeless. And all the crooks are portrayed as psychopaths." It would be safe to say that *Naked City* did not get off to a promising start.

That all changed March 17, 1959. The show needed a face-lift, and the producers did it the hard way. On this particular Tuesday night episode, Lieutenant Muldoon was participating in a car chase with an associate, Sergeant Frank Arcaro,

played by Harry Bellaver. To the shocked surprise of the viewers, the police car rammed right into a gasoline truck and both blew sky high. Incredibly, Arcaro survived, but Muldoon did not. This realistic ploy worked. From then on, there was renewed interest in the flagging series.

In came Horace MacMahon as Lieutenant Mike Parker, Muldoon's replacement. MacMahon was an excellent choice, for he embodied the nature of a grizzled, tough, yet understanding New York cop. The Parker role was basically an extension of the Monaghan role he had in the 1951 movie production of the award-winning play *Detective Story*.

Franciscus and Bellaver were bent on vengeance for the rest of the season, tempered by MacMahon's wisdom. *Naked City* left ABC at the end of the season and was replaced by *Philip Marlowe*, a series that will be examined later.

But in 1960, *Naked City* was back on the New York streets, sporting new characters and new quality. The program was now an hour-long Wednesday night fixture starring MacMahon, Bellaver, and Paul Burke as Detective Adam Flint, a darker, more intense character than that of Franciscus.

With them came a crew of writers and directors intent on mirroring the excellence of the movie the series was based on. Among the talents working toward this goal were such notable directors as Arthur Hiller, Stuart Rosenberg, and Lamont Johnson. According to critic Jack Nolan, the *Naked City* episodes produced between October 1960 and June 1963 "were among the quietest, most literate hours ever written for TV!"

As with many other fine TV productions, it is not always literacy that gets the

Lloyd Bridges, as he appeared in his huge TV hit Sea Hunt.

most reruns or is the best remembered. It is often the faddish, the sophisticated, and the fun series that are clamored for. There was one of each in 1958.

Sea Hunt turned out to be the faddish effort. It was one of the last series made by Ziv Productions and it made Lloyd Bridges' star ascend almost overnight. Ziv was the brainchild of Frederick W. Ziv and under his aegis made *Highway Patrol,* the most successful independently produced action-adventure series bought by the networks. Next to *Highway Patrol, Sea Hunt* brought in the most money before Ziv sold the company for over $20 million in 1960.

Viewers at that time may have remembered Bridges for his solid work in movies like *Here Comes Mr. Jordan* (1941), *High Noon* (1952), and *The Rainmaker* (1956). Bridges was not famous but was a capable actor relegated to B-movies. *Sea Hunt* changed all that.

By the time its 155 episodes had finished their first run in 1961, Bridges was a household name. And as those programs were successively rerun, underwater troubleshooter Mike Nelson impressed a whole new generation of fans.

Ivan Tors produced the series, filmed mostly in Florida at Silver Springs and Marineland. In every show, Mike Nelson would be hired or get involved with an adventure which would require him to strap on tanks, strip down to a bathing suit, and ram a regulator in his mouth. *Sea Hunt* opened up the wonderful underwater world to viewers and they were suitably grateful. Such a role would criminally typecast a lesser talent, but Bridges later managed to keep working in films and on television minus his face mask and flippers.

The sophistication for 1958 came from the fertile mind of Blake Edwards, who had graduated from creating *Richard*

Diamond for Dick Powell to create *Peter Gunn* for himself. *Gunn* was a fascinating show for several reasons. No one seemed sure what the series was intended to be—either a program about a hard-boiled detective or a program about a suave, intelligent detective.

The concept and opening seemed to lean in the hard-boiled direction. Peter Gunn was a Los Angeles private detective who lived at 351 Ellis Park Road but spent most of his time at a waterfront jazz nightspot called Mother's run by a character called Mother (Hope Emerson). She looked like—you guessed it—a mother. One of the club's singers was a sexy but good-hearted gal named Edie Hart (Lola Albright) who monopolized Gunn's time when he was not tracking down criminals (and sometimes when he was). Gunn's L.A.P.D. contact was the gruff but beneficent Lieutenant Jacoby (Herschel Bernardi). The background was established after the exciting, brilliant opening theme music written by Henry Mancini.

After all that, Edwards was not sure just what kind of hero to place within the framework. After a lot of auditioning, Edwards settled upon Craig Stevens, then a 40-year-old actor who had not been lighting up the screen with his performances. In fact, his last role before getting Gunn was in *Abbott and Costello Meet Dr. Jekyll and Mr. Hyde* (1955). Edwards demanded Stevens cut his hair to near crew-cut length, outfitted him with a snappy wardrobe and a snub-nosed revolver, then set the series loose on NBC. Even after Stevens began proving himself in the part, the producer had his doubts.

"We've done 20 episodes and I'm still not sure," Edwards said at the time. Whether he was not sure about Stevens' ability or the combination of hard-hitting action and clever banter is a moot point. *Peter Gunn*'s very quirkiness added to its watchability. Directors Jay Gordon and Lamont Johnson made the series known as much for its elaborate camera angles as for its thrilling plots.

This odd combination of styles worked well for the series, which produced several best-selling records for Mancini based on the *Peter Gunn* themes. At the end of the 1960 season, the show switched to ABC, with Minerva Urecal playing Mother. The rest of the cast had become familiar and pleasant to watch. When Herschel Bernardi was hospitalized with a broken bone, Stevens saw to it that the Jacoby character was still included in the episode. (A double moved in front of a brick wall for establishing shots and Bernardi was filmed in close-up from his bed with a brick backdrop behind him.)

The series lasted only a season on ABC, but it was enough to get everyone off and running. Craig Stevens became a TV fixture as a guest star, did a few more series which proved less successful than *Peter Gunn*, and returned to the detective fold by co-starring with Jo Ann Pflug in a one-shot TV movie called *Nick and Nora* in 1975. Seymour Berns directed this videotaped revival of the *Thin Man* characters Nick and Nora Charles for ABC. In it, the happily married sleuths attempt to prove that a corpse found in the swimming pool of a Los Angeles hotel was actually murdered. The whole effort was less than engaging.

Blake Edwards, meanwhile, set the celluloid world afire with his subsequent feature films. After directing *Breakfast at Tiffany's* (1961), *Experiment in Terror* (1962), *Days of Wine and Roses* (1962), writing and directing *The Pink Panther* (1963), then writing, directing, and producing *The Great Race* (1964), the man hit a dry period. During this dry period Edwards produced and directed a feature-length version of the series that had established him.

Gunn was released in 1967 to a less than enthusiastic response. There was a bit of overkill involved in the movie's production, Edwards probably figuring that a large-screen translation of a small-screen triumph needed more violence to placate the crowds. The *New York Daily News* gave it two stars. New York-based critic Leonard Maltin gave it one and a half stars, saying, "Herschel Bernardi and Lola Albright are missing, and sorely missed, along with the wit that made the show memorable. The movie is a tasteless whodunit." The final irony was that when the film was shown on television, the ratings were not good. So perhaps it is best to remember *Peter Gunn* at its best—as a TV series.

The series that received the most acclaim was the "fun" show of the year, *77 Sunset Strip*. Warner Brothers, the makers of some of the most popular television westerns at that time, was looking to expand its base to other genres. They came up with *77 Sunset Strip*, which not only brought detective teamwork to new

*Hard times for Craig Stevens as **Peter Gunn** (NBC, ABC). Even harder times for the camera crew. Some of their shoes can be seen in the second mirror from the left. (courtesy of United Press International, Inc.)*

heights, but established the now cliché device of setting the action in a famous urban locale.

The detective agency, the locus of the action, was run by Stuart Bailey, an ex-OSS officer and Ph.D. graduate of an Ivy League school. His partner was Jeff Spencer, a former secret agent with a law degree. For such supposedly intelligent men, they used their fists and guns more often than they used their brains. Their office was located at 77 Sunset Strip, Hollywood, California.

Bailey was played by Efrem Zimbalist, Jr., the son of the famous violinist and the renowned soprano Alma Gluck. Spencer was played by Roger Smith, who had been coached in the ways of acting by Jimmy Cagney when they both worked in *Man of a Thousand Faces* (1957), the film biography of Lon Chaney. Their first case, and the series' pilot, was called "Girl on the Run" and featured a young, hair-combing killer played by Edward Breitenberger, later Edd Byrnes.

The greatest response was not to the new show or to the two stars, but to that hair-combing killer. When *77 Sunset Strip* went on as a regular hour-long Friday night feature on ABC, the two detectives had a restaurant called Dino's next door and that restaurant had a parking attendant who wanted to be a private eye. The parking attendant was named Gerald Lloyd Kookson, III, otherwise known as Kookie. And Kookie was played by none other than Edd Byrnes.

Bailey and Spencer may have been the cogs in the *77 Sunset Strip* machine, but Kookie was the grease that made the show work. While actors Zimbalist and Smith were featured every other week, Byrnes always seemed to be there no matter what, helping both men with their

cases. Kookie represented the hip teen-age world while the two private eyes were essentially straight arrows. Always combing his hair, Kookie was more apt to pull out a comb than a gun. It was not long before a record called "Kookie, Kookie, Lend Me Your Comb," recorded by Edd Byrnes and Connie Stevens, was a big hit.

Another Kookie mannerism that sat well with audiences was his use of colorful language. Kookie did not get sick, he got "buzzed by germsville," for which he did not take aspirin, but "headache grapplers." He did not think people were confused, he thought they had "smog in their noggin," for which he did not suggest they sleep, but that they "pile up the Z's."

It was the Kookie gimmick that got the program into the top ten and Edd Byrnes knew it. He was content to be the jack-of-all-episodes for awhile, but by the third season he wanted more. More money, more attention, more billing. Warner Brothers did not want to give it to him, so the actor walked out. The program's popularity plummeted enough to convince the producers to give Byrnes what he wanted, so they made Kookie a fully licensed and recognized private eye—a partner to Bailey and Spencer.

Robert Logan was hired to play J. R. Hale, the new parking man at Dino's, while other series regulars—Louis Quinn as Roscoe the racetrack tout, and Jacqueline Beer as Suzanne the sexy switchboard girl—clamored for atten-

---

"The Fonz," 77 Sunset Strip style. Edd Byrnes played "Kookie," the parking attendant cum private eye with the fastest comb in the West. (ABC)

tion. The show was getting so crowded that Zimbalist was quoted as saying, "Bob Logan has all the teen-agers crazy, Kookie is making inroads with the young married set, Roger Smith appeals to mature women, so I guess that leaves me with the grandmothers, derelicts, and nonwalking patients."

The humor in that statement masked some deep-down bitterness. The show, which had been doing well with its original concept, deteriorated once Kookie was promoted. He no longer had the zest and charm of an "innocent bystander." Now he was right in the middle of it, and things were not the same.

Warner Brothers figured that if one team of detectives in a readily identifiable locale worked, then a lot more would work, too. The studio began churning out 77 Sunset Strip clones. Things did not stop there, either. If one of the shows did not make it, but one of the characters seemed to ring audiences' chimes, that was all right. Just shove him into 77 Sunset Strip!

When Bourbon Street Beat, a 1959 show (to be discussed later) died, Warners made Rex Randolph, played by Richard Long, the fourth partner in 77 Sunset Strip.

The shuffling between shows got pretty ludicrous as time went on. Troy Donahue of both Surfside Six (1960) and Hawaiian Eye (1959) dropped in while Zimbalist guested on Hawaiian Eye, and people from Bourbon Street Beat went to Surfside Six and on and on. The height of these incestuous goings-on was achieved when the Sam character from Richard Diamond lent her legs for an episode of 77!

Things were getting too stupid and pedestrian and the series was paying for it with a diminishing audience. Finally Warners decided to do something, so they brought in Jack Webb to take over production of the series in its sixth season. He responded by eliminating everyone but Zimbalist and made Stuart Bailey an international operative. The studio spared no expense in its attempt to breathe new life into the program, but it was a lot like trying to turn Sam Spade into James Bond at the last minute.

Even though the plots and production values were greatly improved, viewers could not adjust to the change from whimsical, Hollywood-bound 77 Sunset Strip to Stu Bailey's globe-trotting efforts to maintain world equilibrium. The show was better than it had ever been before, but it was different, and people just did not want to watch. ABC TV kept showing 77 Sunset Strip until September 1964, but the last season was made up of reruns of the program in its original form.

1959

In the real world Fidel Castro became the premier of Cuba, ending a brutal civil war. On television Dobie Gillis and The Twilight Zone appeared while The Phil Silvers Show, a.k.a. You'll Never Get Rich, disappeared. In the realm of the TV detective, 77 Sunset Strip began to molt look-alike action series.

The most successful, in terms of critical acceptance, was the least seen because it was an NBC summer replacement for The Tennessee Ernie Ford Show. It had all the requisites for detective success—a handsome leading character; a young and eager assistant; a sexy female associate; and a clever jack-of-all-trades aide who worked outside the main office—all set in a recognizable locale.

In this case, the private detective agency was at *21 Beacon Street*, which, like *77 Sunset Strip*, served as the program's title. The handsome hero was Dennis Morgan, a former singer and movie lead, who played brilliant strategist Dennis Chase. The eager, able assistant was Brian Kelly, playing the similarly named Brian, a law student turned peeper. Lola, the sexy girl, was Joanna Barnes, who then went on to a career in films. The handyman Jim, played by James Maloney, was also a master impersonator.

Taking these stock types and making them and the show interesting was difficult, but the makers of *21 Beacon Street* managed to pull it off. "It's a how-to-do-it!" one reviewer happily bubbled. "The show is loaded with suspense, excitement, and imagination." All three ingredients were supplied by the scripts, which had David Chase using mind more than muscle to get his clients out of elaborate fixes.

But the series did not have what it took—be it an audience, network backing, or executive interest—to get a regular berth on the fall schedule. It was rerun once on ABC, then disappeared. ABC TV in the meantime was giving sanctuary to two other recognizable *77 Sunset Strip* spinoffs, *Bourbon Street Beat* and *Hawaiian Eye*.

Bourbon Street Beat—first seen Monday, October 5, 1959—had Andrew Duggan as Cal Calhoun, a lanky, blond private eye who made his headquarters in New Orleans. Joining him was Richard Long as partner Rex Randolph, the character later to be shuffled over to that address on Sunset Strip. That was not the only similarity: since no locale/team detective series could be complete without the up-and-coming youth who longed to be just like his detective idols, this show found handsome Van Williams for Kenny Madison, a snooper with a future.

When *Bourbon Street* bombed, Williams was also recycled, but not for an already existing series like Long, for one of his own.

The role of "the beautiful girl," in this case secretary Melody Lee Mercer, was played by Arlene Howell. Even though it seemed to be sticking to the successful formula of *77 Sunset Strip*, *Bourbon Street Beat* never gained the former show's popularity and was canceled after a season.

On October 7, *Hawaiian Eye*, premiered. Initially called *The Islander*, Warner Brothers planned it as a combination of *77 Sunset Strip*, *Adventures in Paradise* (1959) and *Maverick* (1957).

Robert Conrad, an actor who emerged from the ranks of stunt men, played Tom Lopaka—one half of the detective team—while Anthony Eisley, another newcomer, played Tracy Steele, the other half. Their female friend was Cricket Blake, a rather bubble-headed singer and amateur photographer played by the then-pert Connie Stevens. Their office was at the lush Hawaiian Village Hotel where Cricket sang with the Arthur Lyman Band.

Hawaiian actor Poncie Ponce, who played cabbie Kazuo Kim, was Kookie's counterpart in *Hawaiian Eye*. He seemed to be always wearing a crazy straw hat, strumming his ukelele, and making bad jokes. Whenever the detectives needed something or got in a spot, Kim had a relative with the specific talent necessary to help out.

The combination of action, sophomoric humor, and music seemed to do the trick since *Hawaiian Eye* matched its daddy, *77 Sunset Strip*, year for year until 1963 when the former was canceled and the latter went into reruns. Before its demise, however, new characters appeared in *Hawaiian Eye*. Grant Williams, the talented leading man of the science-fiction classic *The Incredible Shrinking Man* (1957), came on board in 1960 as Detective Greg MacKenzie. Troy Donahue showed up in 1962 as hotel social director Philip Barton after not making it at *77 Sunset Strip* or *Surfside Six*. And since the series had come under fire for having Kim as just the token Hawaiian, actors Mel Prestidge and Doug Mosam were added as helpers Quon and Monk. In the final season, Connie Stevens left the show, only to be replaced by Tina Cole in the new role of Sunny Day.

The stories on *Hawaiian Eye* were "nothing to write home about," according to one critic who then, as an afterthought, said, "Nicely mounted though." This was true of all the shows Warners and others made in the likeness of *77 Sunset Strip*. They have a very small place in TV history, as do most of the season's other detective shows. Originality was not 1959's strong suit.

Congressional Investigator proved, once again, that some people would do anything to ride on *Dragnet's* coattails. Dramatizations of the Congressional in-

vestigation files lasted for one syndicated season. Actors William Masters, Stephen Roberts, Edward Stroll, and Marion Collier took turns seeking out evidence for use in Congressional hearings. A show like this could have been popular during the Watergate era, but since it was only a few years since the Army's McCarthy hearings, the series had to tread a bit more carefully.

Not for Hire, another one-season syndicated effort, starred Ralph Meeker, filmdom's best Mike Hammer, as Sergeant Steve Dekker of the United States Army Criminal Investigations Division. At first glance, the series' concept seemed strikingly different, but in watching it, one discovered Dekker's port of call: Honolulu. Many viewers passed over it, thinking it was just more fun in the sun, a la *Hawaiian Eye*, while those who stayed to watch found Dekker's cases of desertion, black marketeering, and sabotage less enjoyable than *Hawaiian Eye's* affable adventure. Any way it was approached, *Not for Hire* was a mass turn-off.

Staccato, another series rife with good intentions, just did not pay off, either. The show starred John Cassavetes, an actor with theater and film experience known for his intensity and conviction. As originally conceived, the program would not be just common shoot-'em-up stuff but a story about a jazz pianist named Johnny Staccato who would jam with a bunch of musicians at Waldo's, a Greenwich Village club, when he was not getting involved in other people's lives.

Hollywood rebel John Cassavetes was lured into the Johnny Staccato series, but even his intense acting style failed to keep the show alive.

But things often change between the good intentions of a concept and the reality of doing a weekly series. As time passed, Cassavetes found his character called upon to do more and more private-eye stuff. Somewhere between September 1959, when it premiered, and March 1960, when it was canceled, *Staccato* was renamed *Johnny Staccato* and the character was officially considered a jazz pianist turned private eye.

But even that did not help things much. "Although earnestly performed," judged a reviewer, "the show suffers from a near-fatal similitude to *Peter Gunn*. Cassavetes seems to believe in what he's doing, though." "Near-fatal" soon became terminal and *Johnny Staccato* was no more.

As was the case with *Peter Gunn*, not to mention *77 Sunset Strip*, the soundtrack played on. The theme songs of these three shows took America by storm. The Sunset Strip show had a clever, finger-snapping theme by Mack David and Jerry Livingston, while *Staccato* had an effective score by Elmer Bernstein, who wrote the music for *The Magnificent Seven* (1960).

Henry Mancini, the composer of the *Peter Gunn* music, also penned another hit theme in 1959 for *Mr. Lucky*, a fondly remembered series based on the 1943 movie that starred Cary Grant. In the film, Grant was a professional gambler who originally intends to bilk a beautiful society girl, only to fall in love and go straight. Blake Edwards adapted and produced the television version with the help of co-producer Gordon Oliver and director Jack Arnold.

Together they whipped up an engaging mixture which, despite its cult following,

failed to last beyond one season on CBS. Handsome John Vivyan starred as Joe Adams, commonly known as Lucky or Mr. Lucky, the owner of a California Club called The Calico Cat. Then, in a card game, he won *The Fortuna*, a combination yacht, supper club, and gambling casino.

Anchoring the ship just outside the 12-mile limit, Mr. Lucky enlisted the aid of his clever sidekick Andamo in running the place and keeping the operation clean. Much of the program's charm derived from the interplay between Lucky and Andamo, played by Ross Martin as if it were an audition for his later, more famous role as Artemus Gordon in *The Wild Wild West*. Even in 1959, Martin was making extensive use of disguises and dialects to get his friends out of scrapes.

There was intrigue and danger almost everywhere Lucky turned and when the going really got tough, he could always expect to see Lieutenant Rovacs of the L.A.P.D. covering him. Tom Brown played Rovacs, while Jed Scott played the ship's maitre d' and Pippa Scott played Lucky's girl friend Maggie Shank. The big winner of the series, however, was Henry Mancini, who parlayed his score into two more big-selling albums—*Music from Mr. Lucky* and *Mr. Lucky Goes Latin*.

Also based on a famous movie was the series *Five Fingers*, but there the similarity to *Mr. Lucky* ends. Producers Herbert Swope, Jr., and Martin Manulis had the misfortune to be at the helm of a show that all but scuttled the successful film it was based on. The 1952 espionage film, directed by cinema great Joseph L. Mankiewicz, was based on L. C. Moyzich's book *Operation Cicero*. It starred James Mason as Cicero, the valet of a British ambassador to Turkey who sold secrets to Germans during World War II.

The 1959 series was directed by Gerald Mayer and Montgomery Pittman, as well as others, and was based on nearly nothing. David Hedison starred as Victor Sebastian, an undercover American agent during the Cold War. Using a theatrical agency as a cover, the spy traveled all over Europe in the company of Simone Genet, a fashion model played by the beautiful Luciana Paluzzi. The show's only connection to the movie was Sebastian's code name, Five Fingers. This unsuccessful attempt to capitalize on a fine film lasted only 16 episodes, less than a half year.

During the rest of the year there were more lawyers trying to be Perry Mason and more private eyes trying to be Peter Gunn. *Markham* tried to satisfy both detective and lawyer lovers. Ray Milland starred as Roy Markham, an independently wealthy attorney who got a private-eye license in order to stop crime before it came to the courtroom. But the way the show was played, it appeared that Markham was doing his private detecting simply because he was bored and wanted action.

"This is run-of-the-mill private eyeball stuff," said one critic. "The plots come out of a meat grinder." The meat grinder kept *Markham* rolling along in two different time spots on the network. The Welsh-born actor had an illustrious film career and received an Academy Award for his performance in *The Lost Weekend* (1945). After *Markham* he starred in *Premature Burial* (1962), *Panic in the Year Zero* (1962), and *The Man*

with the X-ray Eyes (1963)—all went on to become minor cult favorites.

Macdonald Carey also came from film to TV, although his film work was not as notable as Milland's.

For two seasons and 78 syndicated episodes, Carey played real-life Philadelphia lawyer Herbert L. Maris, a champion of the underdog. The show about Maris's exploits was called *Lock Up* and it was created specifically for Carey after the cancellation of his prior syndicated show, *Dr. Christian* (1956).

Some critics found the show a breath of fresh air among the copycat dramas that were on the air. "It's nice to see a hero who isn't a pretty boy or a muscleman," said one critic. While that assessment might not have done much for Macdonald Carey's ego, it was good for the series and led to the actor's long-running leading role on NBC's soap opera *Days of Our Lives* (1965).

The D.A.'s Man, a little-known Jack Webb production—and for good reason—also wanted to have the best of both worlds: a little court action and a lot of private-eye action. So they created Shannon, a rock-hard private detective, played by John Compton, who was recruited by the New York district attorney's office to be their decoy, investigator, and all-around pigeon.

Webb had Compton do what he has had almost all his actors do before and since: say their lines in a veritable monotone. Unfortunately, not many actors have the inner energy Webb himself seems to possess, so they come across as lifeless. Such was Compton's fate. The critics were fairly unmerciful to him and the show, which fought its way through 26 episodes and one season.

Perhaps to make up for the lack of action in Shannon's character, Webb loaded the series with fights and shoot-outs. The number and intensity of the fights was so high that reviewers could not help but point it out—even with the likes of *Richard Diamond* and *Mike Hammer* still on the air. "It's larded with pointless violence and timeworn dialogue," said *TV Guide*.

This was not the only show cited for overdone nastiness. Producers Clarence Greene and Russell Rouse had their wrists slapped by viewers and worried executives for mounting the *Tightrope* series. It was of a kind with *The D.A.'s Man*, given that the lead was an under-cover operative. Only this spy worked for the cops instead of the court.

Having the simple name Nick in the lead role must have been a blessing for *Tightrope*'s star, who was born with an Armenian name, Krekor Ohanian. When he first came to Hollywood he changed it to Touch Connors and appeared in movies like *Sudden Fear* (1952). But by the time he was given the lead in *Tightrope*, he was was known as Mike Connors. And the series was known for its comic strip-like excesses. In some quarters it is believed that this overkill is what endeared the show to its audience.

"It's good far-fetched fun," declared one review, while another said, "It's loaded with stock situations and the dialogue could be out of Raymond Chandler by way of Jack Webb with inroads to *Peter Gunn*." Actually, there was not that much dialog to work with. At its best, the series was like a full 15-chapter action serial condensed into 30 minutes. It did not really have to make sense, it just had to move. And move it did, *very* quickly.

In the operative's effort to infiltrate and eradicate organized crime, he was aided by his nifty holster which held his snub-nosed revolver in the small of his back, so if villains frisked him they would not find it. Imagine their surprise when he went to scratch his back and whipped the gun out. The "tightrope" of the title signified the balancing act he had to do to convince the bad guys he was just as bad as them without getting killed by the police.

By the middle of the first season, the series was known for "killing, plus," and parents were getting worried. Senator Estes Kefauver had called for a Congressional hearing into TV violence in 1954 when the special-interest antiviolence groups came into flower. By 1959 their influence was felt. *Tightrope*, a brainless but entertaining action show, fell victim to pressure. Even though it was in the top 20, it was canceled at the end of the season.

One CBS insider attributed its demise to "network politics and the station's overall plans." When pressed for those overall plans, the man admitted to an attempt to tone down violence, brainless or not. ABC also saw the handwriting on the wall and took what could have been the best of all the hard-boiled detective shows and turned it into pablum.

Philip Marlowe was a series whose time had come. The character's fame had been established in books and films starting in 1939. Raymond Chandler, the slight, sensitive Chicago-born writer of great detective fiction, published *The Big Sleep* that year. The hero of that work, Philip Marlowe, became one of the greatest private-eye characters ever.

The *Philip Marlowe* television series

failed at being as memorable as the books or the many films based on the character, so it lasted only six months.

Marlowe's character traits of being tough and slightly bitter were all but eliminated—aced out by the weariness that had all but taken over his TV personality. Actor Philip Carey was a good choice to play the hero; he was rugged and could be sardonic when the script called for it.

This Man Dawson, a mediocre syndicated police series, tried to attract attention with its odd title. Otherwise it was a lightweight half-hour show about Frank Dawson, an unnamed city's police chief. It starred actor Keith Andes, who had worked in films since 1947 and guested on TV series since 1955. *This Man Dawson* kept Andes away from auditions for only 39 weeks. After its cancellation he returned to bit television and film roles, coming back as a series regular in 1963 for the comedy *Glynis*.

Many of the 1959 detective shows had ingredients that spelled success for previous series. A good example of this is *Brenner*, an unpretentious effort that was not produced for very long but still managed to stay on the CBS schedules for four years. *Brenner* patterned itself on *Naked City*, doing extensive on-location filming in New York and attempting to emulate the program's realism and character depth.

It was successful for the most part. Edward Binns, a truly fine character actor with a solid, gravelly voice and demeanor, played Detective Lieutenant Roy Brenner of the N.Y.P.D.'s Confidential Squad. James Broderick, an equally effective charactor actor who gave much the same visual impression as Binns,

played Officer Ernie Brenner, who just happened to be Roy's son. This device worked well, adding an emotional dimension to their investigations. First, there was the matter of experienced Roy trying to pass on his knowledge to Ernie before he retired or was killed. This led to the ongoing concern of both characters for each other's safety. Also concerned about the pair was Captain Laney, their superior, played by Joseph Sullivan.

The series was enhanced further by decent scripts. Even with all this going for it, CBS only ordered about 16 episodes to be used as a summer filler. Then they repeated those programs in the summers of 1961 and 1962. Finally, when they decided to run them once more in 1964, they magnanimously asked the production company for about nine more, just as a change of pace. Surprisingly, those extra episodes were available and a total of 26 *Brenner* shows were broadcast.

One police series which seemed to have delusions of being *Naked City* would have been dismissed by its viewers if it were not for its star, Robert Taylor.

In *The Detectives* Taylor played Captain Matt Holbrook, the leader of a band of New York plainclothes detectives. Viewers saw very little violence on this program, and they did not hear a jazzy music score, either. The stories were as lean and unassuming as Taylor.

Taylor signed on to do his first TV work after 25 years in the movie business. His most memorable work was in such films as *Camille* (1936), *Bataan* (1943), *Quo Vadis* (1951), and *Rogue Cop* (1954). Even with dozens of films to his credit, he found himself starring in his first (and last) TV series. (He did return to host *Death Valley Days* in 1966 and did a guest-star spot in *Hondo* during 1967.)

"I'm only going into it for the money," he told a reporter when asked why he came to television. When the same reporter asked, kindly, if he considered the new medium a challenge, Taylor's reply was, "Oh, nuts."

Well, if *The Detectives* was not a challenge to Taylor, it did serve as a showcase for younger actors. During its two-season run on ABC and its one-season switch to NBC (complete with a title change to *Robert Taylor's Detectives*), there was Russell Thorson as Lieutenant Otto Lindstrom and Lee Farr as Lieutenant James Conway, neither of whom achieved any acting fame. But there was Mark Goddard as Sergeant Chris Ballard, who went on to co-star in the awful, but popular science-fiction TV fever dream *Lost in Space* (1966), produced by schlock-master Irwin Allen. There was Adam West as Sergeant Steve Nelson, who went on to star in *Batman* (1966), developed for TV by schlock-master Lorenzo Semple, Jr. And there was Tige Andrews as Lieutenant Johnny Russo, who went on to co-star in *Mod Squad* (1968), executive-produced by schlock-master Aaron Spelling. Looked at in this light, *The Detectives* seemed to be the gateway to the schlock stars.

During its run, it provided unpretentious viewing, replete with grim-faced Robert Taylor, who would have made a terrific Dick Tracy at that time of his career. There was hardly a gaze that was flintier or a chin as strong and jutting.

Syndicated throughout 1959 was *Manhunt*, which was labeled a "San Diego *Dragnet*." It starred Victor Jory, one of the crustiest-looking actors then around, as Lieutenant Howard Finucane of the San Diego Police Department,

who usually found investigative reporter Ben Andrews, as played by Patrick McVey, dogging his tail. Together, they investigated crimes thought to be mob-related. These two were well-suited to their jobs. McVey was remembered for his reporter role in the *Big Town* series, while Jory paid his detective dues by co-starring in *Bulldog Drummond at Bay* (1937), *Charlie Chan in Rio* (1941), and *Meet Nero Wolfe* (1936). He even starred as "The Shadow" in one of the several Shadow serials.

In April 1959, a funny thing happened. Two action dramas were televised, both about the same topic, both mounted on a dark, realistic fashion, and both based on the experiences and recollections of a famous real-life gangbuster.

NBC's *The Lawless Years* dealt with the exploits of Detective Barney Ruditsky of the N.Y.P.D. during the Roaring Twenties—when booze was banned though plentiful, and the mob ran the whole show.

James Gregory, a fine actor in the Victor Jory-Wendell Corey mold, starred as Barney Ruditsky, with Robert Karnes playing his assistant Max. The two seasons' worth of episodes appeared sporadically over three seasons.

On April 20, 1959—just four days after *The Lawless Years* premiered—*The Untouchables* blasted its way on to the air as a two-part gangster adventure on *The Desilu Playhouse*.

The show was narrated by Walter Winchell, the columnist whose own three television shows had not caught on. Winchell had done a weekly commentary show in 1955, then followed up the next year with a half-hour variety program, then settled on *The Walter*

Winchell File in 1957. He hosted, narrated, and actually appeared in these dramatizations.

It was generally accepted in Hollywood that Winchell was on his way out. But Desi Arnaz liked the man's voice and thought it would be perfect for the gangland drama. The producer of the first *Untouchables* was Quinn Martin, who pushed for authenticity and all that could mean. The director of this two-part show was Phil Karlson, an uncompromising director known for his hard-hitting crime movies like *The Phenix City Story* (1955).

What these people slaved over was a screenplay based on *The Untouchables*, the memoirs of federal Treasury agent Eliot Ness, who was instrumental in bringing the notorious Al Capone to justice. His book, written with United Press International veteran Oscar Fraley, was Ness's recollection of the Capone era. Arnaz, Martin, and Karlson brought that story to television and made it a success along with the man chosen to play Ness.

Robert Stack was not the producers' first choice. Initially they wanted either Van Heflin or Van Johnson as the hero. Heflin had just received great reviews for his work in the film version of Rod Serling's award-winning TV drama *Patterns* (1956). Johnson had just starred in a clever mystery film about a blind writer turned detective, *Twenty-three Paces to Baker Street* (1957) and guested on *I Love Lucy* the same year.

*Federal agent Eliot Ness in his natural habitat—ankle-deep in illegal hootch and fanning the joint with a Thompson submachine gun! Robert Stack starred as the legendary Ness on **The Untouchables**. (ABC)*

Since neither of those leading men wanted the job, they settled on Robert Stack, the man who began his film career as "the first boy to kiss Deanna Durbin" in *First Love* (1939). Stack followed that with a string of earnest performances in films like *Eagle Squadron* (1942), *Mr. Music* (1950), *Bwana Devil* (1953), *The High and the Mighty* (1954), and garnered an Oscar nomination for *Written on the Wind* (1957).

Stack had become a tall, muscular leading man as he proved in the title role of *John Paul Jones* (1959). He followed that up by taking the Eliot Ness role, perhaps thinking it would be a one-shot deal so he could get back to movies.

The real untouchables were a crew of seven federal agents who worked for the Treasury Department and were so dedicated and intent on ridding Chicago of its underworld element in the late twenties and early thirties that they were considered unbribable. Therefore, a Chicago newspaper dubbed them "The Untouchables." Ness liked the name and, like it or not, it stuck. In the *Desilu Playhouse* production, Ness and four men moved in on Capone and his mob, their job complicated by a traitor in the ranks, played by Keenan Wynn.

This effort proved so popular with audiences that it led to the series and a feature film that was compiled from the two-part opener. Desi Arnaz retitled the film *The Scarface Mob* and released it abroad, but it made its way to America in 1962. But while U.S. TV and overseas audiences were lapping it up, critics were less than thrilled. One of the grander raves said, "It's pleasant in an unwholesome way." Another complained that it had "no acting dynamics."

Once *The Untouchables* became a se-

ries on October 15, 1959, there was nothing critics could do to stop it. There was Stack, steely-eyed and tight-lipped as Ness, with future comedy director and producer Jerry Paris—*The Dick Van Dyke Show* and *Happy Days* (1974)—as agent Martin Flaherty, Anthony George as agent Cam Allison, Abel Fernandez as agent William Youngfellow, and Nick Giorgiade as agent Enrico Rossi. Together, they started perforating the bad guys with their .38 caliber revolvers and banjo sub-machine guns.

The small screen was lit up as it had never been before. Watchers could be assured of brutal shoot-outs at least once every half hour, and usually there were more. In addition to the clashes between the good and bad guys, people could delight in the tortures visited upon the various innocents who got caught in front of the mob steamroller.

The Untouchables' cameras did not flinch, no matter what. One outstanding bit of nastiness: a frightened young wife finds her husband hanged in an alleyway—the noose tied to a fire escape—and then she herself gets mowed down in a hail of lead.

Actors Paris and George left the show and were replaced by Steve London as agent Jack Rossman and the greatly loved but underrated Paul Picerni as agent Lee Hobson. It was then that Ness's famous cry, "Rico! Lee!" was heard across the land.

A rare photo—inasmuch as The Untouchables *were rarely seen smiling. Robert Stack (right center) is flanked by his core of top agents. From the left: Abel Fernandez, Nicholas Georgiade, and Paul Picerni as, respectively, Youngblood, Rico, and Lee.* (ABC)

The *Untouchables* showcased new acting talent, and many actors went on to the bigtime. People like James Caan, George Kennedy, Robert Redford, Telly Savalas, Robert Duvall, Peter Falk, Lee Marvin, and Charles Bronson marched across the screen, usually to be killed or maimed by the time the hour was up. There were also semi-regular villains to be looked forward to, like Frank Nitti, Al Capone's second in command. Capone was played by Neville Brand while Nitti was enacted by former *Behind Closed Doors* host Bruce Gordon.

Gordon was a big hit on the show and hindered Ness's fight for justice throughout the series' run. In the final season the two adversaries finally had it out, Ness mercilessly cornering the crushed and broken Nitti in a railway tunnel. But by then, the confrontation was anticlimactic. *The Untouchables* had been defeated by a power greater than all its villains put together: the sponsors.

Here is why. The violent fantasy of the show disturbed one segment of the audience while its authenticity disturbed another. The antiviolence groups complained, but it was the Federation of Italian-American Democratic Organizations that was really effective. It was also very smart. Instead of complaining to the networks or studios—which did little good if the show was a hit—it went right after the advertisers. The Federation was not unduly upset by the program's violence; what it did not like was that nearly all of the people committing the violence and getting killed by Ness were of Italian descent. The predominantly Italian-American dockworkers threatened to strike and boycott the sponsor's product.

Although the advertiser, Liggett and Myers, said their subsequent action had nothing to do with the threats, they withdrew their sponsorship from *The Untouchables* (as well as from some other shows) at the close of the 1961 season. ABC declared that the pullout would not bother them, but behind the scenes things were happening. These things (*read* pressure and counter-pressure) led to an agreement between Desilu Productions, ABC TV, and the Italian-American League to Combat Defamation.

On St. Patrick Day, 1961, the three parties involved agreed to these new rules: first, "There will be no more fictional hoodlums with Italian names. . . ." second, "There will be more stress on the . . . role of 'Nick Rossi,' Ness's right-hand man. . . ." third, "There will be an emphasis on the 'formidable influence' of Italian-American officials in reducing crime and emphasis on the 'great contributions' made to American culture by . . . Italian(s)."

While they were at it, the producers also deemphasized the sadism. Leonard Freeman and Jerry Thorpe took over as executive producers while Fred Freiberger and Howard Hoffman became producers. The show continued to have its effective music score by Wilbur Hatch and Nelson Riddle, and the visual brooding quality was sustained by such directors as Stuart Rosenberg, Robert Butler, and Ida Lupino. But the show's soul had leaked out through its many pressure-made bullet holes. Somehow its change signaled a change in viewer response. It actually seemed as if audiences were looking for quieter, less bloody thrills.

In fall 1961 *The Untouchables* was scheduled opposite *Sing Along with Mitch* and *CBS Reports*. Even against such seemingly lightweight competition, its ratings began to falter. The next year ABC moved the show to fight it out with the Dick Powell, Jack Benny, and Garry Moore shows, but its ratings still lagged. Finally, after 114 pounding episodes and four seasons on the air, *The Untouchables* called it quits in September 1963.

Robert Stack tried to get back into the movie swing of things, only to be disappointed at almost every turn. He just could not shake the Ness persona. He would take parts in television and film, thinking it was his big break, only to have the producer or director tell him "give me Eliot Ness."

"When you do TV," Stack said tiredly in 1979, "people seem to insist on confusing you with the part you play. I played Ness as a cold-eyed, dour, authoritarian figure. That sure as hell is not me."

Stack is a colorful, witty, enjoyable man who got his revenge on 20 years of typecasting with the release of his memoirs and his leading roles in Steven Spielberg's *1941* (1978) and the comedy hit of 1979, *Airplane*.

For better or worse, Stack and *The Untouchables* have carved a niche for themselves in TV detective history. It remains the best gangbuster series ever.

Growing Pains

It is probably safe to say that in the sixties the TV set truly became the new hearth before which the family sat. Only this new hearth seemed intent on jarring rather than comforting us.

1960

During the year 1960 nothing much of note occurred in any of the TV genres, including detective shows. It was one long year of rehashes and reruns with only a few pale glimmers of quality. The first and best known of the rehashes was *Surfside Six*, which was mentioned earlier in conjunction with its other relatives in the Warner Brothers' family: *77 Sunset Strip, Bourbon Street Beat,* and *Hawaiian Eye*.

The character of Ken Madison, played by Van Williams, had come to Miami Beach by way of New Orleans, where he had been the low snooper on the Bourbon Street totem pole. But on the houseboat which served as the private investigators' office, Kenny was top dog,

shepherding fellow detectives Dave Thorne (Lee Patterson) and Sandy Winfield (Troy Donahue).

Taking no chances, the studio supplied them with good-looking girlfriends. Diane McBain played Daphne DeWitt Dutton and Margarita Sierra was nightclub singer Cha Cha O'Brien. The big difference between this series and its predecessors was that a houseboat basin did not need a hip-talking parking attendant. Instead, *Surfside Six* had two police contacts with weird names: Lieutenant Plehn and Lieutenant Snediger, played by Richard Crane and Donald Barry respectively.

So when D. D. Dutton was not acting like she was in a screwball comedy, and Cha Cha was not coming on like Charo, and one of the three detectives was not slugging it out with a bad guy, we could all snigger at the cops' names.

"The whole razzle-dazzle is so consistent," said *TV Guide*, "that the moral values are as invisible as the motives. The series is expertly put together, but lifeless." It appeared that the team detective-interesting locale formula was already wearing out its welcome, so *Surfside Six* lasted just two seasons. In its and *Hawaiian Eye*'s wake, however, were shows that tried to find success in combinations of sun, surf, and sand.

The Islanders premiered in 1960 with a few original wrinkles of its own. William Reynolds and James Philbrook starred as Sandy Wade and Zack Malloy, charter pilots who operated a one-plane airline. Spinning their propellers was Wilhelmina Vandeever, also known as Steamboat Willie, played by Diane Brewster. But rather than being as kooky or cute as her nickname suggests, Willie was a cunning little devil who served as the boys' business manager even though she was never really out for anyone but herself. Through her ploys, mystery and danger always entered the pilots' lives as they flew all over the place.

More like *Sea Hunt* than *Surfside Six* was *The Aquanauts*, which tried to double ocean lovers' fun by giving them two salvage divers for the price of one. At the beginning of their one season on CBS, Keith Larsen played Drake Andrews while personable Jeremy Slate played Larry Lahr. Larsen, the former star of *Northwest Passage* (1957), left the show during the year and was replaced by Ron Ely as Mike Madison, Larry's new partner. Then, when that failed to get the ratings up, the show's location was moved from Honolulu to Malibu, where the boys opened a scuba store.

That didn't work either. Jeremy Slate went on to a movie career that included *The Sons of Katie Elder* (1966) and *The Devil's Brigade* (1968), while Ron Ely came back to TV as *Tarzan* (1966) and

made a fine movie, *Doc Savage: The Man of Bronze* (1975).

A combination of the preceding series could be found in *Coronado 9*, Rod Cameron's third attempt at a series following the disappearances of the unsuccessful *City Detective* and *State Trooper*. Here the battered old pro played Don Adams, a retired naval officer who found new challenges as a private detective in San Diego. Coronado 9, Adams' telephone exchange number, was made the title of the show for obvious reasons. After one syndicated season, Adams was called no more.

Johnny Midnight, another one-season syndicated filler, was a series reminiscent of *Johnny Staccato*. This mystery starred movie favorite Edmond O'Brien as Johnny, an ex-actor turned private peeper. At first glance, it also seemed reminiscent of the radio serial *Johnny Dollar*, which was about an insurance investigator. Some viewers tuned in *Midnight* expecting to see that insurance man because Edmond O'Brien had played him at one time. The radio program proved to be longer running than the TV series, but that did not stop O'Brien. He was back on movie screens later that year, adding to his list of memorable roles.

Johnny Midnight soon had company on the cancellation route: *Dan Raven*. The series was uncomfortably close to *77 Sunset Strip*, although Raven was a cop, not a private eye. Skip Homeier—a cleft-chinned, long-browed actor who had started in films as a child star in *Tomorrow the World* (1944) playing a Nazi youth—played loner Raven on loan to the Los Angeles sheriff's office. And being so close to the entertainment capital, it wasn't unusual for Dan's cases to be involved with actual stars.

People like Paul Anka and Buddy Hackett guest-starred on the hour show, sometimes playing themselves and sometimes playing other characters. Sometimes stars appeared in surprise cameos, other times they were the sun which the plots revolved around. Helping these people, and occasionally Dan, out of trouble were Sergeant Burke, Raven's associate (Dan Barton) and publishing photographer Perry Levitt, the Rona Barrett of picture-takers (Quinn Redeker).

Although it was a clever use of locale and an interesting mixture of fact and fantasy, the series lasted three months on the NBC network. Another series which proved only slightly more successful in an out of the ordinary local was *The Brothers Brannigan*, set in Phoenix, Arizona. The leads were Steve Dunne and Mark Roberts, playing the likable Mike and Bob Brannigan. These two private eyes did what all real-life brothers do: think alike, have slight cases of sibling rivalry, joke a bit, and fall in love with the same girl. Even though they were brothers and even though they worked in Phoenix, their scripts were not much to write home about, so they exited after a single syndicated season.

The series with the most far-out use of locale in the 1960 season lasted just as long as *The Brothers . . .* , but certainly had more to commend it. *Royal Canadian Mounted Police*, made in Canada with full R.C.M.P. cooperation, starred local talent, with Gilles Pelletier as French-Canadian Corporal Jacques Gagnier, John Perkins as Constable Scott, and Don Francks as Constable Mitchell.

Of the three, Francks became the most famous in America, starring in the war series *Jericho* in 1966 and co-starring in the Francis Ford Coppola-directed *Finian's Rainbow* in 1968. Perhaps the hardships involved in filming in the Great North drove Francks to find fame in the United States. Filming on location is never easy, but filming in the frozen wilds of Canada was more difficult than the crew had expected.

Need a rabid fox? In Hollywood, a producer can call one of several animal training services that will happily supply almost any creature for a price. But no amount of money could get the Canadian crew what they wanted, so for one show they actually disguised a cooperative dog to get the rabid fox effect on camera. And even though canines were available, they weren't always the most cooperative. In one scene, a dog team was supposed to pull a sled. They would not do it, no matter how many whips were cracked or how hard their trainer begged and pleaded. So the crew pushed the sled while the cameraman filmed the driver in close-up.

But the series' biggest problem was not reluctant dogs, but a reluctant public. First, the various TV listings all over the country were not eager to fit the full title, *Royal Canadian Mounted Police*, into their schedules, and usually shortened it to *R.C.M.P.* Somewhere along the line, the producers agreed to the title change, so the show officially became *R.C.M.P.* But after one season it was gone.

Just across the Atlantic Ocean from the R.C.M.P. was *The Man from Interpol*, the man being New Scotland Yard Inspector Anthony Smith as portrayed by Richard Wyler. Interpol, short for the International Police Force, was created at the beginning of the industrial age to combat the international forces of organized crime. And Inspector Smith was assigned to the organization by his commander, a superintendent played by John Longden, to do just that.

Some critics liked the results. *TV Guide* called the show "superior to most. The location shots are excellent, giving it an aura of authenticity, but the scripts are riddled with clichés." The clipped British tones of Longden and Wyler did much to improve on these clichés, but it was not enough. *The Man from Interpol* stopped fighting international mobsters at the end of the 1960 season.

Halfway around the world from Inspector Smith was reporter Glenn Evans, described in the advertising as a "two-fisted American correspondent assigned to crowded Oriental and international *Hong Kong!*" Rod Taylor, a tough, brawny Australian-born actor, played Evans with assurance. Backing Evans up were Police Chief Neil Campbell, played by veteran TV actor Lloyd Bochner, and nightclub owner Tully, played by equally experienced stage comedian Jack Kruschen.

The contrast between gaunt Bochner and jolly, husky Kruschen made the show interesting, while Taylor's bashing his way through pushers, killers, smugglers, and spies made the show entertaining. The token Oriental character at the beginning of the ABC show's one-year run was Fong, Evan's houseboy, played by Harold Fong. He was soon replaced by Ling, played by Gerald Jann.

It was not *Hong Kong*'s year, given its quick cancellation, but it was Rod Taylor's, given the 1960 premiere of George Pal's classic film version of *The Time Machine* in which he starred.

Between this great science-fiction movie and the recognition the TV show

gave Taylor, his acting career was launched. He made a number of successful films in the ensuing years before returning to TV for a 1971 series called *Bearcats!* and a 1976 TV movie pilot called *A Matter of Wife or Death*.

Back in 1960 there was more than one series based on a character from another medium. *Dante's Inferno* was unique in that Dante originated on a past TV show. In addition to doing Philip Marlowe on the *Climax* production of *The Long Goodbye* and producing *Richard Diamond*, Dick Powell also served as producer on *Four Star Playhouse* (1952), an interesting omnibus which featured four stars—Dick Powell, Charles Boyer, David Niven, and Ida Lupino—alternating as hosts/actors. Although the dramas each actor presented were different, Powell would often play a character called Willie Dante, who ran a nightclub called Dante's Inferno. Blake Edwards created the concept, and its popularity on the anthology show led to its production as a series.

Powell cast Howard Duff, famous as radio's Sam Spade, as Dante. He is also remembered for his roles in *Brute Force* (1947) and *Naked City* (1948), and for a TV comedy series called *Mr. Adams and Eve* in which he co-starred with Ida Lupino, his then-wife.

The *Dante* series had the wonderful actor Alan Mowbray playing Stewart Styles, the maître d' who knew more about the criminal element than the element itself. Tom D'Andrea, a fine comic foil, played Biff, Dante's assistant, who loved nothing better than stirring up past and present dirt. The trio took on *Mr. Lucky*-like plots for the one season they were on NBC.

Syndicated stations were responsible

for televising *The Third Man*, a travesty of the great film by the same name. The movie, directed by Carol Reed, starred Orson Welles as Harry Lime, a slimy man who had faked his own death in postwar Vienna in order to continue his wicked ways unbothered. Joseph Cotten played a writer who came to solve Harry's "murder," only to discover what a crumb Lime had become. The "third man" of the title refers to the third witness to Harry's hit-and-run death—who turns out to be none other than Harry himself.

Viewers who turned to television's *The Third Man* expecting to see quality were shortchanged. Harry Lime had become a "business tycoon, troubleshooter, and detective [who] aids people in distress." Michael Rennie gave the role his brand of panache, as he did in his many film roles, but the series' creators did a bad job recreating the film.

Despite its misleading title, *The Third Man* was a decent program, aided immeasurably by Rennie and co-star Jonathan Harris, who played Lime's dour aide, Bradford Webster—but given the exceptional screenplay by Graham Greene, the striking photography by Robert Krasker, and the haunting musical score, many movie lovers would prefer to think that *The Third Man* was never on TV.

Michael Shayne may not be as revered as *The Third Man* film, but the famous character of books and movies is loved by millions. Davis Dresser created the character and published his first Shayne novel under the pseudonym Brett Halliday in 1939. With *Dividend on Death*, the private eye was off and running on a career that spanned more than 60 volumes and a dozen movies. In the books,

Shayne started out as a tall, coarse redhead who worked out of Miami Beach. He was as tough, competent, and moral as Philip Marlowe, but without the weariness or self-pity. He liked to plow into things, clean them up, then wipe off his hands and get on to the next case.

Twentieth Century-Fox brought Shayne to the screen in the person of shorter, jauntier Lloyd Nolan for *Michael Shayne, Private Detective* (1940). Although different from the books, the movie's mixture of murder and mirth worked, so sequels were called for. Six more followed with Nolan before 20th Century-Fox put the series to rest in 1942. PRC Productions picked up the ball in 1946 by starring Hugh Beaumont as Shayne in *Murder Is My Business*. Four more Beaumont Shaynes were released in just two years before the film series closed for good with *Too Many Winners* in 1947.

By the time Jeff Chandler was playing Michael Shayne on radio, author Dresser had written many other books pseudonymously, created *Mike Shayne's Mystery Magazine*, owned his own publishing firm, and became one of the founders of The Mystery Writers of America. Dresser had gone from being just an author to being a mover—a power—in the entertainment business.

And by the time *Michael Shayne* got to television, Dresser was ready to be technical consultant to the series. Under his guidance, the Shayne character more closely resembled the original and the location was definitely Miami. Picked to play the detective was veteran Richard Denning, already well known to viewers as Mr. North, of *Mr. and Mrs. North*. Movie audiences also remembered him from films such as *The Glass Key* (1942)

Richard Denning is back, this time as Mike Shayne, giving some pointers to actress Carol Omhart—who proved to be both a help and a hindrance during the "Man with a Cane" episode. (courtesy Theater Collection, Free Library of Philadelphia)

and *Creature from the Black Lagoon* (1954).

Readers of the Shayne novels had much to like in this television version. Will Gentry, the chief of Miami Police, was played by Herbert Rudley. Lucy Hamilton, Shayne's noble and noteworthy secretary, was played by Patricia Donahue. Tim Rourke, a reporter for the *Miami Daily News*, was played by former "Untouchable" Jerry Paris. These actors were time-tested and successful. It was too bad that the scripts were not the same.

"There are lots of rich and wonderful personalities," said *TV Guide*, "but it is still a dreary hour of mayhem and lust.

All in all, *Michael Shayne* is one of the lesser epics we've viewed." Normally a review such as this would give the network hope, since "mayhem and lust" usually spelled success, but in this case it only served to keep the series afloat for one NBC season.

Well, so far, so bad. The detective shows were suffering from lackluster execution.

Harrigan and Son, a boisterous ABC series about two lawyers, was basically *Brenner* played for laughs. Harrigan and son fought in court to get their clients free, and fought each other as to the proper way to do it. Roger Perry, a personable actor who went on to appear in soap operas and vampire movies (the Count Yorga series), played James Harrigan, Jr., who, with the support of his prim secretary Miss Claridge (Helen Kleeb) went strictly by the book.

Pat O'Brien, veteran film actor, played James Harrigan, Sr., who, with *his* beautiful, lively secretary named Gypsy (Georgine Darcy), fought for success by any means. Harrigan Senior's methods were humanistic, moralistic, and victorious rather than cunning, nasty, and vicious, and he usually taught his son a lesson—which sonny often ignored so they could clash again next week—at the end of each half-hour session. These sessions ended after a season.

Along more traditional lines was ABC's half-hour *The Law and Mister Jones*. It was traditional in the sense that it concerned a noble, honest lawyer who fought like the dickens for his clients. James Whitmore, a fine actor often compared to Spencer Tracy, played attorney Abraham Lincoln Jones, a man who had to be honest or give up his first two names. This man was not merely dedicated to truth, justice, and the American way, he was passionate about them. This passion was contagious, inspiring his trusty law clerk. C. E. Carruthers (Colin Carter) and his adoring secretary, Marsha Spear (Janet De Gore).

This passion also infected the series' viewers, who were vocal and adamant about their love for Mr. Jones. ABC found out just how much when they tried to take it off the air at the end of the season. The viewer response was so great that the network brought the program back in the middle of 1962. But hell hath no fury like a network crossed. ABC hardly gave the show a chance to regain its audience;

reviving it in April and canceling it in October of the same year.

Whitmore did not suffer unduly. He is now well known for his one-man shows as Harry Truman, Theodore Roosevelt, and Will Rogers and for his character roles.

The Law and Mr. Jones was not the only surprise of the year. *Diagnosis: Unknown* was pretty interesting both in concept and cast. Patrick O'Neal starred as a mustachioed and goateed pathologist named Dr. Daniel Coffee who worked at a large New York hospital. Pathology is the science of the origin and nature of diseases, and so far as this show was concerned, the ultimate disease was death. Aiding Coffee was Dr. Motilal Mookerji, an Indian (from India) medicine man played by Cal Bellini. Abetting him was Doris Hudson, his friend and love interest, played by Phyllis Newman. Asking him for help was N.Y.P.D. Detective Max Ritter, played by one-time Boston Blackie star Chester Morris.

The show served its purpose as a summer replacement for *The Garry Moore Show*. It was certainly a strange choice for the executives to make—replacing the funny Moore with a subject and star which could hardly be termed accessible. If they had chosen to replace the *U. S. Steel Hour*, for example, *Diagnosis: Unknown* might have stood a chance of becoming "Diagnosis: Fall Scheduling."

A. Dunster Lowell must have been somebody's idea of the return to TV of the "gentleman detective," but it is a show to be cherished only for its eccentricity. Here's how they put *A. Dunster Lowell* together. First they got Robert Vaughn—then 28 years old, a well-educated actor who had started his acting career in *Teenage Caveman* (1958). Then they cut his hair to Peter Gunn length. Then they outfitted him in the finest Ivy League clothes. Then they plopped him down in New England where he could become a criminologist.

But they didn't stop there. They provided him with a 1948 Jaguar convertible, a terrier, and something no good detective should be without: extra sensory perception (ESP).

Once this crazy combination reached the tube, it was not so much canceled as rejected—in the manner of a new heart after a transplant operation. But the Muse bless you, *A. Dunster Lowell!* While we shall see Robert Vaughn again in more congenial surroundings, we shall not see your like again.

The best series of 1960 did not go as far as giving its detective ESP, though it did strive for intelligence. The show was *Checkmate*. The creator was Eric Ambler.

Ambler largely defined the literary spy genre in the same way Dashiell Hammett and Raymond Chandler defined the private-eye genre. Ambler's early novels—*Epitaph for a Spy* (1938), *The Mask of Dimitrios* (1939), and *Journey into Fear* (1940)—paved the way for the likes of Ian Fleming and John Le Carré. After World War II, Ambler became more involved with the production end of things, although he continued to write fine books like *The Light of Day*, which became the famous caper film *Topkapi* (1964).

His *Epitaph for a Spy* became just one of several notable mystery adaptations brought to television by *Climax!* during the mid-fifties. But it was not until 1960

that his first original creation for television was aired. *Checkmate* was all about preventing crime, not solving it. Master criminology teacher Dr. Carl Hyatt was intent on stopping the villain before he committed the dastardly deed. To this end, he collected two prize pupils—Don Corey and Jed Sills—and opened a San Francisco investigations agency called Checkmate, Inc. Its aim and motto: "To thwart crime and 'checkmate' death."

The creation of a series is one thing, but the realization of it is another. To its credit, *Checkmate* was appropriately atmospheric and had fine production values. A major plus was the casting of Sebastian Cabot as Hyatt. Cabot was the very picture of intelligent individuality and an extremely capable performer who knew how to ingratiate himself whether he was playing a hero or a villain. He would have been a fine choice to play Rex Stout's famous fat detective Nero Wolfe, but sadly, Cabot died of a heart attack in 1977 at the age of 59.

Doing most of the actual detecting on the program were Anthony George, a former "Untouchable," who played Corey, and Doug McClure, a baby-faced actor known mostly for his TV work on *Court of Last Resort*, *Johnny Midnight*, and in a few Westerns. George was happy for this chance to play the lead. He parlayed this role into some movie roles, then settled into parts on soap operas.

McClure and company did all right with *Checkmate*, getting it through two seasons on CBS before the network checkmated it. Then McClure went on to *The Virginian* (1962), Cabot to *Family Affair* (1966), and Eric Ambler went on to books like *Dirty Story* (1967) and the

Mystery Writers of America's Grand Master Award in 1975.

The television detective year of 1960 won no awards from critics or viewers, but the nice thing was that the only direction it could go from there was up.

1961

Things were better in 1961, but that is not to say the season did not have its share of clinkers. Most of the failures were at least curious in either casting or conception. Take, for instance, *Tallahassee 7000*. (If Henny Youngman were writing this book, he would say, "Take *Tallahassee 7000*, please!") This was either the most ill-conceived series in the genre or the cleverest secret comedy show of the century.

When the title first appeared in the television listings, everyone pretty much assumed it was just another program in the *Hawaiian Eye/Surfside 6/Coronado 9* mold. The show's description gave support to this view. It was about "the investigations of Lex Rogers, special agent troubleshooter for the Florida Sheriff's Bureau." *Tallahassee 7000* happened to be the phone number of the sheriff's office. It all seems remarkably familiar so far.

But instead of seeing Lex Barker, or Rod Cameron, or Jock Mahoney, or some other rugged leading man playing the rough-and-tumble Rogers, viewers saw Walter Matthau. Here was Matthau, with his hunched posture, loping walk, heavy jowls, and New York accent invading the land of surf, sun, and orange juice as a "special agent troubleshooter." One can imagine its few viewers staring at their sets, mouths agape, either loving every

minute of it or never watching it again. Whatever the reason, only one season's worth of *Tallahassee 7000* appeared.

The Florida sun must affect producers very strangely because the Matthau show was not the only oddly conceived show that year. Just when people thought they were safe from another series set in the Florida sun, there came *Miami Undercover*, which was intentionally sophomoric and moronic. At least, one has to assume so, considering the cast and plot. Lee Bowman, the former Ellery Queen, played Jeff Thompson, while ex-boxer Rocky Graziano played his partner Rocky. It was a pretty sad state of affairs with Bowman, now over 50, playing punching bag to the barely comprehensible Graziano.

The network's description of *Miami Undercover* made things worse. "*Posing* [italics added] as a sophisticated man-about-town, Jeff Thompson, a troubleshooter hired by the Miami Hotel Owners Association, attempts to eliminate the sources of trouble that invade Florida." By the sound of it, retirees and Cubans were in for a hard time at the hands of Jeff and Rocky. To add insult to injury, the producers provided what they called "one honey a show" to hang on the arm or around the neck of the urbane, aging Bowman. *Miami Undercover* was an embarrassment and mercifully short-lived.

These two programs gave viewers a hint of just how unusual the new TV year would be. It seemed that none of the syndicated detectives would be satisfied to be run-of-the-mill cops or snoopers. George Nader, another former Ellery Queen, returned to a starring role in *Shannon*. In *The D.A.'s Man*, the character Shannon was an undercover private eye working for the New York district attorney. Here, he's Joe Shannon, an insurance investigator for the Transport Bonding and Surety Company. His boss, Bill Cochran, was played by Regis Toomey, who served as *Richard Diamond*'s police pal Lieutenant McGough.

It was old-home year all over the syndicated schedules. *Highway Patrol* man Broderick Crawford starred as John King, a private eye specializing in jewel cases, on *King of Diamonds*. Ray Hamilton played Casey O'Brien, his aide. Both this show and *Shannon* were produced to fill only one season.

Another year's worth of syndicated episodes was provided by *The Case of the Dangerous Robin*, which has to rival *Royal Canadian Mounted Police* as a lengthy title. The dangerous robin of the title was Robin Scott, another insurance investigator. He was played by Rick Jason, who was used to little effect in movies, then abused the same way when he got a co-starring role with Vic Morrow in *Combat* (1962).

Before he was swept away among the many lost TV stars, Jason had the good fortune to have beautiful Jean Blake playing his investigative partner Phyllis Collier. They made a handsome pair as they sought to nab those they termed "The Cheaters"—the miserable swine who tried to bilk the upstanding insurance companies with false claims.

Insurance investigation seemed to be an idea whose time had come, since *The Investigators* was the third series in 1961 that dealt with it. Only this show was a full-fledged network endeavor rather than a syndicated effort. CBS put it on Thursday nights opposite *Dr. Kildare*

(1961) and *My Three Sons*. *Naked City* casualty James Franciscus played Russell Andrews, while James Philbrook was Steve Banks; both men were partners in "Investigators, Inc.," a New York-based insurance company.

On TV no detective office was complete without the junior operative and the cool, beautiful girl Friday, so *The Investigators* had one of each. Al Austin played Bill Davis and Mary Murphy was Maggie Banks. All four characters' talents were called upon to prevent the insurance company from being cheated.

Claims cops aside, 1961 was big on detailing the investigations of selfless, dedicated men who were after organized crime. *The Lawless Years* was not enough! *The Untouchables* was not enough! Barney Ruditsky and Eliot Ness did their best, but the underworld continued to flourish. By the early sixties, organized crime was seen as a cancer that had to be excised—on every crime show.

One man was ready to operate on that cancer: Nicholas Cain, a criminal lawyer who once had had many well-known (fictional) gangsters as clients. But he had grown so soul-sickened by their evil ways that he offered himself as an undercover agent for the federal government. He knew how the mob worked and he knew which mobsters were important and which were not. He pledged to infiltrate and ferret out those awful men. Those people went on his own personal "most wanted" list. But it was not just the ten most wanted. It was *Cain's Hundred*.

Nick Cain had the use of any and all of the government's operatives in his attempt to rid the world of its hundred most dangerous men. The way the network

Mark Richmond, playing the cold undercover attorney Nicholas Cain, stands before his scorecard for Cain's Hundred. *According to it, he has a long way to go. (NBC)*

and studio figured it, *Cain's Hundred* could be the TV equivalent of "The Bear Went over the Mountain." In that children's song, a pitiful bear went over mountain after mountain only to see another one ahead of him. In the same way, it would take Cain at least four seasons to get all one hundred villains, assuming that he brought at least one to justice every week. By then, another hundred could have come to power and the Cain process could start all over again.

Everyone agreed it was a great idea for a TV show. So no one could understand why it failed so fast. What happened? When Dick Powell, whose production company was responsible for the show,

was asked about it, he seemed to blame the show's star, saying he "lacked color." That star was Mark Richman, a multipurpose actor in the Lloyd Bochner mold who had done a good job in movies like *Friendly Persuasion* (1956) and *The Crime Busters* (1961)—the latter probably had a lot to do with his being cast as Cain.

No doubt hindsight caused Powell to say what he did, because Richman was *supposed* to be a humorless avenger who lived to arrest gangsters. Even his biblical name, Cain, held special implications. In effect, Powell blamed him for a job too well done. Richman was pretty cold, and the entire show was annoyingly one-note—and that note, for the most part, was awfully strident. Cain brought thirty out of his hundred to justice before being put on NBC's cancellation list.

Ten days after *Cain's Hundred* premiered on NBC, *Target: The Corrupters* started on ABC. Stephen McNally, who played investigative reporter Paul Marino, teamed with Robert Harland, as undercover agent Jack Flood, to infiltrate one mob-controlled business a week. This was not as dangerous as it sounded. Prostitution, drugs, and gambling were not the only things that greased the underworld's wheels. Marino and Flood would also get involved with phony charity rackets and protection schemes, and one week they even ran afoul of a garbage conspiracy. That is right, the mob had gotten the trashmen of the city under their scummy thumbs.

Target: The Corrupters lasted only a month longer than *Cain's Hundred*. It seems people were not ready to enjoy seeing just how much was under the mob's control. Even so, producers kept trying to show them, sometimes sneaking the message in under the title of a famous movie that concerned something else. *The Asphalt Jungle* (1950) was a taut, exceptionally written (by Ben Maddow), beautifully directed (by John Huston), solidly acted (by Sterling Hayden, Sam Jaffe, Louis Calhern, Marilyn Monroe, and Jean Hagen) study of a gang coming apart at the seams. It was a thriller and a character study of criminals turning on each other.

MGM-TV took the title for a television series and did a *Five Fingers/The Third Man* to it. In other words, they took the title and chucked everything else. They did not base it on either the movie or the original 1949 novel by W. R. Burnett. Instead, they made up their own story and

the series paid for it by flopping. Jack Warden, an otherwise fine actor, was cast as Deputy Police Commissioner Matt Gower, who was entrusted to create a whole team of Cainlike avengers to destroy underworld influence in New York City. His number one Cain was Captain Gus Honocheck of the N.Y.P.D., played by Arch Johnson. Together, they would do anything a real-life commissioner and captain would let their underlings do. This unfortunate and ultimately unrealistic adaptation of a good movie lasted a little over three months.

Remarkably similar, but set on the West Coast, was *The New Breed*. It had Leslie Nielsen as Lieutenant Price Adams, the head of the L.A.P.D. Metropolitan Squad, whose duty (you guessed it) was to eradicate organized crime. They were called *The New Breed* because they were supposed to use new scientific methods to do their job. John Beradino, a former infielder for the now-defunct St. Louis Browns baseball team, played Sergeant Vince Cavelli, while John Clarke and Greg Roman were officers Joe Huddleston and Pete Garcia. It lasted a little longer, but was essentially the same show as *The Asphalt Jungle*.

A good movie was not the only thing to get TV treatment this year. A series of fine, award-winning books were adapted with slightly better results, the "87th Precinct" novels by Ed McBain (pen name of mainstream novelist Evan Hunter). McBain gave his detective stories a certain depth by declaring at the outset that the action did not take place in New York, but then went on to detail a place which was obviously Manhattan. The entertaining and ironic novels started in 1956 with *Cop Hater*, and by the time the *87th Precinct* TV series was mounted, 13 more books and two movie adaptations were completed.

Hubbell Robinson Productions and MCA-TV did not want to fool with Mc-Bain's fantasy aspect of a New York that was not New York, so they declared at the outset that the 87th Precinct was in Manhattan and the detectives that inhabited it were New Yorkers. Detective Steve Carella and his deaf-mute wife Teddy made the transition from novels to TV. Robert Lansing played Steve. Lansing had the ability to look grim, tired, hard, and almost vulnerable at the same time. Unfortunately he could not bring out that vulnerability or sensitivity as his performances progressed, so the audience was left with a Mark Richman type.

This left the field wide open for Gena Rowlands, who played Teddy. In addition to being one hell of an actress, she is the wife of actor/director John Cassavetes. She acted rings around everyone else on the show without saying a word. Everyone else on the show included Norman Fell, who played one of detective literature's most beloved characters, Detective Meyer Meyer ("My parents had a sense of humor") and Ron Harper, who played perennial rookie Detective Bert Kling.

It did not help matters that the writers and directors handled the action like a regular cop show until the Teddy scenes. Then, all of a sudden, the pace was lovingly slowed to highlight her infirmities. While there was trouble on the set because of her great notices and the men's mediocre ones, critics generally had good things to say about the entire show. "It's a well-made piece of machinery," said one critic. "Moves rapidly," said another. Scheduled opposite the Danny

Thomas and Andy Griffith shows, *87th Precinct* moved rapidly off the air.

The second to last new show of 1961 had more than its share of technical difficulties, but they were all intentional. The series' theme song told it all:

There's a hold-up in the Bronx;
Brooklyn's broken out in fights;
There's a traffic jam in Harlem that's backed up to Jackson Heights;
There's a scout troop short a child:
Khrushchev's due at Idlewild;
Car 54, Where Are You?*

These words were written by Nat Hiken, the creator, writer, producer, and director who went from making that masterpiece of service comedy, *You'll Never Get Rich*, to making this fondly remembered, much-beloved police force farce.

The Andy Griffith Show, which concerned a sheriff and his deputy, could hardly be termed a cop comedy. The big difference between it and *Car 54* was that, in most cases, Griffith's Andy Taylor could have been anything—a mayor, a barber, a candlestick maker. If the characters on *Car 54* were anything but cops, the show would not have been as funny.

The comedy centered around two men: Officer Gunther Toody and Officer Francis Muldoon. Toody was a garrulous, pea-brained but kindly gnome played by Joe E. Ross. Ross, an experienced vaudeville comedian, had a voice that sounded like Brillo being rubbed on charcoal and a face like Yogi Berra's. Muldoon was a quiet, gawking giant with a face that al-

*Copyright-Emil Ascher, Inc.

ternated between a soulful expression and a catatonic glare. He was played by big-boned Fred Gwynne, a stage actor.

They were a mixture of Abbott and Costello, Laurel and Hardy, and Burns and Allen. They would sit in their patrol car or in the locker room of New York's 53rd Precinct station house with Toody babbling away and Muldoon stoically listening. Each had a cross to bear. Toody had a wife, Lucille (played by Bea Pons), who must have taken spouse lessons from Lucy Ricardo and Alice Kramden. Muldoon had a mother (Ruth Masters), a sister (Helen Parker), and a girlfriend named Bonnie Kalsheim (Alice Ghostley).

They both had Captain Martin Block, their long-suffering superior officer who had to deal with them and the chaos of a Manhattan station house. Paul Reed played the man as if he was not sure which was worse. Within this framework, Toody and Muldoon would go about their business, eager, well-meaning, bumbling, and hardly believable for a second. Interestingly, the Euopolis Productions crew worked on location in New York and all the police uniforms were real.

This realism occasionally caused problems, like the time a woman was so sure she was watching the real New York's Finest in action that she ran to them to complain that her husband was beating her. But most of the problems came from actual officers who felt that the actors' antics within such a realistic environment were belittling them and the work they did. Real cops who had the misfortune to drive a "Car 54" had to suffer innumerable jibes. One police force even went so far as to eliminate their

patrol car with that number—the way an architect will eliminate the 13th floor in a building.

Although the police had to take it seriously, most of the program's viewers took it as intended. *TV Guide* happily reviewed the show: "It is all lunatic! . . . It's more a laugh at TV cops than real cops. Toody and Muldoon are more than lovable incompetents, they are aggressively good and extremely lucky. The whole show is done briskly."

The briskness was attributable to Hiken and the cast he collected. While he was serving as guardian angel—writing and directing many episodes while supervising the others—some of the best talent at broad comedy was traipsing before the cameras. In addition to Gwynne, Ross, and Reed, there were Al Lewis (Grandpa of *The Munsters*), Charlotte Rae (of *The Facts of Life*), Nipsey Russell, Molly Picon, Carl Ballantine, and Larry Storch doing comic turns.

But while the show was amusing and the reviews good, not enough people watched it. Perhaps the problem was that while everyone secretly suspected deep-down that all the lower echelon military men stationed out in the boondocks acted like Sergeant Bilko and his men, New York City police work was too "close" and too real for audiences to willingly accept Toody and Muldoon. Perhaps if Hiken had put his comedy cops in a more innocuous locale, their existence would have been more readily acceptable.

Car 54, Where Are You? had a loyal, though relatively small bunch of fans, so NBC canceled it after two seasons. Hiken's creation lived on with reruns and then syndication to local stations, but it never attained the fame and popularity it perhaps deserved.

One show this season *did* get the fame and popularity it deserved because it was one of the finest, most intense, most thought-provoking dramas ever produced. In addition, it was relevant, hard-hitting, controversial, and—most surprising—successful. It lasted four seasons on CBS, becoming a Saturday night ritual for many during its first three years.

It was *The Defenders*, an example of the TV detective genre at its best. On this show the characters sought answers to believable problems that most of the audience could identify with. Reginald Rose, a playwright who found ample work during the "Golden Age" of TV drama, and Herbert Brodkin, a producer of quality drama (*Studio One, Playhouse 90*), got together, producing *The Defenders* under the aegis of their own production company.

Rose wrote scripts and supervised the work of other writers. Brodkin managed the technical end of things. Around this core was added considerable acting and directing talent. E. G. Marshall, a veteran of films since the mid-forties and a contemporary of James Whitmore and Jack Warden, was cast as liberal trial lawyer Lawrence Preston. Marshall, a small but intense package, was extremely believable when playing a man who lived by and for his convictions. When taking the job, Marshall said, "I've always hated lawyers. I thought they were smug, banal people." *The Defenders* was Marshall's revenge on them and the legal industry's boon.

Picked to play his son, Kenneth Preston —another lawyer in the firm of Preston and Preston—was the fairly inexperienced Robert Reed, an actor who had played minor roles on TV shows like *Father Knows Best* and *Men into Space*. But Rose and Brodkin were not looking for stars, they were looking for people who could do the job, and Reed could play the part of a crusading young attorney very well. He was not as intense as Marshall, but he had a haunted, worried look about him that made an effective contrast.

Among the directors of *The Defenders* were men who would go on to film fame: Buzz Kulik (*The Hunter*—1980), Stuart Rosenberg (*The Amityville Horror*— 1979), and Franklin Schaffner (*Planet of the Apes*—1968, *Patton*—1970). There are also TV talents like Paul Bogart, David Greene, and the all-but-blacklisted Michael Powell, who made the shocking *Peeping Tom* (1960) after making such classics as *Stairway to Heaven* (1946), *Black Narcissus* (1947), and *The Red Shoes* (1948).

Such directors brought effecting dramas to an appreciative TV audience. *The Defenders* was an answer to shows like *Perry Mason* and *Harrigan and Son*. It took the preconceptions and clichés and turned them inside out. The courtroom was a place where the good-guy lawyer did not always win and where justice—but not morality—always prevailed. "The Attack" episode, written by John Bloch, started with the defense of a man who said he killed a boy who attacked his daughter. On any other show, it might have been enough to prove that the boy was a rapist, pusher, or murderer. But on *The Defenders*, it was found that the boy was innocent and that the man being defended was a murderer.

In "The Quality of Mercy" episode by Reginald Rose, Preston and Preston defended a man accused of murder because he performed a mercy-killing on a Mongoloid child. In "The Benefactor" episode by Peter Stone, the question of abortion was dealt with. There was even a show where the Prestons returned to the laws of the nineteenth century to cite a precedent for cannibalism.

The Defenders also set a precedent of its own in having its heroes not only lose, but fail. If they lost a case for a client they knew was guilty, they still would have "won." On *The Defenders*, however, nothing was black or white. It existed to spotlight the large expanse of gray.

Curiously enough, for all its apparent realism, *The Defenders* was almost as unrealistic in its way as *Perry Mason*. For example, the Prestons' style of questioning and objecting would be faulted in an actual court of law. If a real-life lawyer tried some of the things the Prestons succeeded with, he would probably be reprimanded faster than he could say, "Reginald Rose made me do it."

Through the four years the series was on the air it remained fresh and thought-provoking. At the end of the third season, Reginald Rose left, but his noble work continued for one more season—until September 9, 1965.

1962

Networks maintained the status quo with such established successes as *Hawaiian Eye*, *The Untouchables*, *Naked City*, *Perry Mason*, and *77 Sunset Strip*. In other genres, premieres in 1962 included the "notable" *McHale's Navy* and *The Beverly Hillbillies*.

That year the *New York Herald Tribune* commented: "The quality of television during this season casts doubt on the industry's position as the leading source of entertainment." The *World-Telegram and Sun* was even harsher: "The networks trot out the tired, painted Jezebel of economic determinism to justify the egregious bad taste of their stock and trade."

Critics responded favorably to the one new detective show of the year. "There's a great deal that's likeable here . . . never a dull moment," said one reviewer. The series that provided the likability and lack of dull moments was *Sam Benedict*, which seemed to be part *Perry Mason* and part *The Defenders*. The latter contributed to the concept. The cases of Jacob W. Ehrlich, a noted San Francisco lawyer, were dramatized and Ehrlich himself became adviser to the series.

Edmond O'Brien took the lead role after *Johnny Midnight* left the air, and *TV Guide* described the actor's on-screen persona perfectly. "He's famous yet unknown, dynamic yet colorless, friendly yet distant." He was also burly and capable like his acting colleague Raymond Burr. Thinking Jake Ehrlich a little too German-sounding, the producers renamed the character and the show *Sam Benedict* and filled in the missing clichés.

Richard Rust played Hank Tabor, Benedict's young assistant, while Joan Tompkins played Trudy Wagner, Sam's secretary. Although entertaining, it seemed as if audiences had had their fill of jurisprudence, so *Benedict* lasted no more than a year on the NBC network.

1963

On November 22, two months after the start of the new TV season, President

John F. Kennedy was assassinated. And then, on November 24, Lee Harvey Oswald—the accused killer—was murdered live on television. This was TV acting as the nation's eyes, showing what we would not have seen otherwise . . . and perhaps did not want to see. Little did anyone know then that the news departments would soon be racing against each other to show the audience the worst the world had to offer.

TV had ceased to be a toy. It had become a guest. A guest who could be loving, entertaining, and helpful, but also one which could be unknowingly cruel.

If the Neilsen ratings were any evidence, it would appear that viewers sought relief from the shocking events of John Kennedy's assassination and its aftermath in *The Beverly Hillbillies*, the highest rated half-hour show of all time. Its old-fashioned sensibilities and cartoon-like approach soothed a rattled America. The same could be said of the successful TV detectives of the year. Those that made it were ones which were not too hard-hitting.

One of the most notable casualties of the time was *East Side/West Side*, which, technically, is not in this genre at all. Its leading character, Neil Brock as played by acting giant George C. Scott, was a social worker in the New York slums who fought poverty, ignorance, and disease. He would often face crime situations, but unlike TV detectives could find no ready solutions to the problems. *East Side/West Side* was a demanding, angry show which the masses turned away from. Given what the real world was like that year, only fantasy held any appeal.

We ran. And so did someone else. Someone noble, honest and good who had been misjudged and sentenced to die. Someone who would fight that judgment and beat the odds. But first he had to run, to escape, to get some breathing room. This was Richard Kimble: *The Fugitive*.

Producer Quinn Martin hit real pay dirt. Coming from his *Untouchables* success, Martin, through his company QM Productions, mounted Roy Huggins' concept impeccably. Richard Kimble had an argument with his wife in their home in Indiana. Upon returning from a calming drive, he discovers a one-armed man hastily exiting his home and his wife brutally murdered. The authorities accuse him of the murder and sentence him to death. In the company of Lieutenant Philip Gerard, Kimble is taken by train to the place of execution. But the locomotive derails, giving Kimble the chance to escape. He takes off in search of the one-armed man and Gerard goes after him. It is like *Les Misérables* all over again. Lieutenant Gerard is a worthy counterpart of the relentless Inspector Javert. As played by Barry Morse, a well-respected Canadian star, Gerard was a humorless, obsessed arresting machine—a man out to solve the world's problems even if he has to destroy the world to do it.

Kimble, on the other hand, was a sweetheart. He was moral and caring, but somehow still the kind of moody man who might have an innocent fight with his wife. He was played by David Janssen, who succeeded in eclipsing his past success in *Richard Diamond* with this role. Janssen's energetic weariness was perfect for the long-distance runner Kimble.

During the four years he was running on ABC, *Fugitive* mania gripped the country. It got so bad that people accused Barry Morse almost everywhere he went. More than once he was slugged by women wielding pocketbooks while telling him, "Why don't you leave that nice man alone!" Directors like James Goldstone and Mark Rydell were continually given good scripts to do, so Gerard kept pursuing and Kimble kept running. In 1965 *The Fugitive* was awarded an Emmy for the "Best Dramatic Series."

As Kimble went from social problem to family melodrama to chase scene, more of the tapestry was exposed. Diane Brewster played Kimble's late wife Hellen in flashbacks. The one-armed man was seem more and more, played by actor Bill Raisch, who lost an arm during World War II. Jacqueline Scott played Donna Kimble Taft, Richard's married sister with whom he touched base occasionally to see where he stood in terms of his quest. By the middle of the fourth season everyone agreed there were very few places left for Kimble to hide. The producers are to be commended for deciding to end the series with a definite conclusion, rather than leaving Kimble in limbo.

What they are not to be commended for was the vacuous, limp, irrational, and unrealistic conclusion they finally telecast. On August 22, 1967, the first part of "The Judgment" was aired; in it, the one-armed man, Fred Johnson, was arrested. Both Kimble and Gerard head for the man in custody; the former because he wants to clear himself, the latter because he knowns Kimble wants to clear himself.

The ploy works. Kimble is taken into custody. History repeats itself in that there is another escape under Gerard's nose, only this time the one-armed man

gets away. Here is where the finale begins to fall apart. On August 29, the final episode of *The Fugitive* is televised. More than 70 percent of all the people watching TV at that moment are watching this program. All they want is for Kimble to be let off the hook. He is, but in such an incredibly moronic fashion it is almost an insult to all the fine work of the preceding episodes.

Kimble convinces Gerard to let him go after the escaped Johnson. Reluctantly, Gerard agrees (first absurdity). Kimble manages to find the one-armed man in a deserted amusement park. They confront each other, which leads to another quick chase. And where does the one-armed man go? Where else but to the one place in all the carnival he couldn't escape from: a high tower (second absurdity).

Not only does Kimble have to capture the sucker, he has to get him to spill the beans as well. Johnson, in the meantime, seems intent only on spilling Kimble's guts. The one-armed man beats Kimble unmercifully, forcing him to pull out a snub-nosed revolver.

"You won't use that," Johnson says with evil assurance. "You need me alive." He then continues to pummel the hapless Kimble until the gun is dropped and Johnson gets his hand on it. He retreats until he is at the very edge of the unfenced tower, then tightens his finger on the trigger—the barrel pointed right at Kimble's chest.

There's a gun report, all right, but it is the crack of Lieutenant Gerard's rifle, hitting the one-armed man in the back just before he can kill Kimble (third absurdity). Johnson falls all the way down to Gerard's feet. Incredibly, he has just enough life in him to clear Kimble of the crime (fourth absurdity).

The vast majority of the public was grateful for little things, however. Viewers were so used to series simply disappearing that any conclusion was better than none.

The Fugitive made QM Productions over $30 million and all three *Fugitive* men—Janssen, Huggins, and Martin—went on to bigger and better detective things.

Two men who would go on to become giants of the TV mystery genre made their writing debut in 1963. Richard Levinson and William Link, who met at the University of Pennsylvania's Wharton School of Business, decided to become writers rather than become the greatest entertainment accountants of all time. Some of their early television credits included scripts for *Alfred Hitchcock Presents* (1955) and *The Third Man*. They started contributing to the best straight detective series that premiered in 1963. It was a series well suited to their talents. It called for a definite murder mystery complete with clues, suspects, red herrings, and a definite solution; it called for clever dialog; and it called for a touch that would make the nasty art of killing acceptable to the entire family. They pulled it off and so did *Burke's Law*.

Like *Richard Diamond* and *Dante* before it, Burke was created under the auspices of Dick Powell. And as before, Powell played Burke first. But though he played Diamond on radio and Dante on *Four Star Playhouse*, he portrayed Burke on *Dick Powell Theater*, the last of the actor's many TV series. The show premiered in 1961 and ended in 1963, nine months after Powell's death from cancer on January 2.

In 1962 Powell played Captain Amos Burke in "Who Killed Julie Greer?" es-tablishing the format and character. Burke was a homicide detective of the L.A.P.D. who did not complain about the long hours and low pay. First, because he loved his work, and second, because he just happened to be a multimillionaire. He also just happened to be the best detective this side of Sherlock Holmes.

After Powell's death, Four Star Productions took the Burke concept to ABC, who bought it, and then they produced the program in conjunction with Barbety Productions. Their choice as Powell's successor in the role was a good one: Gene Barry.

Barry turned in a good performance in George Pal's *War of the Worlds* (1955) and then became familar to TV watchers as a guest star on *Science Fiction Theater* (1955), *Alfred Hitchcock*, *The Millionaire*, and *Our Miss Brooks*. He hit his stride by starring in *Bat Masterson* (1958), a Western about a dapper Western do-gooder.

Barry also had appeared on the *Dick Powell Theater* episode "Seeds of April" in early 1962, so he was a natural to take up Burke's character when the show went into production. Barry had a strong face, solid body, and an attitude which said "urbane." And he was not averse to fighting when he had to. If only the producers had kept to the original format.

When *Burke's Law* premiered on September 20, 1963, it started, as most of the episodes did, with an elaborate murder. Then the scene quickly shifted to the mansion of Amos Burke. As usual, Burke was in the midst of his rich life style—either having a party or wooing a beautiful girl. Also as usual, just before Burke could move in for the romantic kill, he was interrupted by his Oriental servant, Henry, seen holding the phone.

The dialog usually went like this:

Henry: For you, boss.

Burke *(taking phone):* Burke here. What? Where? *(Pausing with a regretful look at the beautiful girl by his side.)* I'll be right there. *(Hanging up.)* Bring the car around, Henry.

The car was a Rolls-Royce and Henry chauffered his boss to police headquarters, where crusty Detective Sergeant Lester Hart awaited him in the company of eager newcomer Detective Tim Tilson. Those two would follow the suave Burke around on interrogations of the suspects—almost all played as cameos by big-name guest stars—Hart doing the leg work and Tilson getting beaten up, until Captain Amos found the solution.

Regis Toomey made Hart his third supporting detective series role in six years, while Gary Conway used his Tilson part as a stepping stone to other ventures—most unfortunately the lead in Irwin Allen's execrable *Land of the Giants* in 1968. Leon Lontoc played Henry. In the second season a little spice was added with the casting of Ellen O'Neal as Sergeant Ames.

For two seasons the producers were content to mix death and wit, in episodes with titles which started "Who Killed. . . ." Levinson and Link wrote "Who Killed Mother Goose?" and "Who Killed Everybody?"—among others— while Burke tangled with acid-splashing murderers and poison on the wrong end of matchsticks (the victim was a man who chewed matchsticks incessantly). It was a popular show that was easily and often lampooned.

In 1965, the heyday of James Bond and other cinematic secret agents, someone got the bright idea of making Burke a super undercover operative. At the be-

ginning of the series' third season, the title and concept was changed to *Amos Burke—Secret Agent*. Gone were the L.A.P.D. people and the single murders. Gone was Amos' habit of spouting Charlie Chan-like aphorisms and dubbing them "Burke's Law." In their stead was an unseen government boss called "The Man" who gave an uncomfortable Burke his new globe-trotting assignments.

Gene Barry seemed embarrassed on screen and was also defensive in interviews. "ABC is running out of gas," he was quoted as replying when asked about the switch in format. Then, when queried about how television could possibly match the multimillion-dollar action of the movies, Barry supposedly replied, "U.N.C.L.E. is more Mickey Mouse [referring to absurdity or cheapness] than we'll be." It was a half-hearted defense at best. While *The Man from U.N.C.L.E.* (1964) may have been "Mickey Mouse" at times, it was not conceived as a clever, entertaining whodunit, as *Burke's Law* was. U.N.C.L.E. continued while *Amos Burke—Secret Agent* died in four months.

In 1963, there premiered an interesting series with an engaging idea, but its dumb execution secured its own execution. The year before, Universal Studios took the beloved Western form, which had proved so successful for Warner Brothers, and devised the 90-minute *Virginian*. It was a seven-season success that led the way for 1963's mystery attempt.

The logic probably went like this: Lawyer shows are occasionally popular and detective shows sometimes work, so why not combine them for a sure thing? *Arrest and Trial* was the result, a new attempt by Universal's TV department to fill the airwaves.

The first half of the show was taken up with the crime and the manhunt. The second half was concerned with the defendant's trial. This seemed good, even a bit inventive and innovative. But the flaws soon appeared.

Given that the cop arrests the right man, that means the defense attorney is on the bad guy's side. Even if there are extenuating circumstances, it would not sit well with viewers if the guy the cop has been slaving to capture for 45 minutes gets off free. But if the guy does not get off, that makes the lawyer look pretty stupid. And if the guy turns out to be innocent, that not only makes the cop look stupid, it also means the guilty party is still roaming around. So, unless there were multiple episodes or the suspense was maintained by the crime being committed in the first 15 minutes, the cop bagging the wrong man in the second 15 minutes, the lawyer freeing the wronged man in the third 15 minutes, the cop getting the right guy in the next quarter hour, and the lawyer getting him hanged in the final quarter hour, with 15 minutes left for commercials, somebody is going to be the goat.

It would have been a lot smarter to have the lawyer be the district attorney, so the man the cop bagged could be driven into jail without problem. And it would have been smarter yet if the producers had not cast Ben Gazzara as Detective Sergeant Nick Anderson, and—wonder of wonders—Chuck Connors as attorney John Egan. The roles would have been fine if switched, but as it stood, no one accepted diminutive Gazzara as the rough cop when hulking Chuck Connors was waiting at the courthouse for his nabbed client. Both men did their parts well—Connors prov-

ing he could act beyond *The Rifleman*—but it still looked funny.

Still, it was mediocre scripts that proved the show's undoing, and it died after one season.

Among all the network drivel of 1963, there was a syndicated wonder, *The Saint*. Local channels showed this crack-

The world-famous symbol of bon-vivant mercenary Simon Templar (better known as The Saint*). (ITC Entertainment, Inc.)*

ling good action series imported from England by the same company who brought us *The New Adventures of Charlie Chan*—the Independent Television Corporation (I.T.C.).

Simon Templar, otherwise known as the Saint—gentleman, adventurer, thief— was created by Leslie Charles Bowyer Yin, the son of an Englishwoman and an Oriental doctor. By the time the first novel about the Saint, *Meet the Tiger*, was published in 1928, the author's name had legally been changed to Leslie Charteris. And as Leslie Charteris, he wrote more than 40 books featuring the character.

The Templar of Simon Templar referred to the Knights Templar of the twelfth century. He was called the Saint because of his initials, S.T., and the fact that he loved aiding people in trouble. His nickname suggested his calling card: a wordless image of a stick figure complete with halo. This image not only identified him to the crooks and cops in his stories, but also to his fans all over the world.

So when the Saint started appearing on TV, the character was already known, as was the actor playing him—Roger Moore.

Moore, who appeared in *The Last Time I Saw Paris* (1954), *Interrupted Melody* (1955), and *The King's Thief* (1955), started showing up on American television in the late fifties as an urbane hero. On *Maverick* in the 1960/1961 season he played Beauregard Maverick, an English cousin.

As the Saint, Moore was following in the footsteps of George Sanders, Louis Hayward, and Hugh Sinclair, who starred as Templar in a series of nine B-movies made from 1938 to 1954.

Sanders was the best of these Saints, but even he was unable to suggest both the sophistication and physical strength Simon was supposed to possess. Sanders' brother, Tom Conway, played the Saint on radio, as did Brian Aherne and Vincent Price.

Moore successfully conveyed the character's high life as well as his fighting abilities. He could project cosmopolitan polish as well as masculinity. And when the script called for it, he could even get across an emotion or two. Moore was a limited actor, yet he was well aware of his limitations and was eager to improve himself.

Once, during *The Saint*'s run, he was asked by a critic if he felt he was a significant actor. "Yes, I'm significant," Moore replied, "if there is any significance to mediocrity. I'm probably not a very good actor. The Saint should have a strong hairline, blue eyes, and be muscular." When queried further on why he was so hard on himself, he replied, "It's better to knock yourself than him (the Saint). That way no one does it for you."

Despite Moore's harsh words about himself, it was his charm and eagerness to do his best that propelled *The Saint* to success. After three syndicated seasons and 71 black and white episodes, the NBC network was so impressed with the show's track record that they asked I.T.C. for more.

With a new bankroll, the production crew made 43 more hour-long episodes, this time in color. *The Saint* hung his halo in ports all over Europe, getting mixed up in spy and crime adventures everywhere. Templar's long-suffering nemesis, Chief Inspector Claude Eustace Teal of Scotland Yard, was played by Winsley Pithey, Norman Pitt, and Ivor

The most famous Saint of stage and screen, Roger Moore. Though professing little faith in his own talent, the actor has played some of the greatest screen heroes. (ITC Entertainment, Inc.)

Dean—the latter being most identified with the role.

The Saint was a renewed success on NBC in 1967, running in prime time to unprecedented ratings—at least according to I.T.C. It continued running, no matter what the ratings, over three NBC seasons, even replacing *Star Trek* when the series was canceled for the last time in 1969.

The Saint was such a long-running success that its effects are still being felt today. Somewhere in the country the show is still playing, and a movie made up of a two-part episode called *"Vendetta for the Saint"* (1968) is constantly being scheduled in syndication. Roger Moore, of course, went on to international superstardom, replacing Sean Connery and George Lazenby in the James Bond movie series. In addition, he has made other entertaining films: *Gold* (1974), *The Wild Geese* (1978), and *The Sea Wolves* (1981).

The Saint, too, went on to other things. In the late seventies, I.T.C. gave the character a rebirth under the production control of Anthony Spinner. Replacing Moore was Ian Ogilvy, who had amassed some good credits—including a part in the PBS/BBC's *Masterpiece Theater* presentation of *"I, Claudius."* And Ogilvy looked like a young Roger Moore, talked like a young Roger Moore, and fought like a young Roger Moore. In this new version of Templar's adventures, how-

In 1979, the Saint's halo was given to Ian Ogilvy, star of **The Return of the Saint.**
The short-lived series' producers gave him plenty to do besides car chases and gun
fights. (ITC Entertainment, Inc.)

ever, suspense was stressed more than violence, with on-location filming helping enormously.

Again, American executives were impressed, so they brought the new series over here for late 1979 airing. And late it was. *The Return of the Saint* was scheduled for CBS-TV airing every Friday night at 12:40 A.M.! In addition, the network added ten more minutes of commercials in between breaks, making viewing difficult at best, torturous at worst.

A series plus was an animated opening that carried on the tradition of the Saint's being introduced to someone and then a halo appearing over his head—only this time the credit sequence went on to show the haloed stick figure doing a lot of things, like riding a horse, driving a car, and diving off a boat. When the figure kisses a beautiful woman, she then throws the halo away.

Although the opening was clever and Ogilvy capable, the shows were not as solid as the original TV *Saint.* During 1980 they were canceled.

1964

With the great success of *The Beverly Hillbillies,* studios kept churning out, and the networks kept displaying, more and more moronic sitcom fodder. *Bewitched,*

The Munsters, and *The Addams Family* premiered in 1964. In the action adventure area, the public had something else to save them from the rigors of everyday life: James Bond.

Bond went from being a slightly outrageous book hero to an unspectacular TV hero (in the person of Barry Nelson) to the biggest movie series moneymaker of all time.

Where movies lead, television follows. But it usually is not the fault of television producers that shows are so derivative. The producers come up with great ideas—it is the network executives who want tangible proof that the proposed show will be a guaranteed success. Because of this, many groundbreaking proposals are turned down or shelved simply because the networks would rather ape something established than set their own standards.

It is not surprising that the concept that was to become *The Man from U.N.C.L.E.* had a rocky road to the small screen. It all started in 1963 when producer Norman Felton—whose credits included *Robert Montgomery Presents* (1950) and *Studio One*—visited Ian Fleming, the author of the James Bond books. Fleming had long been involved with the media, so he was responsive when Felton asked if he would create a superspy specifically for TV. According to reports, Fleming simply recycled a minor Sicilian character in his *Diamonds Are Forever* (1956) and came up with Napoleon Solo.

For every TV detective show that appears on the air, there are usually at least three pilots which are made but not sold. Such was the case with Norman Felton's *Solo* in 1964. Felton, by now an experienced hand at series—having mounted *Dr. Kildare* (1961)—did not let the matter

rest there. He turned to Sam Rolfe, a noted writer/producer who worked on *Have Gun, Will Travel.*

Rolfe did the trick, taking the loner Solo, giving him a "franchise," as it's called, and giving the franchise depth. In most action shows, the franchise is a police department, or private detective office, or a newspaper or legal firm. In this case, the franchise was U.N.C.L.E.—an acronym for United Network Command for Law and Enforcement—a supersecret intelligence agency.

U.N.C.L.E.'s headquarters were in New York in the East Forties. The agent's entrance was in the changing room of a tailor's shop. The nation's greatest secret agents would enter del Floria's Tailoring, go into the back room, twist a hanger after the tailor had pushed down his ironing machine, and the changing room wall would swing back to expose the front desk of the greatest intelligence agency the world would ever know. The agents would get their triangular ID badges with the U.N.C.L.E. insignia, then go about their business.

U.N.C.L.E. was made up of eight sections. Number one was Policy and Operations; number two was Operations and Enforcement; number three was Enforcement and Intelligence; number four was Intelligence and Communications; number five was Communications and Security; number six was Security and Personnel; number seven broke the system by being Propaganda and Finance; while number eight was Camouflage and Deception.

U.N.C.L.E. even had its own gun. It was based on a P.38 automatic, given a mounted scope, a long bullet magazine extension, a silenced barrel extension, a shoulder stock, and a muzzle break. Four

Author Ian Fleming, the ex-spy creator of James Bond, Agent 007 of Her Majesty's Secret Service; and Napoleon Solo, the Man from U.N.C.L.E. (courtesy of Richard Shenkman and the James Bond 007 Fan Club)

of these weapons were actually made for the show at a cost of $35,000. Sometimes the pistol could be used without the additions. Then the end of the barrel was cut off and a cage was substituted.

This was the stuff that created audiences. With James Bond/Agent 007 raking it in at the box offices, NBC gave a go-ahead for the series. The Fleming/Rolfe/Felton creation premiered Tuesday night, September 22, 1964, as *The Man from U.N.C.L.E.* "The Vulcan Affair," the first episode, was conceived by Ian Fleming.

Nothing happened. The world went about its business with only a small percentage acknowledging that the series had ever started. Everyone wondered what could be wrong. The stories, some conceived by Ian Fleming, were good. The production quality was high. The action and thrills were abundant. The gimmicks were engaging. So why were so few people watching? All the executives knew was that when they switched the time period from Tuesday at 8:30 to Monday at 8:00 in January of 1965, *The Man from U.N.C.L.E.* caught on.

The atmospheric introduction of Napoleon Solo, used in the pilot, then during the first season credit sequence of The Man from U.N.C.L.E. *(NBC: courtesy of the Bob Short Collection)*

Above, U.N.C.L.E. in action, utilizing the final version of the "U.N.C.L.E. gun," during "The Prince of Darkness Affair" episode. (NBC: courtesy of the Bob Short Collection)

A portrait of the U.N.C.L.E. family: David McCallum holding the gun as agent Illya Kuryakin; Robert Vaughn as Solo holding the "cigarette-case communicator"— which was used the first season, before the radio-pen was introduced; and Leo G. Carroll as U.N.C.L.E. head Alexander Waverly. (NBC)

By the time the summer reruns started, 50 percent of the audience was tuned to NBC enjoying the antics of Napoleon Solo and company. Robert Vaughn, who had hardly been seen as A. Dunster Lowell, parlayed the Solo part and an Academy Award nomination for best supporting actor in *The Young Philadelphians* (1959) into a career. His fine performance as the bitter gunfighter in *The Magnificent Seven* (1960) also led to his casting as the suave Solo.

Joining him on the merry U.N.C.L.E. ride was David McCallum as Russian agent Illya Kuryakin—another big reason the series made it. McCallum started his career as a child actor in Scotland and went on to good performances in *Billy Budd* (1962) and *The Great Escape*

(1963). His boyish good looks gave Kuryakin an attractiveness that Solo didn't possess. That, and the fact that he single-handedly started a whole new fashion trend, made him the more popular U.N.C.L.E. star.

Illya had a habit of wearing turtlenecks instead of a shirt and tie. What started as a character trait soon blossomed into a fad and then a sartorial staple. Fancy restaurants' "coat and tie required" soon turned into just "coat required," as Hollywood biggies all followed McCallum's example and the nation followed suit (but not tie). A poster depicting Illya in his turtleneck and pointing the U.N.C.L.E. gun became one of the sixties' best-sellers.

The Man from U.N.C.L.E. television

Just a small example of U.N.C.L.E. mania. In addition to the U.N.C.L.E. sweatshirt, pajamas, button-down shirt, and socks, there was an U.N.C.L.E. game, magazine, books, and a radio which turned into a rifle at the flick of a switch.

show almost became secondary to *The Man from U.N.C.L.E.* industry. Besides fads, it also gave birth to an entire line of toy products based on the gadgets used in the series: cigarette cases that were disguised communication devices, radios that were disguised as pens, and gas-spouting alarm clocks, cameras, canes, and fountain pens.

U.N.C.L.E. was not the most brilliant drama ever produced. In fact, it was considered more a spy spoof than an espionage adventure. The millions of youngsters and teens who made

U.N.C.L.E. a hit ignored the fact that Vaughn and McCallum were shorter than almost everyone else on the show. They ignored the inconsistencies of the increasingly outlandish episodes. All they cared about were their heroes and their comic strip-like battles against the evil organization THRUSH.

Like Sherlock Holmes with Professor Moriarty, U.N.C.L.E. had THRUSH, an insidious organization that sought to take over the world, or destroy it in the process. THRUSH was created in response to the James Bond adversary SPECTRE, in-

This black bird was the insignia of THRUSH, the international organization of evil, dedicated to destroying U.N.C.L.E. and the free world. The letters spelling THRUSH didn't stand for anything until the main U.N.C.L.E. fan club suggested a title which the show's producers accepted. (courtesy of the Bob Short Collection)

troduced in *Dr. No.* THRUSH was never an acronym for anything, even though the U.N.C.L.E. fan club asked if it could stand for the Technological Hierarchy for the Removal of Undesirables and the Subjugation of Humanity, and the producers said okay. It was reaching, but there it is.

James Bond had his superior M, and the U.N.C.L.E. agents had Alexander Waverly, a brilliant old gentleman played by Leo G. Carroll. Carroll gained fame as the star of the sitcom *Topper* (1953) but was pleased to spend his final years working. His only complaint? "I'm stuck behind a table all the time! All I do once a week is press a couple of buttons to send the agents on their way." Still, he did even that very well, garnering reviews like "classy and charming" from *TV Guide.*

The Man from U.N.C.L.E. died in 1968, not from old age but from an overdose of high spirits. Soon after agent 007's star had burned down to nova level, *Batman's* star went *super*nova. Viewers responded to this new hero who

was outrageous, campy, and knowingly stupid. Sadly, the U.N.C.L.E. producers thought that their show's longevity would be assured by following suit.

The NBC network probably had a lot to do with the change because they wanted a success on the level of ABC's *Batman.* Norman Felton created a campy spinoff called *The Girl from U.N.C.L.E.* in 1966. It was based on a *Man from . . .* episode called "The Moonglow Affair," which starred Norman Fell as an aging agent teamed up with a beautiful girl. It was a decent melodrama, with Fell showing he still had what it took at the finale.

In the spinoffs, Fell was nowhere to be seen. Instead Noel Harrison, Rex's son, played Mark Slate, a hip, blond English agent who was teamed with vivacious April Dancer, played by Stephanie Powers. Together they stumbled through adventures that made the far-fetched *Man from . . .* plots look like *War and Peace. The Girl from U.N.C.L.E.* was an absurdly ludicrous show and deserved its fate of cancellation after one season.

From **The Man from U.N.C.L.E.**'s rib came **The Girl from U.N.C.L.E.**, starring
Stephanie Powers as April Dancer—taking over the role from Mary Ann Mobley
who played the part in the pilot. This photo gives an example of how moronic this
spinoff was and why it failed so badly. (NBC)

If NBC had not been so eager to tamper with its success, U.N.C.L.E. would probably have been going strong when 1966 rolled around. There were two big-selling record albums based on the U.N.C.L.E. themes (composed by Jerry Goldsmith and Lalo Schifrin) as well as five theatrical features put together from two-part TV episodes. The network was not swayed. *The Man from U.N.C.L.E.* got campier and campier.

The U.N.C.L.E. audience was diminished by the stupid stories and the switch to a Friday time slot. At the beginning of the 1967 season, it was returned to its Monday berth with a large dose of realism injected, but it was too late. The series said "uncle" on January 15, 1968, after more than one hundred episodes.

For years Norman Felton and MGM-TV sought to revive *The Man from U.N.C.L.E.* as a TV special or theatrical film, but although announced in negotiation several times, nothing has come of it. Vaughn went on to other things; McCallum worked on stage and in some disappointing films before returning to TV for the equally disappointing *The*

Invisible Man (1975). Even the reruns remain in the MGM vault while lesser efforts are syndicated constantly.

U.N.C.L.E. was not the only genre offering of 1964, but it was the only successful one. *The Reporter* was a run-of-the-mill show created by Jerome Weidman, the author of *I Can Get It for You Wholesale*. Presented by Richelieu Productions on CBS, it was just another newspaper drama featuring a tough but tender news hound.

Harry Guardino—a far from mediocre actor—played Danny Taylor, the reporter. Gary Merrill, a dependable actor, played Lou Sheldon, his crusty but understanding editor. George O'Hanlon played Artie, the cute but clever cabby, and Remo Pisani played Ike Dawson, the manager of the Press Box bar and grill. Up against *The Jack Paar Show* on Friday night, *The Reporter* only made it through 13 weeks.

Sophistication and entertainment quality were the hallmarks of Four Star Productions, the organization Dick Powell

The Rogues, framed for a publicity photo. From the left: Gig Young, Charles Boyer, and David Niven. (NBC)

so influenced. After Powell's death, as previously noted, the company sprang *Burke's Law* on everybody. In 1964, they set *The Rogues* off to do their thing. Their thing included being better gentlemen thieves and con artists than the Saint, Boston Blackie, and the Lone Wolf rolled into one!

Tom McDermott, a former advertising executive, took Dick Powell's place on the business side while Four Star acting veterans David Niven and Charles Boyer went to work in front of the cameras, playing (respectively) Alec Fleming, the greatest criminal of them all, and Marcel St. Clair, the head of the clan on their French mother's side. Rounding out the on-screen family—descended from a British knight and a French countess—was Gig Young as their American relative, Tony Fleming, Robert Coote as Timmy Fleming, a jack-of-all-cons, and Gladys Cooper as the matriarch Margaret Fleming, the real brains of the clan. Adding conflict was John Williams playing Inspector Briscoe of Scotland Yard.

The New York Times called *The Rogues* "a joyous outing! Superbly played, deftly written and mounted with sophistication." But it seems the audiences of 1964 were not interested in deft writing and sophistication. Even against such thin competition as *Candid Camera* (1948) and *What's My Line?* (1950), it still failed to last more than one year.

Network television was now almost 20 years old. Its maturity was beginning to show, not necessarily in the programs it chose to air, but in the new concepts and formats it was creating for itself. In 1964, NBC-TV and Universal Studios created the Project 120 concept; the latter would

produce motion pictures *made specifically* for TV and the former would air them. Today, the made-for-TV movie— or teleflick or "Big Event" or just plain TV movie— is an accepted format much beloved by viewers. Back then, it was an audacious idea that bore watching.

Curiously, the television audience did not see the first Project 120 effort first. Don (*Dirty Harry*) Siegal's *The Killers*, starring Lee Marvin and Ronald Reagan, was deemed too violent for the tube and was given a theatrical release instead. (President Reagan played a slimy villain responsible for the death of John Cassavetes.) The second Project 120 was aired on October of 1964 and starred John Forsythe. *See How They Run* was about some kids stalked by hit men because they had evidence damaging to the underworld.

1965

In 1965, ABC-TV was having a bad year. The idea of dropping truly miserable shows and replacing them before the end of the season was nothing new, but this year ABC President Thomas Moore set aside a specific period for that purpose. Thus, the "second season" was born. Now, somewhere between the end of one year and the beginning of another, networks could ax the clinkers and let the public pass judgment on a whole new set of shows.

The modern era of programming chaos truly began. The changes, although not felt until a few years later, seemed to have a positive effect on the mystery genre. There were more mysteries this year, and by and large they were better. For example, *Trials of O'Brien* was an entertaining and unusual lawyer series. The title was a pun on not just the actual cases of lawyer Daniel J. O'Brien, but also the "trials" of his private life. He seemed to be one of the most slovenly, and disorganized attorneys in New York.

High on O'Brien's list of personal problems to resolve was desire to get back with his beautiful ex-wife Katie, played by Joanna Barnes. His next priority was his gambling problem. All the money he made seemed to pass right into the hands of his bookie and the Internal Revenue Service. Yet all was not as it seemed. For O'Brien may have looked sloppy, but he lived in a sumptuous apartment and ran a very successful firm.

Peter Falk played O'Brien: that helps to resolve some of the incongruities. The image of the rumpled, diminutive actor playing a fellow who looks as if he cannot tie his shoes but happens to be one of the most brilliant detectives in the world seems familiar. Of course it is familiar, but it did not work in 1965. *The Trials of O'Brien* did not fall victim to the second season, but it did not last more than one year, either. Falk was to reproduce the O'Brien personality for another franchise a few years later, making a much bigger noise, as we shall see.

In the meantime, the cancellation of *The Rogues* did not slow down Four Star Productions. During *The Rogues* run, they introduced a female private eye on an April episode of *Burke's Law*. They gave her her own series in the fall of 1965. *Honey West* was a TV rarity—it

Anne Francis, introduced as an ingenue in the classic science-fiction film **Forbidden Planet** *(1956) looks a little older, but much better armed as* **Honey West.** *(ABC)*

had a female hero. What could have been a ground-breaking show settled into being just another short-lived effort mimicking *Batman* and James Bond.

Honey West, played by Anne Francis, was partnered with the aptly named Sam Bolt, played by rugged, squinty-eyed John Ericson. When Honey got into a fix she couldn't kick or shoot her way out of, Bolt would bolt from here to there to save his partner's sexy skin. The show had a ludicrous number of gimmicks. Honey had a four-wheeled electronic detective lab in a van marked H. W. Bolt & Co., TV Service. She had a pet ocelot named Bruce. She had an annoying aunt played by Irene Hervey.

Honey was loaded down with gadgets which never helped when the going got rough. Besides the .38 in her handbag

and the derringer tucked elsewhere, Honey had a compact which exploded, a garter-belt gas mask, tear-gas earrings, and a lipstick microphone. Anne Francis played Honey as best she could given the circumstances, but it is doubtful if even Raquel Welch could have saved this show. It disappeared from the screen after a year.

Lawyer shows and private-eye shows were not doing so well in 1965, but Westerns were. *Bonanza* premiered and was shooting up everything including the ratings charts. Ford Motors was kind of jealous of Chevrolet's sponsorship of the Western, so they countered by sponsoring Quinn Martin's new show, *The F.B.I.*. The producer of *The Untouchables* and

Stephen Young (left) and Efrem Zimbalist, Jr., try to get the goods on the bad guys as agents of **The F.B.I.** *(ABC)*

The Fugitive wanted to make a flag-waving, trumpet-blowing, unquestioning glorification of the Federal Bureau of Investigation. J. Edgar Hoover, ever the master media manipulator, liked the idea and opened certain files to Martin.

The F.B.I. succeeded in entertaining America for nine years while serving as the best public relations possible for the bureau. Efrem Zimbalist, Jr., played Inspector Lewis Erskine, as devoted an agent as one could wish for and the foe of assorted public enemies.

Zimbalist finally got into the spotlight after having shared the *77 Sunset Strip* space with almost everyone Warner Brothers ever created. Critics approved of the choice; one said that he was "as fine a lead as any this year." They weren't as easy on the show itself. The unabashed patriotism made some uneasy. "It's all played *too* straight," said one review.

Essentially, that was both the failure and saving grace of the show. It could hardly be considered a "textured" program. Most episodes started with a crime. Just before the opening credits, there would be a freeze frame and the criminal's name and crime would be emblazoned on the screen. Then, after the initial commercial, Erskine and company would get into their fleet of Fords and methodically, dispassionately, professionally run the criminal to ground.

In the first season, color was added with Lynn Loring playing Erskine's daughter, Barbara. She was eliminated after the first season as a distraction to the main order of business: catching public enemies. Retained were Erskine's boss, Assistant F.B.I. Director Arthur Ward (Philip Abbott), and younger assistant agent Jim Rhodes (Stephen Brooks). Play-

ing partner to Erskine was a thankless job. Zimbalist was a good enough actor to completely fill the screen whenever he was on, but when Brooks left he was replaced by William Reynolds, a supporting lead who had done the same sort of work in *Pete Kelley's Blues* (1959), *The Islanders*, and *The Gallant Men* (1962). Here he played special agent Tom Colby until 1973. Then he too got fed up.

"They treat me like a middleweight and I want to be a light heavyweight," he complained. Following his exit came Shelly Novack as agent Chris Daniels. Throughout the cast changes Zimbalist remained Erskine and Erskine remained the same arrest automaton he had always been. A source of satire was Erskine's ability to spy a criminal, shout "Hold it! F.B.I.!" and then—no matter how far away, no matter how heavily armed, no matter what the obstruction—shoot him *only* in the shoulder without batting an eye. Erskine, like the Royal Canadian Mounted Police, always got his man.

While *The F.B.I.* maintained the TV detective status quo, *I Spy* was revolutionary. Nothing seemed unusual about *I Spy* at first. Besides having the same name as the Raymond Massey-hosted anthology of some years earlier, it seemed to be the simple tale of a tennis pro and his trainer who were actually a pair of secret agents for the United States government. But producers Sheldon Leonard and David Friedkin had thrown a couple of wrenches into the works.

First, *I Spy* was about as traditional a spy series as Truman Capote is a traditional writer. Second, the role of Alexander Scott, the tennis trainer, was played by comedian Bill Cosby. No big deal? Perhaps not today, but in 1965 it was a *huge* deal. *The Nat King Cole Show* had been dropped in 1958 because no one would sponsor it. Even though there are still racial problems now, they do not compare to the bigotry and ignorance of just a few years ago.

It helped that Cosby was not cast because Scott *had* to be a black. He was cast because he was best for the role. Further aid was apparent in the form of co-star Robert Culp, playing undercover tennis pro Kelly Robinson. Culp was a young but excellent actor who got his start on the late fifties drama anthologies. He did his first film work in 1963 for *PT 109*. During *I Spy*'s run he was to exercise his talents as a director and writer as well.

David Friedkin supervised the worldwide on-location shooting for the *I Spy* crew. In conjunction with Mort Fine, he wrote many of the scripts while such talents as Tom Gries, Paul Wendkos, and Richard Sarafian directed them in Greece, Hong Kong, and other exotic locations. The writers created compelling dramatic scripts, but none of them were responsible for the clever banter that went on between Robinson and Scott. Culp and Cosby kept up their own friendly patter, which went a long way toward making viewers love them.

The Academy of Television Arts and Sciences loved them, too, but the society's members seemed more intent on pointing out the crossed color barrier than did the show itself. For three years in a row they awarded the Emmy for the Best Actor in a Drama to Bill Cosby and seemed to be oblivious to the exceptional work of Culp. Cosby openly admitted that Culp "taught me everything I

know." It is not that Cosby did not deserve it, but three years in a row was a little obvious and a little ridiculous.

After three seasons on NBC, the two actors had just about had it. The shooting schedule was murder and it was getting more and more difficult to maintain the level of quality. The series had already accomplished what it set out to do: entertain while raising some questions about the morality of the government and espionage work (Robinson and Scott had both been on the verge of quitting at one time or another), so everyone agreed to call it quits. *I Spy* became a landmark in television history for being the first series with a black lead—and it is remembered as one of the best TV spy shows.

But just one of the best. If push comes to shove, *Secret Agent* would have to be called the best. It had a strange and wondrous history which goes back to 1961. CBS replaced *Wanted: Dead or Alive* (1958)—the Western starring Steve McQueen as bounty hunter Josh Randall—with *Danger Man*, an English import produced by the Associated Television Corporation (ATV) and distributed by I.T.C.

Danger Man starred American-born Patrick McGoohan as an operative for the North Atlantic Treaty Organization (NATO) named John Drake. Considering the series had its United States premiere a year before *Dr. No* was released, Drake's outlandish adventures the world over were fairly groundbreaking. He was a suave but extremely dangerous sort, with one of the hardest right crosses on television. If his fist connected, his adversary would be knocked out at the very least, or across the room at the very most.

This half-hour program left in September with hardly a word of publicity or

review. The John Drake character stayed off the air until 1965 when CBS brought him back as a summer replacement. This was a new John Drake, no longer prone toward fisticuffs. He had a new boss in the British government. He was now on her Majesty's Secret Service as a *Secret Agent*.

This was the show that got the attention. Critics invariably compared it to *The Man from U.N.C.L.E.* and consistently found the American show wanting. "The plots are tricky, not hokey," said a reviewer. "And the dialog sizzles with believability. All the scripts abound with complexities." Star McGoohan and producer Ralph Smart were mostly responsible. The stories ranged from seemingly mundane missions to find out why an agent had not contacted London lately to infiltrating a school for Russian spies.

There were gadgets and plenty of action, but never outside the realm of possibility. Drake's most outlandish machinery was a typewriter that incorporated a camera and an electric shaver that was actually a tape recorder. Drake now did not like to fight if he could use his brain instead. He professed to never carrying guns ("Ugly, oily things. They could hurt someone."), but he could use one effectively when he had to.

These newly made, stark, realistic hour-long adventures impressed everyone who watched, including CBS. They scheduled new episodes of *Secret Agent* to replace *The Trials of O'Brien*, which they moved to Friday nights in December

The many faces, hats, shirts, and jackets of John Drake—as played by Patrick McGoohan—the Secret Agent. *(ITC Entertainment, Inc.)*

1965. John Drake got through another year in America before they canceled him again.

"They decided," Cleveland Amory fumed, referring to CBS, "in their infinite idiocy, to take *Secret Agent* off the air. And against, mind you, the specific, utterly systematic advice of this critic. Still, they wouldn't give us back the peerless Patrick McGoohan."

Amory had only to take heart and hold on for two more years. On June 1, 1968, John Drake was brought back by CBS as a summer fill-in for *The Jackie Gleason Show*. In this third incarnation, Drake's series was called *The Prisoner*.

But was it John Drake who Patrick McGoohan was playing? At the beginning of this first episode (and almost every episode that followed) there is a thunderclap and the view of a dark storm cloud. Then, from down a long flat road comes a man driving furiously in a convertible sports car. He drives to London and parks in an underground garage. The next thing we see is the man walking purposefully down a dark hallway. He flings open two doors and glowers at a man behind a desk. The music from the sound track (by Ron Grainer) builds dramatically. Finally, he slams down a paper which we assume is his resignation since his identification card is plucked from the active files, defaced and refiled under RESIGNED."

When next we see the man he is back in the streets, driving toward his apartment. He is unaware that a large hearse-like van is following him. At home he quickly packs—travel brochures lying about suggest a vacation in the tropics. But then the hearse pulls up outside and shortly thereafter gas pours through the apartment door keyhole. The man stiff-

112   TV DETECTIVES

ens. Taking one last look about him, he falls, unconscious, onto his bed.

This is just the first part of the opening. The man is Patrick McGoohan, and by what he does and the way he does it we can only assume that he is still a secret agent. And if a secret agent, then inevitably John Drake. After a quick fade, we see the man awakening in his bed in his room. But when he groggily goes to the window he sees outside a strange medieval environment rather than a city.

As he investigates his new surroundings, the credits start and a dialog is heard. (McGoohan was not only the star, but the series' creator, executive producer, and often the writer and/or direc-

tor of the episodes.) The voice-over dialog is strange and representative of the series as a whole.

McGoohan: Where am I?
A Different Voice Each Week: In The Village.
McG: What do you want?
Voice: Information.
McG: Whose side are you on?
Voice: That would be telling. We want information . . . information . . . information!
McG: You won't get it.
Voice: By hook or by crook, we will.
McG: Who are you?
Voice: The new Number Two.
McG: (*flatly, metallically*) Who is

It looks like "Number 6" has usurped the "Number 2" position of guest star Eric Portman in the "Free for All" episode of The Prisoner—*created, executive produced, and starred in by Patrick McGoohan—but nothing is what it seems in "the Village."*
(*ITC Entertainment, Inc.*)

Number One?
Voice: *You* are Number Six.
McG: (*shouting*) I am not a number! I am a free man!
Voice: (*laughter*)

It was a stunning opening to a stunning show. It stands as one of the most audacious, infuriating, challenging, confusing, inventive, and exciting series of any kind ever televised. Number Six becomes the ultimate detective. All the different Number Two's attempt to find out why he resigned while he foils them in order to maintain his individuality.

The Prisoner was not only different in theme, it was different in structure. McGoohan made only a set number of episodes—19 at last count—and no more. These episodes detail his arrival, his many battles with The Village hierarchy and residents, and then his escape. Producer David Tomblin and script editor George Markstein saw to it that these battles involved a range of activities: science fiction clashes of dream stealing, brainwashing, and computers; to satires of *Secret Agent* serials and James Bond movies; and Pinteresque conversations.

Finally, The Village exhausts all its domination techniques and in the last episode offers Number Six leadership of The Village. By way of reply, he mounts a revolution and goes off to confront Number One. Once he corners the cowled figure, McGoohan throws back the hood to see a rubber ape mask. When he pulls off the mask he sees the distorted, hysterical face of himself.

The Prisoner left two major questions unanswered. Was Number Six John Drake? And what the hell did it all mean? As for the second query, perhaps Patrick McGoohan's remarks about television

might offer a clue: "There's a brainwasher for you. All that advertising . . . the preoccupation with the trivial . . . with the way things and people look rather than how they really are."

The Prisoner, then, might be a very serious joke—a celluloid pie in the face of the medium presenting it.

As to the Drake question, it can never be completely answered. There is said to be an episode of *Secret Agent* never shown in this country with John Drake investigating the story of a brain transferal device in Europe. The story is that Drake lets the inventor get away and is reprimanded by his superiors. Some feel that Drake resigns after that as a matter of principle, and the prime evidence for Number Six being Drake comes in a *Prisoner* episode called "A Change of Mind." That's where a brain transferal device made by a captured scientist is used on Number Six.

Whether true or false, it hardly makes a difference. What does make a difference is that *The Prisoner* was made and rebroadcast several times on CBS and PBS stations.

A 1965 CBS show that combined the best of Westerns with the best of action-oriented espionage was *The Wild Wild West*.

Created by Michael Garrison for Bruce Lansbury Productions, the program was a crazy framework to display the talents of two government agents in the late nineteenth century. Only these men thought they were living in the twentieth century! James T. West and Artemus Gordon, two of President Ulysses S. Grant's best men, lived in an opulently appointed railway car. It had a kitchen, a lab, an arsenal, and a parlor outfitted with an escape hatch in the fireplace. The pair ate, slept and worked out of it, traveling the new nation to right wrongs and fight evil.

TV detective veterans Robert Conrad and Ross Martin played the leads. Conrad played West as a self-assured, smug wild man who would rather mop up a bar with an entire crew of wharf rats than seek out evidence. Martin played Gordon, the more studious of the partners. When he was not inventing a new weapon West could use, he was disguising himself and using a dialect to get after their adversaries.

Their adversaries were very impressive, as were the threats they posed. Lloyd Bochner played Zacariah Skull in one episode. Victor Buono played Count Manzeppi, an evil Magician, in another. But the most famous of the show's villains was Dr. Miguelito Loveless, played by Michael Dunn, an actor who was a dwarf. His size did not stop him from trying to take over the world time and time again.

James T. and Artemus accepted all challenges, using their rustic gadgetry to foil the bad guys. One of West's devices was a derringer that shot a miniature grappling hook with wire attached. They could make a gun or a sword out of nearly anything. They needed this skill, too, as they took on things like a submarine disguised as a dragon in "The Night of the Watery Death" and a missile shaped like a bird in "The Night of the Condor" episode.

While bizarre, Lansbury and his fellow producers (Collier Young, Gene L. Coon, and Richard Landau among others) rarely allowed the humor to be at the expense of the show. Things became campy, but not in the self-conscious way of *Batman*

and *The Girl from U.N.C.L.E.* Conrad and Martin played everything straight while directors Richard Donner (*Superman*, 1978), Bernard Kowalsky, Sherman Marks, Charles Rondeau, and others kept an eye on the goings-on.

No matter what the plot or approach, at least once a half hour (often more), James T. West would hear fighting words and nothing could hold him back. The viewers could settle in and watch the agent beat up whole gangs of ruffians in some of the most elaborate fights since the days of the movie serials. It was these action scenes, almost slapstick in style, that got the show killed—not diminished ratings.

Even after four and a half seasons on the air, and even after Ross Martin was replaced by Charles Aidman as Jeremy Pike, *The Wild Wild West* was still going strong in 1970. In 1969, however, the Surgeon General of the United States was ordered to find out what effects TV violence had on children. Although his report wasn't published until 1972, the very fact that it was being prepared sent shock waves throughout the industry. Dr. Frank Stanton, then president of CBS, vowed to beat the Surgeon General to the punch. His own war on violence included axing *The Wild Wild West*.

In 1979 CBS Entertainment presented a special TV movie, *The Wild Wild West Revisited*. James T. West and Artemus Gordon were back—ten years later—

After 10 years CBS decided to resurrect **The Wild Wild West** *as a 1979 TV movie—***The Wild Wild West Revisited.** *Although a decade older, Robert Conrad (top) and Ross Martin (bottom) returned to the famous roles of James T. West and Artemus Gordon. Their reunion proved so popular that 1980 featured another TV movie—***More Wild Wild West.** *(CBS)*

with older and wiser Robert Conrad and Ross Martin returning to the roles. This time Miguelito Loveless, Jr., was out to take over the world using bionic doubles ("Six hundred-dollar men," he called them) as his army. The humor was broader than it had been in the series and the action was toned down considerably.

Western film veteran Burt Kennedy directed and singer/songwriter/actor Paul Williams turned in a neat performance as the villain. It was entertaining enough to warrant the appearance of *More Wild Wild West* in 1980. This time comedian Jonathan Winters played "daffy, megalomaniacal Albert Paradine II who wants nothing less than to rule the world," according to the press release. The humor was even broader the second time around, and much of it was at the expense of the characters. To give an idea of just how far it was stretched, noted fitness expert Jack LaLanne guest-starred as a character named Jack LaStrange and Dr. Joyce Brothers had a cameo as a "bystander."

The ideas were too cute and the script too thin, so *More Wild Wild West* went into the dumper. No further sequels have been mentioned thus far.

If *The Wild Wild West* was done tongue-in cheek, then *Get Smart* was done tongue-through-cheek, fingers-tickling sides, and elbow-breaking-funnybone. *Get Smart* also shared a kinship with the *West* show in that the villain in Smart's first episode, Mr. Big, was played by Michael Dunn.

In that episode, telecast September 18, 1965, there was a bit of dialog that was the show's high point. Cornered by the villain on a boat, secret agent Maxwell Smart attempts a show of bravado. "Would you believe that seven Coast Guard cutters are converging on us at this very moment?"

Mr. Big: I find that hard to believe.
Max: Would you believe six?
Mr. Big: I don't think so.
Max: How about two cops in a row-boat?

It was a classic piece of comedy that would be repeated in slightly different form throughout the five-year run of the spy sitcom. In the beginning, however, there were only Mel Brooks and Buck Henry. The two humorists, who have both gone on to movie fame, conceived Maxwell Smart, Agent 86 of C.O.N.-T.R.O.L., a super tiptop secret government agency that everyone seemed to know about. Its entrance was a pair of elevator doors that opened onto a stairway that led down to a hall that was interrupted by many swinging and sliding doors which ended in a telephone booth whose floor fell out after Max inserted a dime and dialed.

C.O.N.T.R.O.L. headquarters was located at 123 Main Street, Washington, D.C. There worked the forever nameless female operative, Agent 99, and the long-suffering Chief, who was also known as Thaddeus. Together, they fought the forces of K.A.O.S., an organization as rotten as C.O.N.T.R.O.L. was nifty. To do this, they used as a cover the fake Pontiac Greeting Card Company, where Max was a salesman and the Chief his boss.

As far as viewers were concerned, comedian/actor Don Adams *was* Maxwell Smart from the moment they set eyes on him. Smart's *schtick* was so inseparable from Adams' standup routines, the typecasting hardly mattered. Agent 99 was played by ex-show girl, ex-model Barbara Feldon. The Chief was played by

Unbeknownst to Agent 99 (Barbara Feldon, on the right) a talking doll with a secret message has just piddled on Maxwell Smart, Agent 86 of the supersecret spy organization, C.O.N.T.R.O.L. The look on the face of master comedy actor Don Adams says it all. (NBC)

the very inventive Ed Platt, who took the thankless job and made it continually fresh. "I'm a foil," he said to describe the role. "A frustration symbol who borders on the psychotic."

Maxwell Smart was just the sort of man who would make anyone psychotic. As the series progressed, more and more running gags and recurring characters were introduced. In addition to the "Would you believe . . . ?" line, Adams coined the "Sorry about that, Chief," line for every instance he caused some sort of damage to his boss (which was often). Larrabee, an innocuous agent who seemed to be the Chief's receptionist,

was played by Robert Karvelas. There was the "telephone" shoe, which Max used after taking off the sole and heel. A major change came later when the shoe went from dial to push-button.

There was Fang, Agent K-9, of C.O.N.T.R.O.L.'s dog agents, who failed to sniff out much of anything in the first season. There was the "Cone of Silence," an anti-bugging device which had the effect of making almost everything that was said under it unintelligible. There was Conrad Siegfried McTavish, the German-accented head of K.A.O.S., played by Bernie Kopell (now on *The Love Boat*), and his assistant

Starker who loved motorcycles. King Moody, who played Starker, is now Ronald McDonald on commercials.

Other characters of note were Hymie (Dick Gautier), originally an evil K.A.O.S. robot turned to the side of right by Max; former C.O.N.T.R.O.L. head Admiral Harold Harmon Hargrade, now retired, prone to sudden naps and senility (William Schallert); and Agent 13, who could be counted on to be hiding in lockers, cigarette machines, grandfather clocks, and any other weird contraption the prop people came up with (Dave Ketchum).

Max's apartment was filled with security devices that constantly changed; an invisible wall that invariably knocked the wrong person out remained, however.

The gags were all good and funny, so no one really got tired of the look-alike situations. The problem came when no new gimmicks could be spun off from the old ones. Then, in the fourth season, they attempted to make the spy satire into a domestic comedy by having the long-frustrated love between 86 and 99 bloom. By the end of the season, they were wed—Max making a shambles of the Chief in the process. NBC saw no future for the couple, so it canceled the series.

The CBS network was not so insensitive and picked the program up to fill a Friday night slot. There the happy couple gave birth to a baby boy and their fate was sealed. The show was still funny, but it was not the same. The feeling that secret agents shouldn't have loved ones proved right. *Get Smart* now dealt with family affairs as much as secret missions. It did not work and CBS knew it. *Get Smart* went off the air in 1970.

Just like *The Wild Wild West* before it, cancellation didn't mean it was gone for good. Maxwell Smart returned in 1980 with an eight million-dollar Universal movie that was originally to be called *The Return of Maxwell Smart*. Don Adams was back playing the role, but the heart that was Agent 99 and the soul that was the Chief were missing. Ed Platt had died in 1974, and Barbara Feldon was either not interested or not invited to return.

Worse, the times had changed. Government was no longer funny, thanks to Watergate and the ever-growing awareness of corruption and stupidity in Washington. The movie tried to compensate for this with a plot that had K.A.O.S. threatening to use a weapon that would destroy all clothing. But Max alone was not enough to make *The Nude Bomb*—the new title—even a mildly amusing curiosity piece. Without the Chief, Agent 99, Siegfried, Hymie, and all the others, Don Adams looked truly naked on the screen.

Maxwell Smart is best remembered the way Peter Gunn was—before both were adapted to movies. It is best to laugh at *Get Smart*'s reruns on TV, remembering a time when the word "corruption" only referred to the bad guys and we didn't know all the things we were to shockingly discover through television.

Hip City

The truth was coming out. Like an overeager child anxious to impress his peers (and unmindful of the possible consequences), television seemed to take delight in showing us just how warped our world had become. President Lyndon Baines Johnson got on the tube to announce renewed bombing of North Vietnam. Renewed? Most people did not know there had been *any* bombing at all! Doesn't that word mean the continuation of our favorite shows?

1966

The television programmers were just as anxious to soothe our piqued consciousnesses as the news departments were to provoke them. The Pablum kept coming with *Green Acres, My Mother the Car, Family Affair,* and *I Dream of Jeannie*. But there were signs of cracking. *Hogan's Heroes* and *Star Trek* showed up, altering some people's perceptions of exactly what is popular. Some war series showed up—like *Blue Light* and *The*

Man Who Never Was—and all failed. The super heroes faded—*Batman*'s initial huge popularity fell off fast and *The Green Hornet* seemed to be over just as it got started.

For the most part, the mysteries of the year were dark, brooding, cerebral approaches to detective work. The single entry from the "squared-jaw" school of cop series was *The Felony Squad*, a grim 30-minute ABC effort produced by the 20th Century-Fox studio.

It was cast with an eye to familiar faces—to give audiences a respected, well-known TV detective to hold on to during the trying plots. Leading the way was Howard Duff as Detective Sam Stone (a name obviously patterned on the famous hard-boiled detective Sam Spade, whom Duff played on radio). Right behind him was ex-*Dragnet* partner Ben Alexander playing Sergeant Dan Briggs. Alexander still had the same hound-dog look he had when playing Officer Frank Smith opposite Joe Friday, only now he was heavier. Playing Briggs's son was a newcomer, Dennis Cole. Cole

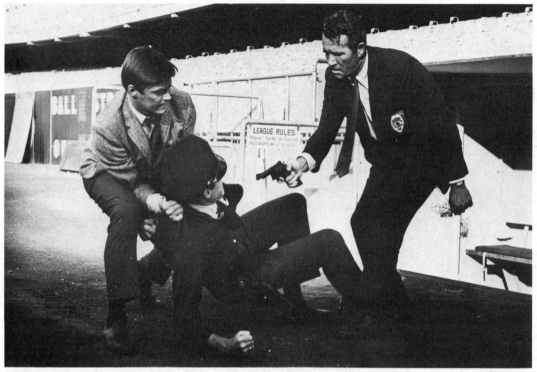

Dennis Cole (left) and gun-pointing Howard Duff bring down actor Kevin Hagen, who's playing a crook in disguise. It's all part of the job for **The Felony Squad.** *(ABC)*

played Detective Jim Briggs, Stone's inexperienced partner.

Rounding out the crew was Frank Maxwell as their superior, Captain Nye. Later he was replaced by Barney Phillips as Captain Franks for a while. Even with this crew to build stories on, the writers had a hard time adjusting to what they read in the newspapers and saw on the newscasts. Crime didn't make sense as it used to. In the debut episode, "The Streets Are Paved with Quicksand," a cop is heard to say, "Today's breed of killer doesn't always oblige with a neat, understandable motive. That's what makes him so lethal and us cops gray before our time."

It is also what gives writers an excuse

to pour on the violence and make viewers gray before *our* time. The reviewers couldn't help but agree. One said tersely: "Top cops, rough toughs, fun guns, thrill kills, but no style."

The whole thing had a vague air of desperation about it as the Felony Squad prowled the Los Angeles streets to capture sweaty swine. Howard Duff was as worried about the show as the critics were. "I thought *Mr. Adams and Eve* was a drag," he said in an interview, "but this is worse. Sometimes I wonder if I've sold out . . . maybe I have." *The Felony Squad* kept Duff selling out for three seasons, but they were rough, ugly years that look sad in the syndicated reruns.

Just up the coast from the Squad was a

detective with a specialty. He didn't go after a murderer, he went after the victim to protect him from the potential murderer! *T.H.E. Cat* was an NBC series that tried to substitute swashbuckling for violence. T.H.E. stood for Thomas Hewitt Edward (get it? Thomas Cat? Tom Cat?), a fact the character repeated just before every opening credit.

The openings were like those of *The Saint*. Thomas Hewitt Edward would either do something neat, or someone would be looking for him, but he would always be asked his name. Then, with smug poise, he would rattle off the four monikers in clipped tones. After that an animated credit sequence like that of *Peter Gunn* crossed with *Suspense* (1949) rolled. The whole format was annoyingly similar to Gunn.

T.H.E. Cat was a professional bodyguard who lived in what was initially termed ''a contemporary metropolis''—which is just another name for the studio back lot. His office was in a nightclub called the Casa del Gato (*gato* means ''cat'' in Spanish), which was owned by Pepi, whose life had been saved by Cat in the past. From there he took assignments to protect life and limb. He did not carry a gun, but he always seemed to have lots of rope and grappling hooks.

Pepi was played by Robert Carricart while Cat was Robert Loggia, another stunt man turned actor. Interestingly enough, he had started in the Steve Carella part in the movie adaptation of the 87th Precinct book *Cop Hater*. The role that probably secured him this series, though, was the Walt Disney production of *The Nine Lives of Elfego Baca* (1959), in which he played Spanish swashbuckler El Gato. The movie was shown on Disney's television show and quite possibly it got producer Boris Sagal's creative juices flowing.

However it was conceived, *T.H.E. Cat* took place mostly on darkened streets and in the smoky nightclub. There was a feeling of claustrophobia in every shot, which did not make viewing comfortable. Even outside, the mood was so oppressive that it made one glad the program only ran 30 minutes. This discomfort was heightened as the weeks went on and viewers discovered that Cat did not seem to be very good at what he did.

He would climb a wall here and there and occasionally jump from hither to yon, but his clients often got killed. And no matter how fine a broad jumper he was, he could not jump bullets. The show went off after about six months.

Across the country from the Felony Squad and the bodyguard was another detective eager to ply his trade. Although he was featured in an hour-long show on NBC, he and Cat had a lot in common. First, both were produced by noted TV directors. Sagal did *Cat*, while Paul Bogart did *Hawk*. Secondly, both characters had a nighttime beat. With Hawk, the ABC publicity said it all: ''Full-blooded Indian . . . cold-blooded job. New York after dark is his beat!''

John Hawk was an Iroquois who was a member of the Manhattan district attorney's special investigative squad. This is where *Hawk* and *Cat* have a third aspect in common: the star of *Hawk*—Burt Reynolds—also used to do stunt work. Since Reynolds' grandmother was a Cherokee, it was not miscasting at all to make him *Hawk*. In fact, it was very nice. Up until then, he had only been in three movies and had character parts on *Riverboat* and *Gunsmoke*.

Burt Reynolds, looking suitably hawk-like for his dour, humorless role of American Indian detective John Hawk. It was the first of two cop shows that used the actor's athletic ability but ignored his inherent whimsical charm. (NBC)

Hawk was Reynolds' first starring TV series and he really put his muscle into it (of which he had plenty). John Hawk was a laconic, almost stolid character until he started fighting. Given the antiviolence edicts that were being handed down, he could do precious little fighting. Left motionless with pedestrian scripts, *Hawk* sank in a little more than four months.

Over at CBS, in the meantime, someone discovered a terrific way to shoo away the reality blues. He did it by creating a team of special operatives who weren't supermen—in fact, at first glance they seemed just like me or you—but still could do anything. The creator was Bruce Geller and the everyman-supermen were called the *Mission: Impossible* team. This long-running series

that rendered homage to team work and good old Yankee ingenuity, was conceived by a man who had written for *Jimmie Hughes, Rookie Cop* and *Rocky King* and had produced *Rawhide* before hitting on this big winner.

"Good morning, Mr. Briggs." Those four words were first spoken on September 17, 1966, and set the framework for the series over the next eight years. On the early shows, however, there were two major differences from later shows in the pre-credit teaser. For the first year the leader of the Impossible Missions Force (the I.M.F) was Dan Briggs, a quiet, chunky, dark-haired brain played by Steven Hill. And the climax line, the one so joyously satirized since, "This tape will self-destruct in five seconds," was not used the first few times out. Instead it was, "Please dispose of this tape in the usual manner," after which Briggs would throw the spool into a furnace, or an acid bath, or something like that.

Following that, Briggs would return to his fancy home and select the agents needed for the assignment he'd just been given, remembering the now-famous warning, "if you or any member of the I.M. Force be caught or killed, the Secretary will disavow any knowledge of your actions." He usually chose to use the services of Barney Collier, an electronics and engineering whiz played by Greg Morris. The role was originally conceived for a white man, and Morris, an ex-athlete who turned to acting after his coach died, joked about the racial situation. He said he was cast because he was

tall . . . and good. Another tall member of the I.M. Force was strongman Willy Armitage, played by strongman Peter Lupus. The final official member of the team in its first year was model Cinnamon Carter, played by cool Barbara Bain. The popular man-of-disguise, Rollin Hand, played by Bain's real-life husband Martin Landau, initially was reserved for a few "special guest star" appearances.

This first season produced a recognizable format that the subsequent seasons would use. Nevertheless, all the muscle and flesh of the first year would be ripped away before long. When the soft-spoken Briggs was in charge, the team was far from infallible and given to showing real feeling. It also acknowledged the morality of what it was doing. When detailing

In the beginning, the Mission: Impossible *team wasn't afraid to get its hands dirty. Then, actor Steven Hill (left) was boss Dan Briggs, shown here with Peter Lupus in the "Snowball in Hell" episode. (CBS)*

a mission to the Force that could have been done quicker another way, Briggs even went so far as to say: "Assassination is out as a matter of policy."

Much of the camaraderie and questions of morality disappeared the following year when Peter Graves, a brother of James Arness, took over the Force's leadership as Jim Phelps. He was a craggy-faced, white-haired, all-business hunk of a leading man. With him as head of the group, the *Mission: Impossible* settled onto the course it would follow for many years. Each week he would be told he had "a mission, should you decide to accept it," and every week, without refusal, he would deliver the goods with the help of his team and an outrageously timed plan which depended on split-second timing and ridiculous coincidences to work.

Making those coincidences seem natural was the job of Geller and his production team. The producer pushed his directors to be as innovative and stylish as possible given the budget and schedule. The dozens of directors—notably Lee H. Katzin, Reza Badiyi, and Alf Kjellin—did a reputable job, while much of the responsibility for the show's success rests squarely on the shoulders of the various film editors and writers. Lalo Schifrin's accompanying music helped a lot as well.

By the third season, *Mission: Impossible* was all over the top-ten ratings chart with husband-and-wife team Landau and Bain leading the popularity parade. Rollin Hand had since been promoted to regular agent along with the rest, and delighted the viewers with his Artemus Gordon-like disguises and dialects. The big difference between the two characters was that Rollin used life-masks to

effect his changes rather than stick little bits and pieces all over his face. A popular I.M.F. cliché was when someone would pull his entire fake face off, revealing someone else beneath.

Things were going great until the 1969 Emmy Awards. Barbara Bain was nominated and won an award for the "Outstanding Continued Performance by an Actress in a Leading Role in a Dramatic Series" (that's the actual category!). Instead of just thanking everyone and getting off, Bain leveled scathing remarks at Douglas Cramer of Paramount, *Mission: Impossible*'s parent company. She followed that with the news that she and her husband were leaving the series. It was a move that did not endear her to those in TV land. The Landaus were almost immediately labeled troublemakers, a designation that followed them through the years and even onto the set of I.T.C.'s awful *Space: 1999* show—in which the pair starred in 1975.

The show was not as good without them, but it was still successful. Rollin was replaced by magician Paris, played by *Star Trek* alumnus Leonard Nimoy, for a few years. When Nimoy left, the producers figured they didn't need anyone to fill the gap. They still had Jim, Barney, Willy, and the various girls. Replacing Cinnamon, at first, was Lesley Ann Warren playing Dana Lambert. Replacing Dana when she left was Casey, as portrayed by Lynda Day George. Other girls the series tested for a few episodes were Barbara Anderson, Jessica Walters, Lee

The I.M.F., season two. Standing are Barbara Bain and Peter Graves—who played new boss Jim Phelps. Sitting, left to right, are Peter Lupus, Greg Morris, and Martin Landau. (CBS)

Meriwether, and Elizabeth Ashley, among others. Sam Elliot also did some work on the show, playing an odd-agent-out named Doug.

Besides Greg Morris and Peter Lupus, the only other actor who lasted all eight seasons was Bob Johnson, the man who recorded all those missions, should Jim or Dan decide to accept them. Those missions changed in the final episodes.

In the early seventies there was a prevailing attitude that this country was in trouble. People were getting angry that billions were being spent on foreign aid but little was being done about the problems at home. The attitude infected the I.M. Force to the degree that they stopped bailing out Third World countries and started going after organized crime, in America.

The mob fights were the death knell of the series, which ended in 1973 after a proud and prosperous run. An even more prosperous run was had by the final new show of 1966—a run that would last, on and off, for 16 years. In England, where the series originated, it lasted for nearly two decades. If a list of the greatest entertainment ever provided to us by Britain were compiled, *The Avengers* would have to rank high—somewhere between The Beatles and *Secret Agent*.

The Avengers started in England in 1960 in an extremely different format. Then called *Police Surgeon*, it starred Ian Hendry as Dr. David Keel, who swore to eradicate crime after his wife was killed by mobsters. Featured on this show was a dapper character called Steed, played by Patrick Macnee. The two teamed up, vowing to avenge crime. Then, under *The Avengers* banner, they alternated as the leading character each week. Steed's full name and occupation were never re-

vealed, but his umbrella and bowler were ever-present.

An English actors' strike initiated the end of *Police Surgeon*, but Brian Clemens, a British writer, liked the Steed character enough to resurrect him with a whole new franchise. The following year *The Avengers* was truly born. This time Steed was an agent of the government Ministry and his partner was Mrs. Catherine Gale, a widow who knew judo and had a habit of wearing leather. Although accused in the press of "catering to leather freaks," this partnership proved a fruitful one and lasted until 1965. Honor Blackman, an actress already in her thirties when success beckoned after a string of minor U.K. films, played Mrs. Gale.

Then, presumably on the strength of her role as Pussy Galore in *Goldfinger* (1964), Blackman left *The Avengers*. She was replaced by then 28-year-old Diana Rigg, playing the part of possible-widow Mrs. Emma Peel, wife of Peter Peel who was lost in the Amazon. Mrs. Peel (never Emma) meets Steed after they have a trifling auto accident together. Once Steed, now with the first name of John, discovers her independent means and adventure-loving nature, he uses her as a freelance partner.

It was this team that American audiences got a glimpse of on March 28, 1966. *The Avengers* went on ABC TV as a replacement for the canceled *Ben Casey* (1963). The initial reaction of the critics was cool and standoffish. They seemed unsure about the wild, humorous, exciting, tightly written, and impeccably played series. The public held no such reservations. In the privacy of their own homes, without anyone having to know, they loved watching the cat-suited

The third and most famous team
of The Avengers. First there was
Patrick Macnee (right) and Ian
Hendry, then Honor Blackman
took over in the role of Mrs.
Gale. Although the British had
been watching the show for
years, the first partner
Americans saw was Diana
Rigg (left) as Mrs. Emma
Peel.
(ITC Entertainment, Inc.)

Mrs. Peel get into all sorts of kinky situations and the Old-World Steed chivalrously coming to her rescue.

Watching the show was like watching James Bond meet The Perils of Pauline. It was all done with wit and high production values, and the English actors knew how to turn a phrase better than anyone in America. It was also played fairly straight, although the series delighted in letting the audience in on the joke. Occasionally they would throw in charming sight gags (like Mrs. Peel becoming the roaring lion of the MGM trademark during an episode where two mad filmmakers plan to snuff her) which somehow did not break the spell. Every week there would be a world-shaking threat which

the Avengers would foil with panache.

By 1968, everyone acknowledged the guilty pleasure of watching the show, the press and public alike. At the height of the show's success, Diana Rigg announced her departure. "I began to feel claustrophobic," she explained. "It was getting increasingly more difficult to leave. Why wait until I was stale?" The resounding audience reply was "Why not?" But it was too late, her mind was made up. On March 20, 1968, Peter Peel was found and returned to London. As he drove away with his rightful wife, we could see the back of his head. He was decked out exactly like Steed—bowler and all.

With Mrs. Peel gone, Her Majesty's

Leggy, enigmatic Joanna Lumley, an actress who had co-starred with Diana Rigg in the James Bond film, On Her Majesty's Secret Service (1969), played Purdey, Steed's fourth female partner. (The New Avengers, Ltd.)

Secret Service assigned another agent to be Steed's partner. Her Majesty's taste must have been suffering that day, because Linda Thorson joined the cast as Tara King. The logic of the choice was apparent. Since Mrs. Peel was slinky and long-haired, why not get a replacement who was voluptuous and short-haired? But while Thorson had bigger lungs, she had less appeal and talent. The character of Tara King was that of a dizzy, mod "bird" (British slang like the American "chick"). She was the most immature partner Steed ever had, which strained the camaraderie the two characters were supposed to have.

To make things worse, the male character of Mother was added, the code name of Steed's wheelchair-bound boss. English comedy actor Patrick Newell essayed the role. It was a new format destined for failure. The scripts were still good, as was the direction by British notables Roy Ward Baker, Don Sharp,

Returning a decade later, Patrick Macnee looks even better as John Steed, the head of The New Avengers. (*The New Avengers, Ltd.*)

Robert Fuest, John Hough and others, but Mrs. Peel had taken most of the audience with her. *The Avengers* was canceled in 1969.

John Steed entered a time machine and emerged 10 years later, looking only a trifle heavier. He took up his bumbershoot and bowler once again for *The New Avengers*. Steed was back at his apartment at Number 3 Stable Mews,

London, for a series of all new adventures featuring a new supporting cast. What had not changed was the series' producer, Brian Clemens. He teamed with Augustine Fennell and composer Laurie Johnson to create an English television force called The New Avengers, Ltd.

What had changed was the British TV industry's approach to violence. They cut back on the outrageousness they were known for, putting a severe crimp in *The*

New Avengers' format. What was left was Joanna Lumley, a svelte, leggy blonde actress who had co-starred in *On Her Majesty's Secret Service* (1969)—the James Bond film starring Diana Rigg—as Purdey, Steed's new partner. And there was also Gareth Hunt, a handsome actor who starred as the callous chauffer in *Upstairs, Downstairs,* as Mike Gambit, the third member of the team.

Gambit had been a racing car driver and was a great shot, while Purdey had been a professional dancer with a great kick. But while everyone had terrific destructive talents, according to the scripts, all they could do was stand around and talk about them. There was precious little action in *The New Avengers* and when it came, it was fairly short and unexciting. The bon vivance of the previous incarnation was replaced with a whimsical solemnity that did not cut the mustard.

CBS TV put the new show on at 11:30 on Friday nights with 10 minutes more commercials (like *The Return of the Saint*) and high hopes. *The New Avengers* didn't deliver. The series dragged itself into 1980, but only as repeats. Once more, the original version is the version viewers should remember. In fact, *The Avengers* of 1966 to 1969 should be the only non-PBS British im-

The big change in **The New Avengers** *was that there was a second male agent: Gareth Hunt as crack shot and race-car driver Mike Gambit. And, although the series is off the air, there are plans to make an* **Avengers** *movie. (The New Avengers, Ltd.)*

port American audiences should remember from this era.

With Steed and Peel's success, there followed a slew of England-based detectives, all of whom wanted a slice of the American pie. In 1966, there came *The Baron*, loosely based on the novels of John Creasy writing as Anthony Morton. In the novels, The Baron was John Mannering, who started his career on the wrong side of the law. Until he met Lourna Fauntley, the love of his life, he was a gentleman jewel thief in the tradition of Raffles and The Falcon. Love changed his ways, and he became a consultant to Scotland Yard.

Producer Monty Berman eliminated Lourna and Scotland Yard, making Mannering an American who was called The Baron because of his Texas family's oil-baron background. On TV, as in the books, Mannering was an antiques dealer who was not above using his store as a cover. But only on TV did Mannering work almost exclusively with British Intelligence—in the person of John Alexander Templeton-Greene, played by Colin Gordon. On the tube, Mannering's love interest was Cordelia Winfield, his antiques assistant and adventure aide, played by Sue Lloyd.

The hour-long episodes were pretty common shoot-'em-up stuff and *The Baron* lasted only seven months on ABC. The series got some renewed life in syndication, while the show's star, Steve Forrest, came back to America and gained fame as another TV detective in 1975. Another famous portrayer of detectives got another chance, thanks to the influx of British shows. Louis Hayward, TV's Lone Wolf and filmdom's The Saint,

came back on local stations as a Scotland Yard policeman in *The Inspector*. Hayward was almost 60 at this point, so he did not seem to mind sharing the show with Ivan, a German shepherd who helped the inspector out.

The Inspector was a forgettable little show, but its inclusion is necessary, if only to say the author did not forget it even if the rest of the nation has.

1967

It was another good year for TV detectives, but a bad year for the real world. Viewers in 1967 were shocked to have their shows interrupted for the news that astronauts Grissom, White, and Chaffee had been killed in a Cape Kennedy flash fire while testing their Apollo spacecraft.

Later that year, Richard Speck was found guilty of murdering eight nurses. It was one of the first modern-day murder sprees to become a media field day. Campus unrest was growing and the young were dissatisfied with the way the country was being run—specifically in terms of Vietnam.

Producer Herbert Brodkin (*The Defenders*) tried to capture the confusion, frustration, and aimlessness of youth in a strange little series called *Coronet Blue*. CBS bought it in 1966, but then canceled the contract after 13 episodes had been filmed. At Brodkin's insistence, the network ran it as a summer replacement for *The Carol Burnett Show*. Then, viewers were able to see for themselves the story of Michael Alden, the name the leading character takes after being shot, dumped into the East River of New York, and awakening with amnesia. All he can remember are the words Coronet Blue.

Trust Brodkin to imbue the series with

class. *Coronet Blue* became a well-received, highly regarded, minor cult show—minor only because it came and went so quickly. Frank Converse, who had guested on one episode of *Hawk* before getting the *Coronet Blue* job, played Alden with confused conviction. As he went around trying to discover who he was while danger came at him from all sides, the young people watched, feeling the same way.

No matter how many letters poured in and how many favorable critiques were written, a TV network does not take kindly to being forced to do anything. *Coronet Blue* never had a chance to be continued and therefore never had an ending. The last time Alden was seen, he was still searching for an answer. That is suitable, I suppose. For so are we.

All our troubles would be solved if only we had super powers. I.T.C. offered us an English show with characters who did. This was *The Champions*, another in the long line of *Avengers* knock-offs. Stuart Damon (now a regular on *General*

The Champions came on like an English Mod Squad. Alexandra Bastedo, Stuart Damon, and William Gaunt (from left to right) played the super-powered secret agents. (ITC Entertainment, Inc.)

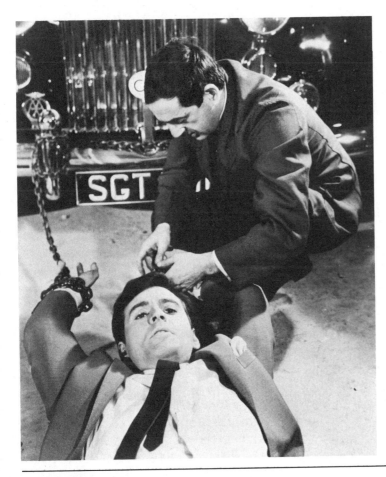

Just one of the delightful predicaments **The Champions** *got themselves into week after week. Lucky their adversaries were all inventive sadists.*
(ITC Entertainment, Inc.)

Hospital), Alexandra Bastedo, and William Gaunt played Craig Stirling, Sharon Macready, and Richard Barrett—three agents for the British intelligence agency called Nemesis.

While on assignment to steal Chinese germ warfare secrets, the agents' plane crash-lands in the Himalayas. There they are rescued by an ancient unknown race and taken to their "lost city." Finding the agents to be the good guys, these people imbue the trio with special powers, making them "super people." Says one character in the pilot episode, "Their mental and physical capacities [have been] fused to computer efficiency, sense and

hearing, raised to the highest, futuristic stage of mental and physical growth."

Vowing to use their powers for niceness (as Maxwell Smart would say), they return to Mother England and Nemesis headquarters in Geneva, Switzerland. From those two points, the trio is sent off on new assignments by their boss, W. L. Tremayne, as played by the burly Anthony Nicholls. Although *The Champions* predates *The Six Million Dollar Man* (1974) by several years, they utilized funny soundtrack noises, exaggerated broad jumping, and slow motion, but with less success. Even with its super powers, *The Champions* was boring and was thrown off the NBC network at the end of its short summer run.

Over on ABC, producer Paul Monash was trying to satisfy all viewing factions with another lawyer who was trying to be a combination of Perry Mason and the lawyers of *The Defenders*. Clinton Judd was the attorney's name and, to satisfy the more conservative watchers, he was the most successful lawyer in the world. To satisfy the liberals, he had enough money to take on unpopular causes. To satisfy the elderly viewers, he was played by Carl Betz, that "nice man" who played Donna Reed's husband on *The Donna Reed Show* (1958). To satisfy the teenybopper set, Judd's assistant was young, handsome Ben Caldwell, played by Stephen Young.

Otherwise, Judd was a flamboyant Texas-based attorney who traveled all over the country to find and defend clients. That was why the show was called *Judd for the Defense*. Something that recalls two previously mentioned landmark legal series occurred in Judd's premiere episode in which he successfully defended his client (like Perry Mason) only to find out the guy was guilty (a plot worthy of *The Defenders*). Judd managed to get him on another charge, though, so justice and morality triumphed. Judd continued to triumph for two seasons.

The rest of this season's detective contributions were all gems. There was not a clinker in the lot. They were not all runaway successes, but they were all damned good. The relative failure was *N.Y.P.D.*, the latest in a string of shows produced by David Susskind's company, Talent Associates. The series came on like a half-hour *Naked City* since it was filmed on location in New York and the scripts concerned realistic police problems.

To heighten the atmosphere, producer Dan Melnick filmed the program with 16mm film cameras, often hand-held. This gave *N.Y.P.D.* the aura of a gritty nightmare. Starring was *Asphalt Jungle* graduate Jack Warden as Detective Lieutenant Mike Haines. Frank Converse, who was about to be left hanging on *Coronet Blue*, played the inexperienced up-and-coming Detective Johnny Corso. That took care of the clichéd camaraderie, but for realism's sake, a black character was added named Detective Jeff Ward, played by stage performer Robert Hooks.

Here was a series that asked, even begged its contributors to be imaginative and inventive. Directors like Daniel Petrie and Robert Butler had a field day with their unusual angles and moving shots. New York actors also had a field day, with the best talent from the stage and commercial world doing stints as criminals or their victims. *N.Y.P.D.* was a dose of salt thrown into the pudding of TV programming, so it was not surprising that it was short-lived. The most surprising thing was that it lasted more than one season, and went off in 1969.

On the West Coast, another group of police officers fared much better. Bucking the odds, they lasted for eight years. To get things started, Universal Studios mounted a two-hour made-for-television movie written by Don M. Mankiewicz and Collier Young. Televised in March 1967, it told of a San Francisco chief of detectives whose legs were paralyzed after an assassination attempt. For the rest of the film, the veteran detective worked out of a wheelchair to bring his assailant to justice.

Taken just as a story, not many would give a crippled cop odds to succeed as a TV detective. But this was more than just any partially paralyzed policeman. This was Robert Ironside. And Ironside was not portrayed by just any old actor; he was embodied (and quite a body it was) by Raymond Burr. "I've switched from the defense to the prosecution," the actor exclaimed. "There's more latitude to the human being because he is not tied down to the courtroom."

Burr proved he could do more sitting down in a wheelchair than dozens of other actors could do standing up. If *Ironside* did not prove once and for all that Burr was a commanding actor, then nothing would. He was the presence that

made the show watchable. The NBC series started September 14, but Ironside's franchise and co-stars were established back with the TV Movie.

Although he was not as mobile as before, his brain was still so sharp that Police Commissioner Randall (Gene Lyons) offered him a position as a special consultant. He flavored the offer by allowing Ironside to actually live in the attic of police headquarters, and gave him the services of two police officers— Detective Sergeant Ed Brown (Don Galloway, co-star of *Arrest and Trial*) and Policewoman Eve Whitefield (Barbara Anderson), whom Ironside had originally recruited. Once Ironside decided to take the commissioner up on the offer, he

The early days of Chief Robert T. Ironside. Raymond Burr filled the leopard-skin wheelchair, giving an apathetic ear to the pleadings of ex-con Mark Sanger (actor Don Mitchell) who was to become his aide. (NBC)

Officer Eve Whitfield (actress Barbara Anderson) wasn't above wearing a see-through blouse to get her man for Ironside. *(NBC)*

found his own assistant outside the force in Mark Sanger (Don Mitchell), a young black man Ironside had arrested in the past. Mark did not want to be the cop's "boy." The cop wanted him to be his "legs" instead.

Mark went on to become Ironside's "pusher"—in that he usually was behind the wheelchair, pushing—and chauffeur of "the Chief's" van, a souped-up vehicle with telephone, tape recorder, and hydraulic lift. All four went on cases that Ironside deemed suitable to investigate, driving all over the city of the Bay (actually the Universal back lot with on-location filming thrown in).

Ironside was basically an above-

average mystery show. In many episodes the Chief's infirmity did not matter. Actually, the wheelchair made him the ultimate "armchair detective" and assured viewers that the show would be more cerebral than sadistic.

In addition, the wheelchair made Burr's action scenes all the more suspenseful. Here was a man who was supposedly helpless, but time after time he proved himself to be as physical as necessary. Over the years, Ironside avoided being thrown down an elevator shaft by grabbing the hanging wires, karate-chopped a few villains, and kept from falling off a wooden raft when stuck out in the bay. None of this stuff seemed unbelievable because Burr made the character seem completely capable. And this made his rare moments of doubt and vulnerability all the more effective.

While Burr was the Rock of Gibraltar, other cast members were not. Barbara Anderson had more in common with Barbara Bain than just a first name. Besides the physical resemblance, Anderson also grew tired of her role and asked the producers for more to do. The producers said no, so she left the program in 1971. Brunette Elizabeth Baur took over, playing Officer Fran Belding.

Once Anderson exited, all the other supporting roles were slightly expanded so they took up more air time. Detective Sergeant Ed Brown went on some undercover operations while Mark Sanger went to law school. Brown seemed content with his secret missions, but Sanger kept on going until it seemed as if Universal was grooming the character for spinoff status. Mark got his degree, got married to Diana (Jane Pringle), moved out of Ironside's wood-paneled top-floor apartment (complete with pool table and ceiling exercise equipment), passed the bar, and became a lawyer.

Nothing came of Sanger's progress other than some legal cases that the group got involved with, and it is just as well. We can be glad that *Ironside* was good enough to keep an inferior spinoff from tarnishing its reputation. And it was Raymond Burr's last big TV success. Although the talented actor would try to capture the *Perry Mason* and *Ironside* magic three more times, it would never quite work out.

The first try was with *Mallory: Circumstantial Evidence*, a 1976 made-for-TV movie with Burr playing Daniel Mallory, a lawyer. Only this attorney had a bad

reputation (undeserved) for doing some unethical things (doubtful). The script by Joel Oliansky and Joseph Polizzi and the direction by Boris Sagal was unimpeachable, but the show never went to series. Next came *Kingston: The Power Play*, just a few months later. In this movie scripted by Dick Nelson and directed by Robert Day, Burr was a hard-hitting investigative reporter. Finally there was *The Jordan Chance* (1978) with Burr as Frank Jordan, *another* unjustly treated lawyer (he was jailed for a crime he did not commit) who wanted to make sure the same thing did not happen to other people. This one was written by Stephen Cannell, a major name in the mystery biz (as we shall discover) but was still deemed unworthy for a series.

Looking back at 1967, we find that the private eye was not doing very well. The last one who showed up was *Honey West* in 1965, and before that it was *Michael Shayne, Dan Raven,* and *A. Dunster Lowell* way back in 1960. The one that premiered in 1967 made up for lost time. Producer Bruce Geller had just improved the spy series by creating *Mission: Impossible*, so he turned his attention to the hard-boiled detective and came up with a winner.

He created *Mannix*, or what would happen if Mike Hammer was hired by Pinkertons. In the original concept, Joe Mannix was an independent, athletic, and unconventional peeper who trusted the evidence of his own eyes and the law of his own fists more than anything. To put food on the table he goes to work for Intertect, an investigative conglomerate controlled by computers and run by the buttoned-down mind of Lou Wickersham.

When the series premiered on CBS in September, it had a format that *TV Guide* called "Taut, tingling, engrossing, original and well written." From the very start, *Mannix* was the best private-eye action TV had to offer. Helping keep it that way was Mike Connors, the man who played Mannix. He had been itching to get back at and on television since the premature rejection of *Tightrope*, so he took the role of Mannix in his teeth and ripped away. He was perfect for the part and became Mannix in the process.

Adding to the dramatic fireworks was Joseph Campanella, a craggy character actor who knew how to hold his own in any scene. He made the cliché Wickersham into a human being, and the conflict between the aggressively independent Joe and the corporate-minded Lou set sparks flying the first season. The emotional confrontations were so hot, in fact, that they burned themselves out before the first year was over. There was a famous episode in which the two came to blows—both of them reaching an understanding because of it.

The understanding included Mannix quitting Intertect, a move explained in the episode that aired March 16, 1968. So, in the show's second year Joe opened his own private detective office at 17 Paseo Verde, Los Angeles. He hired as his secretary Peggy Fair (Gail Fisher), the wife of an old friend who had been killed in the line of duty as a cop. Replacing Lou Wickersham in the eyes of the audience were a team of different L.A.P.D. lieutenants who alternately bugged and benefited Mannix.

There was Lieutenant Art Malcolm (Ward Wood), Lieutenant Dan Ives (Jack Ging), Lieutenant George Kramer (Lawrence Linville, who became the Larry

Linville of *M*A*S*H* fame), and the most popular, Lieutenant Adam Tobias as played by ex-Defender Robert Reed. With or without them, Mannix would track down his adversaries week after week, utlizing dazzling athletic ability. In the first season, one show featured a battle royal between Mannix and a huge guard in a mud puddle. By his eighth and last season Mannix was not even letting things like temporary blindness and broken bones get in his way.

Another justly famous fight scene involved Mannix subduing a gun-wielding doctor and a syringe-waving nurse with both his arms in a cast. Filled with screeching tires, flame-spitting guns, and flying fists, *Mannix* ranks as one of the most thunderously satisfying private-eye fests ever made. It was not just the mindless violence of *Tightrope* or the mindful investigation of *Naked City*, it was a well-balanced combination of the two that worked beautifully.

1968

The worst happened. On April 4, Martin Luther King was assassinated. On June 6, Robert F. Kennedy was assassinated. Both deaths were turned into media events. And on August 25, protestors turned the Democratic Convention in Chicago into one of the bloodiest three-ring circuses ever televised. The demonstrators chanted the motto: "The Whole World Is Watching." They were right. The whole world was watching on television.

With these tragic real-life events taking place, not only was the whole world watching, but it was watching nervously. Most could not help wondering where

The Mannix *cast and crew in action. On the far left, star Mike Connors. On the right, making his 1972 TV debut, is Eddie Egan, the retired cop who actually busted "The French Connection." Gene Hackman won an Oscar for portraying a pseudonymed Egan in the movie of the same name. Egan went on to a continuing role on* Joe Forrester *and* Eischied. *(courtesy of United Press International, Inc.)*

TV fit in and what it was actually doing *to others* watching it. Those who study television violence worry about children, worry about the poor, worry about the "sickies," but then go home and watch their favorite show—be it *Mannix, The Flying Nun*, or *The Lawrence Welk Show*. They can handle it, everybody else cannot.

Among the new genre shows of the 1968 season were some greats. Anything but great, however, was *Hunter*, a pathetic English rip-off of *The Man from U.N.C.L.E.* It starred Tony Ward as John Hunter, the man from C.O.S.M.I.C. That was bad enough, but then COSMIC stands for the *Office Of Security and Military Intelligence.* The front and back C were probably tacked on because Hunter

would feel stupid if he said he worked for OSMI. But not half as stupid as viewers found this syndicated show. It disappeared blessedly fast.

Also doing a quick disappearing act was NBC's *The Outsider*, a series that proved to be the flip side of Mike Hammer. Hammer was an outcast from society because he was a hard man who stood for what he believed in. David Ross was an "outsider" because he was a pathetic little schmuck who got trampled on by life. Darren McGavin played both roles on television with equal ability.

Hammer just got angrier as time went on. Ross got bitter and resigned. Orphaned as a kid, a high school dropout, and framed for a crime he had not committed, Ross happily withdrew into his own haphazard world of poverty and depression. He was an interesting creation, but hardly the stuff of hit shows. NBC hoped the public would root for this bulldog underdog and wrote their press releases to point out his individuality.

"He's a go-it-alone private eye who knows the underworld from the inside," they said. "Rejected by society—and rejecting society—he lives in an off-beat world: often dangerous . . . always fascinating." It was fascinating, all right, and raised some interesting questions like, how does an ex-con get a private investigator's license? And why does he keep his telephone in the refrigerator of his run-down, ramshackle office cum apartment?

When he was not trying to evoke pity in the audience, he would go out on cases that were structured to beat out what little life was left in him. If he was not losing his girl friend in a fatal accident, he was getting beaten up by hoods, suspects, and sometimes even clients. One thing can be said for *The Outsider*: he could really take a punch—lots of them. What could not be said about *The Outsider* was that he lasted more than a season.

The quality and longevity of that season's output was unprecedented. For the failure NBC had with *The Outsider* on Wednesday nights, they had a winner with *The Name of the Game* on Friday nights. This series was a truly fascinating combination of old and new formats. The teamwork series idea—that is, having three stars alternate the lead each week—was not new, but since the last time this device had been used for a mystery show was earlier in the sixties, it seemed new to a fresh generation of young viewers.

What was new was that it came from a successful TV movie. In 1966, Universal continued their Project 120 series with an adaptation of the novel *One Woman* by Tiffany Thayer. Retitling it *Fame Is the Name of the Game*, director Stuart Rosenberg had an interesting script by Ranald MacDougall that told of one reporter's obsession with solving a prostitute's murder. The reporter was named Jeff Dillon and he was played by personable Anthony Franciosa, who started his career in *A Face in the Crowd* (1957), repeating his stage role in *A Hatful of Rain* (1957), and co-starring with Paul Newman in *The Long Hot Summer* (1958).

The character of Jeff Dillon was carried over to the series, as was the character of his girl friday, Peggy Maxwell. Peggy was played by newcomer Susan Saint James in her TV debut. It was an auspicious one that led to an Emmy Award for Outstanding Continued Performance by an Actress in a Supporting Role in a Series (they can not just say Best Supporting Drama Actress, can they?) as well as future TV detective fame. The fact that a successful series was spun off from the teleflick (the second to do so; *The Iron Horse* was the first) led the way for dozens of TV movie pilots.

For some reason, Universal did not want Franciosa to carry the ball alone, so they added two new characters under the banner of Howard Publications, a fictional magazine corporation. Heading the outfit was Glenn Howard, a debonair, dynamic businessman played by Gene Barry. Franciosa's Dillon was the top reporter for Howard's *People Magazine* (predating Time, Inc.'s *People* magazine by several years). Finally there was Dan Farrell, an obsessed ex-FBI agent whose family was murdered by thugs, as the senior editor of Howard's *Crime Magazine.* Robert Stack returned to the investigative fold by playing Farrell with the same intensity he gave to Ness.

Surprisingly, the Farrell segments of the 90-minute show were the weakest, even though they dealt with the most familiar themes. The Dillon segments were interesting as the reporter searched out the truth about some unpopular and relevant themes, but the scripts soon devolved into melodrama. It was the Howard segments, seemingly the most uninteresting of the lot, that really shone. *The Name of the Game's* writers and directors were challenged with making the tales of a filthy rich publisher riveting, so they pulled out all the thematic stops. One episode had Barry playing Howard and a Howard ancestor in a story set a 100 years earlier. Another story had a "Greek chorus" of people made up in whiteface serving as the episode's singing conscience. The viewers could see the chorus but the characters on screen could not!

Probably the most famous episode was the one in which Glenn Howard awoke more than 45 years in the future to find that pollution had forced Los Angeles to go underground. This was "L.A.: 2017," written by science-fiction great Philip Wylie and directed by Steven Spielberg. For that program alone, *The Name of the Game* deserves a rousing cheer. Instead, it got a three-year run, good notices, and an afterlife through repeats.

Over on NBC on Saturday was *Adam-12,* a Jack Webb-Mark VII Production which featured everything that made *Dragnet* famous—the authentic phraseology, the clipped dialog, the bland supporting players, and cases taken from actual police files. The files here were those of patrol car officers, those dedicated cops who drive all over the Los Angeles streets to settle family disputes, chase bank and gas station robbers, and search out missing children.

Martin Milner—the man who had driven along *Route 66* a few years back—got back behind the wheel as Officer Pete Malloy, a bitter patrol veteran whose long-time partner had just been gunned down. Although he was intent on retiring, crusty, understanding Sergeant MacDonald (William Boyett) convinced him to break in patrolman Jim Reed (Kent McCord), described as an "overeager, overbrave rookie." This kid's dedication, industry, and good looks so affect Malloy that the veteran cop stays on—ostensibly to keep the kid alive.

As the seven years of their run rolled on, Malloy and Reed (badge numbers 2430 and 744, respectively—trivia lovers, take note!) were each promoted, and their large audience was entertained by screeching car chases, neighborhood eccentrics, shoot-outs, and cats stuck up in trees, among other things. It was an eclectic show, jumping from the mundane to the maniacal in the space of a radio call.

The funniest part of the show was when the two officers were called upon to have friendly conversations between action scenes in the front seat of their patrol car—code number: A for Adam 12. The camera would cut back and forth between their two faces as they discussed marriage, home, and family with all the passion of Joe Friday reading the phone book. The success of this show probably stemmed from the fact that it had enough action within its half-hour framework to keep the viewer busy, and

*Martin Milner returned to TV
driving after piloting a Chevy along
Route 66. Here he's in uniform for
manning the Los Angeles patrol
car known as Adam-12.
(NBC)*

that these two lifeless cops were maintaining community peace with a professionalism not found on *The Six O'Clock News*.

Yes, reality was still a consideration that determined what people watched to relax. Outside, students were fighting with police and crime was getting worse. This had been true for several years, but the executives did not want to deal with it until they could make it harmless enough to make money from it. Over at ABC, producers Aaron Spelling and Danny Thomas were doing just that. They took a nine-year-old pilot script by ex-policeman Bud Ruskin about his experiences as an undercover narc and

sold it to the networks as *The Mod Squad*.

Ruskin's original was a heartfelt saga about a team of rookies who walked into the fire, but one can visualize the Spelling/Goldberg changes by reading the ABC publicity campaign: "The police don't understand the now generation and the now generation doesn't dig the fuzz. The solution: find some swinging young people who live the beat scene. And get them to work for the cops." Crazy, man. Dig it.

The "swinging young people" recruited by the fuzz were Pete Cochran, the black sheep of a wealthy family, who had been arrested for stealing a car; Julie

Barnes, poor white trash arrested for vagrancy after running away from her prostitute mother; and Lincoln Hayes, one of a ghetto family of 13 who was arrested during a race riot. The actors recruited to play these parts came from backgrounds that were just as colorful.

Michael Cole was a high school dropout before getting the Cochran role. Peggy Lipton was an attorney's daughter from Long Island. And Clarence Williams III, was a numbers runner from Harlem before going out to the Coast to become an actor. The only acting pro among the major cast was Tige Andrews of *Robert Taylor's Detectives* as tough but understanding Captain Adam Greer, the conceiver and control of *The Mod Squad*. He gave the three characters a choice: either work with the cops to defeat the real sources of evil in our society or go to jail and then back to the streets.

Reluctantly the trio agreed and soon joined in as eager, able undercover police. At first they tooled around town in a 1950 paneled Woody station wagon, fighting drug runners and leather gangs, but when the Woody was wrecked in the second season, it was a signal for the gradual deterioration of the show into the regular TV routine of madmen on the loose and personal friends in danger.

"We never thought of being relevant," said Executive Producer Aaron Spelling to reporters who questioned *The Mod Squad*'s entertainment value. "We never used the word." Actor Williams put it more succinctly to an interviewer: "It's all cop stuff, man."

On-line producers Harve Bennett and Tony Barrett kept the cop stuff coming fast and furious while the young actors seemed to get more and more demoralized. As the five seasons wore on, both

Linc and Julie seemed to act less and less, as if somewhere in the second season they had been taken over by pod people from *The Invasion of the Body Snatchers*. In the final two years, they just said their lines as if sleepwalking.

The only time the actors came to life was during action scenes. Although the stunt people did most of the work, the Linc character was written to be as tough as Batman. The height of his ability was shown on one episode when the black man leaped headfirst off a warehouse into a pile of lumber, for gosh sake, then went on to tackle the fleeing crook as if nothing had happened. The final season was almost as ludicrous, since the producers insisted on casting guest stars like Richard Dreyfuss, Sammy Davis, Jr., and Martin Sheen. The on-screen chemistry made the stars look all the more like ventriloquist's dummies while the guests looked like frenetic scenery chewers.

After a spell of six years, the partnership of Danny Thomas and Aaron Spelling was revived to bring Pete, Linc, Julie, and Captain Greer back. *The Return of the Mod Squad* was aired in 1979 as a TV movie, but nothing much had changed. In fact, it had gotten worse. Whether or not the three young leads had become better actors in the interim could hardly be discerned from the boring script and unexceptional direction. The characters were reunited to investigate threats on Adam Greer's life only to discover—through the purest chance—that Frank Webber (Tom Bosley) was out to get them because his son was a retarded drug casualty of the sixties.

It was an embarrassing, nearly unwatchable effort. It disappeared into the TV sea without making a ripple, after which Andrews and Cole continued to

The Mod Squad *in the early years. Clarence Williams III's afro was shorter (far left),*
Tige Andrews was tougher and more commanding, Peggy Lipton was more
attentive, and Michael Cole's ears could be seen. (ABC)

serve as series' guest stars, Williams went back to his stage work in New York and Boston, and Lipton went back to her husband, Quincy Jones, and her family.

Earlier in 1968, ABC had released a second-season action show to take the Tuesday time spot of *The Invaders*, which they were moving to a later hour. The replacement turned out to be a quick hit called *It Takes a Thief*. It took a thief to do special jobs for the government, and the thief it took was one Alexander Mundy, a fashionable cat burglar who was languishing away in San Jobel Prison. He had been arrested by a po-

liceman named Noah Bain, whom he considered to be the only cop who could match him in skill. To facilitate matters, Bain had taken a job as a department head with the Special Intelligence Agency (the S.I.A.), who needed a specialist to lift things from foreign governments and enemies of the nation. Bain suggested Mundy and the plot got rolling.

Bain sprung Mundy from jail and put him under house confinement when he was not on a mission. "I'm no spy," Mundy complained. "You don't have to spy," Bain reasonably replied at the beginning of every episode for one and half seasons. "You just have to steal."

Here's The Mod Squad *in later years. Cole's hair was hippier, while both Lipton and Williams played it like zombies, man. A TV movie reunion in 1980—*The Return of the Mod Squad—*was a disaster. (ABC)*

Malachi Throne, a supporting actor who could easily be interchanged with Tige Andrews, played Bain with the casual, cool Robert Wagner as a fine choice for Mundy. Wagner, the husband of Natalie Wood and co-star of the movies *A Kiss Before Dying* (1956), *Sail a Crooked Ship* (1962) and *Harper* (1966), had played a gentleman jewel thief opposite David Niven in *The Pink Panther* (1964)—the first of the Blake Edwards "Inspector Clouseau" films starring Peter Sellers. It was probably his breezy performance there that made him a shoo-in for the Mundy role.

In 1969 Mundy was changed to Thursday nights with a slightly new format and a new supporting cast. Edward Binns had replaced Throne as Wally Powers, a new S.I.A. boss. In addition, the marvelous Fred Astaire was convinced by Wagner to take the role of Alister Mundy, the greatest of all gentleman thieves, who taught Alexander everything he knew. When the father and son team was not operating together, Mundy would occasionally team up with Chuck Brown, a dippy female kitten burglar played by Susan Saint James.

In this final season, ending in 1970, Mundy was no longer under house arrest. He had proven his worth and was given a free hand by executive producer Jack Arnold. *It Takes a Thief* was short-lived but stylish.

Almost anything would be considered

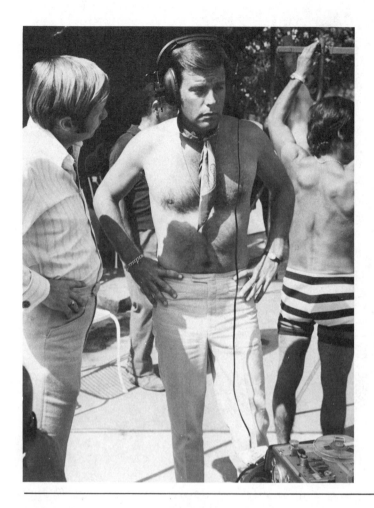

For actor Robert Wagner, starring as Alexander Mundy in It Takes a Thief, it took a sound man to play him a little something in between scenes. (ABC)

short-lived when compared to CBS's blockbuster of the season. The network got things going on September 20 with a two-hour pilot film directed by Paul Wendkos and written/produced by Leonard Freeman. It was the story of Steve McGarrett, the head of a special unit attached to the Hawaii State Police who was given special jurisdiction over everything. As they said in the telefilm: "He takes orders only from the Governor . . . or God. And sometimes even *they* have trouble!"

This was *Hawaii Five-O* and no one

expected it to be the long-running, runaway success that it was. As of 1981, it is the longest-running detective show—12 seasons. More than a decade before, the telefilm had introduced the Five-O team. There was pure Hawaiian Detective Kono, played by island comedian and entertainer Zulu. There was Chinese immigrant Detective Chin Ho Kelly, played by Kam Fong. In the two-hour pilot, McGarrett's assistant Danny "Dan-O" Williams was played by Tim O'Kelly. Producer Freeman was not satisfied so he recruited a young actor he had

Jack Lord as rock-hard super-cop Steve McGarrett, who helmed the Hawaii Five-O squad for 12 seasons. (CBS)

worked with before in the Clint Eastwood picture *Hang 'Em High* (1968), James MacArthur, to play the role in the subsequent series. The pilot's governor was played by Lew Ayres, but he was either unable or unwilling to make the move to Hawaii for the on-location series, so Richard Denning happily took his place.

The man who was McGarrett for the pilot and for the rest of the series was Jack Lord, born John Ryan and known for his villain role in movies like *The Red Menace* (1949). Wanting more, he announced he would no longer consider criminal parts and waited out the producers. His breakthrough year was 1962 when he starred in TV's *Stoney Burke*

and co-starred as James Bond's CIA buddy Felix Leiter in *Dr. No*. Six years later he shrugged on McGarrett's severe blue suit, stuck the revolver in its holster and captured the nation's imagination.

Many critics have called McGarrett emotionless, but actually he was passionate. McGarrett believed in the law, and who he was, and what he was doing—not necessarily in that order. To him, his occupation was practically a divine calling. It was this passion and self-assurance that drew viewers to McGarrett in the same way people are attracted to TV evangelists. McGarrett practically burned with religious righteousness.

People have called McGarrett a fascist.

On the contrary, he was scrupulously law-abiding—to the point that, on several occasions, he was offered ways to make justice prevail illegally and he turned the offers down. Afterward, however, he slaved all the more to bring his quarry in—but always by the book. His eventual triumph was made all the more sweet. When he grinned his death's-head smile and said "Book him, Dan-O," it was hard not to applaud inwardly.

The other factor in *Hawaii Five-O's* success was Leonard Freeman's approach. All filming was done on location and he recruited the best talent for the kind of hard-line cops 'n' robbers thing he wanted. Fred Baum, one of the last in a long line of the show's producers after Freeman's death, summed it up this way: "It has to go back to Freeman's concept and Jack Lord's dedication. The concept allows you to do a show of dimension. We are not locked in or hurt by the antiviolence edicts. McGarrett is a strong character, he is not a caricature. He has dignity. People like the look, the characters, and Jack Lord."

The show's best supporting character was introduced in the pilot movie: Red Chinese Agent Wo Fat (who shared his name with a famous Honolulu restaurant), played by Khigh Dhiegh. Over the next 12 seasons, the insidious villain would appear eight more times to tangle with McGarrett. Their final confrontation came with *Hawaii Five-O's* last original episode, aired on April 5, 1980. Titled "Woe to Wo Fat," it was almost as bad as the previous years had been good.

It was an arbitrarily written, illogical script that was unexceptionally directed. At the finale, McGarrett gets Wo Fat behind bars, but Lord could not resist hav-

ing the villain pull a file out of his slipper—giving the impression that he would escape. It was a cutesy, self-conscious in-joke that had no place on the hard-hitting series.

By that time, there had been some cast changes. Denning had stuck it out, but MacArthur left at the end of 11 seasons and was replaced by William Smith as Keno. Zulu had left after four seasons to be replaced by Al Harrington as Ben Kokua. Kam Fong held out until the 11th season when his character, Chin Ho, was murdered by a mad-dog killer played by Steven Keats. Naturally, McGarrett brought him to justice, but sadly could not take care of him himself because the network had said it was a no-no. Not that McGarrett would have killed him in cold blood. Since there was an edict saying that no hero can kill the villain under any circumstance (they could only die in accidents or by their own hand, and even that was frowned upon), viewers had to be satisfied with a simple arrest.

Trying to forget the limp finale and remember the glory days, we take leave of Hawaii and 1968. As McGarrett would say, "Be there. Aloha."

1969

A man walked on the moon. Television showed us this feat on the morning of July 20, 1969. Neil Armstrong said the words, "One small step for man; one giant leap for mankind," specifically for the TV audience. And would you believe it? There are those who still believe the moon landing was faked by television. There was even a reprehensible movie called *Capricorn One* (1978) which was based on this contention. No one disbe-

Hawaii Five-O's limp finale after more than a decade on the air was the "Woe to Wo Fat" episode. McGarrett got the satisfaction of finally putting the Red Chinese spy behind bars, but viewers got the short end of the script. (CBS)

lieved that students were shot at Kent State University or that William Calley massacred 22 Vietnamese villagers. Television brought both those events into our homes, but there was no group who firmly believed TV faked them. However, when television finally does show something of galactic import, people do not buy it. Death and violence, now that is believable! You cannot win.

The TV detectives of the year did not either. Of little distinction was *The Bold Ones*, NBC's first attempt to duplicate the success of *The Name of the Game*. But instead of three characters alternat-

ing in a 90-minute time slot, it had three series alternating in a 60-minute time slot. The first was "The New Doctors," which one must assume is the sequel to "The Old Doctors" (actually it was given the "New" ID so it would not be confused with the NBC soap opera *The Doctors*), starring E. G. Marshall, John Saxon, and David Hartman.

The other segments were more in the detective line. There was "The Lawyers," which was about the firm of Nichols, Darrell & Darrell. Burl Ives was Walter Nichols while Joseph Campanella played straight-laced Brian Darrell to James

Farentino's laid-back Neil Darrell. These two brothers provided the sibling rivalry while senior partner Nichols played the company's guru.

"The Protectors" was also known as "The Law Enforcers" once NBC noticed that a lot of people were turning *The Bold Ones* off when this segment came on. The secondary conflict here was between white Deputy Police Chief Sam Danforth and black District Attorney William Washburn. Leslie Nielsen was the cop with Hari Rhodes as the district attorney who would squabble over tactics, rights, and race while the city beat up on itself.

TV Guide took a look at all three portions and sniffed: "Little of distinction here." They were right, but NBC tried to rectify matters by getting rid of the cop section and adding "The Senator," starring Hal Holbrook—a political exposé that was ahead of its time (and unwatched). The next season only the lawyers and doctors remained. Finally only "The New Doctors" was left and in the summer of 1973, they followed their friends off the air.

Of no distinction was Sheldon Leonard's *My Friend Tony*, an NBC second season replacement for *The Beautiful Phyllis Diller Show*. James Whitmore played criminologist John Woodruff who befriended an Italian street urchin during the Second World War and later made him part of his private investigations practice. Tony Novello (Enzo Cerusico) was cute, anxious, slightly bumbling, and no fun at all to watch. The difference between the two men was supposed to provide the mundane show with interest and color, but it did not work. It all ended after four months.

1970

The television year was stunning in its mediocrity. The only bright spots were *The Mary Tyler Moore Show* and *The Odd Couple*, and even they were not that good in their first year. The TV detective stuff was achingly bad.

Just edging onto the merely mediocre list was Quinn Martin's production of *Dan August* and that was because of its star, Burt Reynolds. Since leaving *Hawk*, Reynolds had starred in *Navajo Joe* (1967) and *Skullduggery* (1969). With the production of *Dan August*, the rugged actor started appearing on talk shows—especially *The Tonight Show*—where he displayed a charming talent for self-appraisal. He would put himself down or up depending on which would be funnier, and the crowd loved it.

When asked how he got the Dan August part, Reynolds replied, "They asked me if I could jump over a car. I said, 'Sure, I can jump over a car.' They said, 'You're our boy.'" It seems that Martin was not watching these talk shows, for while he had Reynolds jumping over cars, off houses, and down hallways, he kept even a whisper of humor off *Dan August*. Instead, Detective Lieutenant Dan August was a dour cop in Santa Luisa, California, where the sun was hot, the people were Mexican, and a lot of psychos came to visit.

If the producers had only allowed Reynolds to be the macho, wisecracking detective he turned out to be in *Fuzz* (1972) and *Shamus* (1973), they probably would have had a hit on their hands. Instead, the show was dull and it left the ABC air a season later. But when Reynolds went on to become a superstar, CBS bought the rights to rebroadcast *Dan*

Here's Burt Reynolds again, sporting a Dan August crew cap. It's too bad the actor wasn't able to look and act natural on screen. His super-stardom might have come to him earlier. As he had always said, "I succeeded in spite of television, not because of it." (courtesy of Pictorial Parade and Frank Edwards/Fotos International)

August from 1973 to 1975. It was still a mediocre show, but it became evident that Reynolds was straining to burst out from behind the deadpan expression he had to keep.

A throwback to the days of the glorious *Tallahassee 7000* and the interesting *Paris Precinct* was *Paris 7000*, which turned out to be neither glorious nor interesting. Lightweight movie star George Hamilton played State Department agent Jack Brennan, who was sent to the American ambassador's office in France to aid United States citizens in peril. The number to call in Paris was "Paris 7000." It came on in the second season and went off at the summer season.

Viewers only had to look at the remaining genre shows of the year to see that great minds work alike. For instance, on ABC there was *The Young Lawyers*, and on CBS there was *The Storefront Lawyers*. The latter series premiered first, so here goes.

To get an idea of just what *The Store-front Lawyers* was all about and just where it went wrong, one only has to read the synopsis of its permiere episode. "Three young members of a prestigious Los Angeles law firm set up a free legal-aid service for the needy. Their first case is a sensational murder." Well, of course it is! Robert Foxworth, a steely eyed, curly haired actor, played intrepid David Hansen, the instigator of the plan. David Arkin (Alan's son) was Jewish aide Gabriel Kaye, and Sheila Larken was a legal representative for Women's Lib named Deborah Sullivan.

The three toiled in their Neighborhood Legal Services storefront office for four months until the network noticed that no one was watching them do it. They conceptually dynamited the storefront, gave each character a new wardrobe, then brought them back in January under the title *Men at Law*. This probably did not sit well with actress Larken, but a job's a job. This time they were back with the big law firm they had left (Horton, Troy, McNeil, Carroll and Clark Law Offices) to open the clinic with Devlin O'Neil himself (Gerald S. O'Laughlin) serving as their guardian attorney. Either way, the group was gone by the end of the season.

So was *The Young Lawyers*, but at least they kept the same format throughout. The setting was Boston, with crusty old David Barrett (Lee J. Cobb) serving as supervisor, teacher, and mentor for two law students. In Massachusetts, law students are allowed to try cases for those who cannot afford Clinton Judd or Perry Mason, and that is just what Aaron Silverman (Zalman King), and Pat Walters (Judy Pace), did.

One of Aaron's opening lines pretty much summed up the approach of *The Young Lawyers*. "As lawyers, particularly student lawyers, we've got to play it by the book. We play it by the book, but sometimes we miss the fine print. Then we stick our necks out." ABC chopped them off before *The Young Lawyers* could become *The A-Bit-Older Lawyers*.

Astonishingly, these were not the worst of the "hippie" shows the networks foisted on us. There were also *The New People*, about a bunch of marooned teens who set up their own society and, incredibly, *The Young Rebels*, about three Revolutionary War teens!

Almost anything would be better than these shows, and almost anything was, *except* for *The Most Deadly Game*. This ABC show was proof of the horrors that are wrought between conception and presentation. Eric Ambler, the noted novelist, created the concept of master criminologist Ethan Arcane who ran a detective agency with a former intelligence officer named Jonathan Croft and his college-educated ward, the beautiful Vanessa Smith.

So far, so good. The parts were cast with detective pioneer Ralph Bellamy as Arcane, Yvette Mimieux as his ward, and George Maharis as Croft. Fine and dandy. But the scripts were full of so much false, self-conscious modern lingo that they were ludicrous. *TV Guide* reprinted some representative dialog: "Vanessa's a Now girl, Chief. If she met a guy who turned her on, I'm guessing she wouldn't have to dance through fourteen minuets and a sarabande. . . ." That's

---

The television detective genre owes a debt to Ralph Bellamy. Not only did he star as "Ellery Queen" in a series of films, he starred as the Man Against Crime. Unfortunately, he also appeared in the dreadful The Most Deadly Game. (ABC)

Actress Yvette Mimieux was about the only attractive thing about The Most Deadly
Game, *playing Vanessa Smith, crack criminologist. Sadly, all of the dialog was
awful. (courtesy of United Press International, Inc.)*

enough of that. If you think reading it was
bad, try actually saying it with conviction
and you will see what the actors were up
against. *The Most Deadly Game* was bad
news from the title on down and was put
out of its misery after 11 episodes.

Finally, there was *The Silent Force*,
which should have stayed silent. It was a
nice idea: an interracial and intersexual
team of three federal agents assigned to
go undercover and destroy organized
crime. Sort of a middle-aged Mod Squad.
But a lot of time had passed since *The
Untouchables*. In 1970, it was evident
that organized crime was everywhere,

and to eradicate it would weaken, if not
destroy, the nation's foundation. The
syndicate was inside of almost every
union and every local government. It had
grown so powerful that mentioning its
name in conjunction with evil was *ver-
boten* on television.

So *The Silent Force* could not even
mention the word *Mafia*. All they could
say was "The Mob." Ed Nelson was
Ward Fuller, the white agent, Percy Rod-
riquez was Jason Hart, the sophisticated
black man, and Lynda Day George was
Amelia Cole. *The Silent Force* quietly
disappeared at the second season.

The Gimmick Eyes
and the Glory Years

The most auspicious moment of the new television decade came on January 12, 1971. It started with a song. "Boy, the way Glenn Miller played. . . ." It was the opening of *All in the Family* and the show changed completely the way people would approach TV. It hardly made any impression at first, but as the weeks went on, it grew to a power that has not diminished even a decade later.

Producer Norman Lear and his crew had a telling effect on the TV detective. Mystery shows were made that would not have been made but for the ground-breaking themes and dramatic depth of *All in the Family*.

1971

We start with a detective comedy that was as staid in its way as *All in the Family* was revolutionary: *The Smith Family*. Here was a throwback to the "Happy Days" of the fifties' sitcoms, and it starred Henry Fonda. Like *The Andy Griffith*

Show before it, this ABC second season filler had as much to do with crab grass as crime. It was created to realistically portray the life of a policeman, but it got bogged down with melo-dramatic messages.

Sergeant Chad Smith lived at 219 Primrose Lane with his wife, Betty (Janet Blair), his college student daughter Cindy (Darleen Carr), his teen-age son Bob (Ron Howard), and his seven-year-old Brian (Michael-James Wixted). Everything Chad did at work seemed to interrelate with what was going on at home. He would find missing kids, only to think about how Cindy wants to move out. He would help a drug bust, worrying whether Bob was smoking pot, and so on and so forth.

"Underwhelming," decided Cleveland Amory upon reviewing the show. "The timing is off . . . about 20 years off. The morals are delivered with all the subtlety of a sledge hammer." *The Smith Family* moved out of the network neighborhood in the summer of 1972.

Henry Fonda sought to embody the "common man cop" in a supposedly realistic dramatic comedy, **The Smith Family.** **(ABC)**

Speaking of subtlety, when we last left Don Adams on TV, he was a married and child-bearing Maxwell Smart. This season saw him return as Detective Lennie Cook of the L.A.P.D., one half of *The Partners*. The other half was black, cool Detective George Robinson, played by Rupert Crosse. Naturally, Adams was as big a bumbler here as he was in *Get Smart*, only on this cop show he looked stupider because it was not written as well. And they did not have "Would you believe. . ." and "Sorry about that" to fall back on.

The slow-burning foil here was no chief, but a Captain Aaron Andrews played by John Doucette. For a nostalgic flavor, they brought back Larrabee portrayer Robert Karvelas as Freddie Butler, "the man with the compulsion to confess to everything." The buffoonery did not work because they were not satirizing other cop shows, they were simply falling down a lot. *Get Smart* was a lampoon. *The Partners* was a mistake. It was killed in the line of duty at the second season mark.

With these feeble comedies out of the way, we can get down to what this season was all about and what made 1971 the start of the TV detective "glory years." The first trend to examine is the one toward frontier detectives. This can be traced back to the success of *The Wild*

Wild West and all the top 10 Westerns of the past, but it cannot be said that this trend was planned. It just so happened that there were three rustic investigators who showed up on two networks at the same time. It was their success or failure that would dictate whether the trend went on for more than a year.

They all failed, but not without a moment of glory for each. The moment of glory for *Bearcats!* came in April of 1971 with the telecast of a two-hour movie upon which the September series would be based. In the recurring show, as in *Powderkeg*, the teleflick, Rod Taylor is Hank Brackett, a turn-of-the-century mercenary who teams with Dennis Cole as Johnny Reach on a succession of assignments in the Southwest of 1914.

Writer/producer/director Douglas Heyes, who had earlier written and directed a fine private-eye teleflick called *The Lonely Profession*, added some interesting touches here—such as the mercenaries asking their clients for a blank check *before* the mission that they would fill out for an amount they deemed suitable if they survived. Their major mode of transportation was a beautiful Stutz Bearcat, hence the show's name.

The teleflick was clever and engaging, but once the full-scale series started, *Bearcats!* ran into trouble. It was an action show in a medium that had exorcized action. So when Brackett and Reach appeared on the weekly schedule, their Gatling gun blazing, antiviolence groups strongly disagreed with their method of solving problems. Of course, if the show had shown signs of being a hit, CBS might not have considered taking it off, but it did not. *Bearcats!* drove into the sunset for good at the second season, never to return.

Cade's County's moment of glory came during the casting process. The second of three frontier mysteries signed Glenn Ford, star of many great movies from 1939 on. Best known for his work as a detective in *The Big Heat* (1953) and *Fate Is the Hunter* (1964), a teacher in *The Blackboard Jungle* (1955), and cowboy in *The Sheepman* (1958), *Cimarron* (1961), and *The Rounders* (1965), his film career was slowing down in the early seventies.

He did one TV movie, *The Brotherhood of the Bell*, before signing on as Sheriff Sam Cade, whose jurisdiction covered all of Madrid County, California. The series was contemporary, but the sprawling country it pictured looked little different from the Wild West, except that instead of horses, Cade and his deputies rode Jeeps. His deputies included J. J. Jackson (veteran character actor Edgar Buchanan, whose film career started way back in 1940 after a dentistry career), Arlo Pritchard (blond newcomer Taylor Lacher), Rudy Davillo (Victor Campos), and a production in-joke, a character known only as Pete. The joke was that this final deputy was played by Peter Ford, Glenn's son.

With Ford's experience and the on-location photography, *Cade's County* was able to get through a season. After that not even Ford's crinkly smile and twinkly, knowing eyes could get them back on the air. Curiously enough, a TV movie comprised of a two-part episode was released to the stations after the show had gone off the air.

Two years later, Ford would test the TV waters again with *Jarrett* (1973), a teleflick pilot about a sophisticated private detective who dabbled in cases involving fine art. Although produced and written by Richard Maibum, the screenwriter for most of the James Bond films, it did not catch fire.

The third frontier detective show, *Nichols*, had its moment of glory in its very last episode. Other than that, it was similar to *Trials of O'Brien* because there was a failed characterization that succeeded for the actor in question just a few years later. The characterization was that of Nichols and the actor was James Garner. He had just come from making three successful Western comedies—*Support Your Local Sheriff* (1969), *Support Your Local Gunfighter* (1971), and *The Skin Game* (1971). In all of them he played essentially the same part—a cowardly, apathetic drifter who is pulled into trouble against his will. Through con-man skills and an inherent ability with a gun, he always managed to triumph.

And since Garner had his own production company, he figured to combine the popularity of those movies with the memory of him as *Maverick* to come up with a guaranteed winner for NBC. He surrounded himself with talent. Meta Rosenberg, his former agent, was now co-founder of Cherokee Productions (Garner's Company) and his executive producer. They got people like Frank Pierson and Paul Bogart to direct the adventures of "no-first-name" Nichols, who leaves the army after 18 years to return in 1914 to the Arizona town which bears his family name.

He hired Neva Patterson to play Ma Ketchum, the tough, wily matriarch who had taken over the town after the last Nichols left. Stuart Margolin played Mitch Ketchum, a craven swine who became Nichols' deputy after Ma blackmailed Nichols into becoming sheriff for

not being able to pay a fine. John Beck played Ketchum, a burly bully who beat up on Nichols and caused the damage for which he was fined in the first place. And hoarse-voiced Margot Kidder played Ruth, the beautiful barmaid who Nichols was talking to when the jealous Ketchum attacked.

Here was a show that had everything. Everything but enough people who wanted to watch it. After a disappointing showing during the first few weeks, the title was changed to *James Garner as Nichols*, in case people did not know. When that did not work, they all decided that the public apathy was caused by Nichols' own apathy. The leading character spent all his time trying to get rich quick. So an audacious scheme was hit upon to change the direction of the series, seemingly with the full backing of the network.

In the final episode of the first year, Nichols was killed while trying to prevent a barroom brawl. There was no gradual change of character here. No sudden realization that he must take control of his own life. No, they just croaked Nichols and replaced him with his twin brother, Jim Nichols, who comes to town a few days later to pick up the pieces. Jim was played by James Garner, which came as little surprise, and Jim was a capable, brave, heroic sort, which also was no surprise.

The surprise was that NBC canceled the series at the end of the season, knowing full well these changes were taking place. So even though *Nichols* was finally set with a take-charge kind of lead, the network told them all to take off. Garner and company left the airwaves for awhile, but like MacArthur, they would return.

A man who did not return was *Owen Marshall: Counselor at Law*. Once he finished his three-season run, that was it. He first appeared on ABC in a TV movie with the subtitle "A Pattern of Morality," written by producer David Victor and Jerry McNeely. Victor had also created *Marcus Welby, M.D.*, and he visualized Marshall as being that kindly doctor's legal counterpart. He invested both shows with the same ingredients.

Both men were widowers, both were fatherly types, both had offices in their homes, and both had handsome young assistants. Arthur Hill, a respected stage actor who had starred in the original Broadway production of *Who's Afraid of Virginia Wolfe?*, starred as Marshall, while hunky Lee Majors played Jess Brandon in the series. In both the tele-flick and series was Melissa Marshall, Owen's daughter, played by Christine Matchett, and Frieda Krause, Owen's secretary, played by Joan Darling. Missing in the series was Baird Marshall, Owen's son, played by Rick Lenz, in the movie version.

The set of the show would be rife with entrances and exits. Lee Majors left in slow motion when *The Six Million Dollar Man* beckoned. In his stead came David Soul playing Ted Warrick. Soul, in turn, left when another cop show beckoned. Reni Santoni showed up then to play Danny Paterno, Owen's third aide. Even Joan Darling left when an opportunity to direct beckoned. She went on to a notable career behind the camera. In the series' final year, Marcus Welby showed up for the second time to bolster the slipping ratings by having Owen defend his assistant, Dr. Kiley, in a paternity suit.

That sensationalist ploy could not get *Owen Marshall: Counselor at Law* into a higher court. He lost his cancellation case, leaving the air with good reviews. Arguing a worse case for his defense was Jack Webb. The success of *Adam-12* had put the man back into the batting box and he took full advantage of it this year by putting two shows on the fall schedules. Both were preceded by TV movies, both premiered on the same night, and both died early deaths. They even followed one another in their respective time slots.

The first was *The D.A.*, starring grossly miscast Robert Conrad as *Deputy* District Attorney Paul Ryan. Conrad cannot be blamed for the weaknesses of the series. Two TV movies were presented before NBC decided to air the half-hour series. In the first, *The D.A.: Murder One* (1969), Ryan sent a nurse to death row by proving, over the objections of his superiors, that she had been knocking off her family with insulin. In the second, *The D.A.: Conspiracy to Kill*, he got a druggist thrown in the clink for being a robbery mastermind and an accessory to murder.

In his first series episode he went after a father charged with murdering his two-year-old daughter. This and other stories were based on actual cases that Webb had investigated over the years. However, the sight (and sound) of Robert Conrad portraying a studious attorney was not very believable. If he had been a feisty defense attorney who got himself through law school to defend the little guy, maybe. But this man amid a large, politically motivated staff? Not likely, and not watched. *The D.A.* was thrown out of court at the second season.

As a producer, Jack Webb had dug through the files of the plainclothes police (*Dragnet*), uniformed officers

(*Adam-12*), and lawyers (*The D.A.*). It seemed as though the only files he had not gotten his hands on were the government's. Perish the thought. With *O'Hara, United States Treasury*, Webb invaded the ground that Quinn Martin made famous.

As with almost everything else that year, *O'Hara* started in a TV movie— *Operation Cobra*. David Janssen quit running from the authorities to become one in the form of James O'Hara, a mirthless, laconic agent for the Treasury Department. As such, he was after the same game as *The Untouchables*, only later and with a lot less action. Jack Webb himself directed the teleflick, setting the staid pace the series would follow until its demise a season later.

The show was pure misery for Janssen fans, who found their hero not weary or cynical, but nearly catatonic. Happily he would return to TV detective stardom the same year that Garner pulled off his *coup de grâce*.

By now a pattern was beginning to emerge in the 1971 efforts: TV movie pilots filled with old TV hands and respected movie stars. For some reason, the producers waited until the new decade to flood the airwaves with teleflick ideas, and the fading film stars waited until then to give in. Whatever the cause, it would make for a minor golden age of good shows and great characters. With the means of a TV movie to gauge public response, only the concepts with the best response would get on the air.

Such was the case with Sterling Silliphant's *Longstreet*, aired as an ABC teleflick in February 1971. Silliphant had produced *Naked City* and had written the *Route 66* pilot. Here he scripted and executive-produced the story of

Michael Longstreet, an insurance investigator blinded by the booby-trapped bottle of champagne which killed his wife. With the help of his old boss, Duke Paige, his Braille teacher, Nikki Bell, and Pax the seeing-eye dog, he tracks down his assailants (who tried to kill him because they heard he might prove a threat to their upcoming caper).

Although this sounds a little far-fetched, producer/director Joseph Sargent gave the teleflick class and conviction. By the end of the film, Longstreet has opened his own investigations office in New Orleans with Nikki as his companion. In September the series started with James Franciscus returning as the lead. Peter Mark Richman had replaced Bradford Dillman as his ex-boss and Marlyn Mason had replaced Martine Beswick as Nikki. Pax was the same old dog.

At first, Longstreet got by with his brains and an electronic cane that judged distances. He soon found that this was not enough. There were ruffians willing to beat up a blind man. He was a constant victim until Li Tsung was introduced in a two-part episode. After being defeated by some waterfront thugs, Longstreet learned kung fu from Master Tsung, played by real-life master Bruce Lee. By the end of the second part, Longstreet returned to the wharf and gave the thugs what-for. It was *Longstreet*'s grandest moment as a series.

It is a shame that Longstreet was not as proficient as the Marvel Comics' blind superhero Daredevil, because after that fight early in the season, the scripts took a turn toward the mundane. *Longstreet* ended after one season.

But at least it had a high point. *Sarge* did not even have that. What it did have was a February TV movie pilot starring

Academy Award-winner George Kennedy as Police Sergeant Samuel Patrick Cavanaugh, who became Father Samuel Patrick Cavanaugh after the murder of his wife. When sent to a San Diego parish, he discovers the man who had killed his spouse while gunning for him. For his series premiere, *Sarge* was teamed with *Ironside* to find *The Priest Killer* (another two-hour film) and insure good ratings. David Levinson produced and Richard A. Colla executive-produced both films. Although both men were talented writers and directors, *Sarge* was an uncomfortable combination of divinity and death.

George Kennedy was burly enough to be convincing as a policeman and sensitive enough to be convincing as a priest, but the writers did not know whether they were scripting a contemporary drama about urban problems or a bloodthirsty whodunit. The viewers did not know which they were watching, either, so they switched off. *Sarge* went to that big precinct house in the sky at the second season.

About the only shows that did not have made-for-TV movie pilots were the British imports. The best of these was *The Strange Report*, which NBC picked up as a second season replacement for *Bracken's World*. It was a modest, intelligent little thriller with the fine actor Anthony Quayle as Adam Strange, the best criminologist in the Isles. Driving around London in his unlicensed taxi, Strange used the services of Hamlyn Gynt (Kaz Garas) and neighbor Evelyn McLean (Anneke Wills) on special cases the government gave him.

These cases were in the "impossible" category, either because they were too hot for Her Majesty to handle or they had everyone befuddled. No matter, Adam Strange would get the job done. Quite right, too. It is the least we expect from an actor who appeared in both film versions of Sherlock Holmes's tussle with Jack the Ripper—*A Study in Terror* (1965) and *Murder by Decree* (1979).

Strange was not alone in solving the Home Office's nasty crimes. Producer Monty Berman created a government department for that. In *Department S* Peter Wyngarde played the foppish writer Jason King, who lent his consulting services to two of the department's best agents—Stewart Sullivan (Joel Fabiani) and Annabelle Hurst (Rosemary Nicols). To show just how much things were changing, *Department S* had a black boss, and a knighted black boss at that, Sir Curtis Seretse, played by Dennis Peters. One year's worth of episodes were shown.

Saint producer Robert Baker made another action series that year, tailored specifically for the international market. "The original idea sprang from a long line of Hollywood movies," Baker explained, "which had their basis in a clash of two strong personalities. Clark Gable and Spencer Tracy in *Boom Town*. Or more recently Paul Newman and Robert Redford in *Butch Cassidy and the Sundance Kid*. This kind of relationship had always intrigued me, so when *The Saint* was over, I sat down and worked out *The Persuaders*."

Once that was done, Baker got Lew Grade to back it and Roger Moore and Tony Curtis to star in it. It was an old ploy by now. With *The Saint* leading the way, English entrepreneurs discovered that American networks were more apt to buy their products for stateside showing if an American character or actor was featured. And with the combination of

Moore and Curtis, the ABC network "really flipped," in Baker's words.

Moore played Lord Brett Sinclair, a rich Britisher, while Curtis was Danny Wilde, a rough-edged businessman who had to pull himself out of Hell's Kitchen. Meeting on the Riviera, it was aggression at first sight. Not until Judge Fulton (Laurence Naismith) convinces them that they are wasting their lives and their wealth do they become partners against crime. Being a bit less professional about it than Steed and Mrs. Peel, they become known as The Persuaders.

The two actors obviously enjoyed themselves because they were able to ad-lib filler dialog whenever they felt like it. The scripts were far-fetched fantasies that only sought to be slightly coherent, and the action was plentiful. As clever as Moore and Curtis were, they were no Cosby and Culp. Their series just lasted until the summer in the United States. From there they were thrown to the syndicators.

We find the second trend of 1971 becoming clearer. *Longstreet* and *Sarge* were two of a kind, two detectives with an extra bit of spice thrown in to make them unusual. Their genesis can be traced directly to *Ironside*. A crippled detective, then a blind detective, then a priest-detective—you get the idea? Detectives this year had to have a gimmick—a special something to make them different from all the others.

That special something could be as extreme as blindness or as simple as a few dozen extra pounds. When it came time to put an overweight detective on TV, the publicity writers were not subtle about it. "Bigger than life," was the premiere week's catchline. "That's William Con-

rad. As private eye *Cannon*. Big excitement every week."

Just like his gimmicky brethren, private eye Frank Cannon was introduced with a TV movie. His was simply called *Cannon* and it aired in March of 1971. In the Ed Hume-written, George McCowan-directed two-hour pilot, the character is introduced as a fat, expensive investigator who indulges his tastes for almost anything edible with the fat fees he charges. What he had going for him, besides his girth, was Quinn Martin as producer.

Martin had the necessary experience in the television mystery field to get solid scripts and a solid technical crew. The rest of *Cannon*'s attraction came in the large-size container known as William Conrad. Although none of the odds makers thought the cases of an obese, balding, middle-aged snoop would attract anybody, people tuned in to see a change from the usual pretty-boy peepers. And once they tuned in, *Cannon* and Conrad usually held them.

"Kids seem to like the show because they think Cannon is honest," Conrad explained. "Middle-aged people see him as one of their own making it—not some stereotyped Hollywood god, but the guy they see on the street. I don't know why old people like it." Then Conrad laughed. A big, hearty laugh—the kind that makes others feel good.

That was the magic ingredient of the series. With Conrad's big, rich, full voice (the one that played Marshall Dillon on the *Gunsmoke* radio show), many saw the handsome, capable, friendly man who cared. *Cannon* was like everyone's favorite uncle, only this one packed a gun and was not above using it. It was also fun to watch him maneuver through

William Conrad, looking really "heavy" for his role as the overweight detective Cannon. (courtesy of United Press International, Inc.)

scenes seemingly written for Mannix. Thin heroes could get out of trouble easily, but people wanted to see how on earth Conrad would be able to handle it.

To his credit, Conrad handled these action scenes with panache. "Cannon was a very physical role," he elaborated. "It was one of the few series without a regular supporting cast, so the action—the running, the car chases, the battles and the exertion—fell on one man: Can-

non. Me." Even so, everyone knew *Cannon* could not sustain a knock-down, drag-out brawl the way *Mannix* could, so they were not written. That added an extra dose of calm class to the proceedings and pleased the antiviolence groups no end. People tuned in knowing they were not going to see "Tuesday Night at the Fights."

Cannon's initial caseload ran out in five years, but Conrad kept busy within

*But as **Cannon** and actor Conrad proved, flab does not have to get in the way of fistfights. Although still rotund, Conrad professed to being in his best shape for the part. To facilitate matters, he practiced the martial arts at a Los Angeles gym. (courtesy of United Press International, Inc.)*

the TV mystery genre. In the past, he had produced shows like *This Man Dawson, Klondike*, and a season of *77 Sunset Strip*. After *Cannon* left the airwaves, he starred in two interesting whodunit tele-flicks: *The Murder That Wouldn't Die*, with Conrad as a college football coach solving a murder in Hawaii; and *Turnover Smith*, with Conrad in the title role of a university criminologist who uses a computer to solve a mass murder.

Then, on November 1, 1980, QM Productions resurrected Cannon in a one-shot TV movie suitably titled *The Return of Frank Cannon*. In it, the detective comes out of retirement to investigate the mysterious death of an old friend who

supposedly committed suicide. When asked if the film would lead to a renewed series, Conrad replied in the negative. And no wonder—he was already cast as the lead in a new series about the third greatest literary detective after Sherlock Holmes and Ellery Queen!

The remainder of 1971 is taken up with three great series, one loosely based on a movie; one loosely based on a series of detective stories, films, and a prior series; and one based on a previous TV character. Now I will come clean. I lied about last year. There was one more series I failed to mention that premiered in 1970: *McCloud*.

McCloud showed up in the company

of three other nondetective shows, all presented under the banner of *Four-in-One*—another NBC variation on *The Bold Ones* format. The series, in turn, was foreshadowed by a TV movie called *McCloud: Who Killed Miss U.S.A.?* People tuning into this February 1970 broadcast expecting to see a rip-snorting thriller about a psycho loose in a beauty pageant saw instead a story that vaguely resembled the one for Clint Eastwood's *Coogan's Bluff* (1969), directed by Don Siegel.

In that film, Eastwood played an Arizona lawman who comes to New York to extradite a particularly slimy creature who gets away and leads him on a merry chase. In the teleflick, Dennis Weaver plays a Taos, New Mexico, lawman who comes to New York to extradite a subpoenaed witness, only to see the witness shanghaied and find himself handcuffed to a fence along a highway.

From there he gets involved with the murder of a pageant contestant and runs afoul of the N.Y.P.D. in the person of Chief Peter B. Clifford, a man not so far removed from the Chief on *Get Smart*. *McCloud* is not a bumbler, he is just an affable, matchstick-chewing, cowboy-hatted and booted Westerner who carries a walnut-handled six-gun and says "There ye go" a lot. It was as if Deputy Chester Goode of *Gunsmoke* (who Weaver played) had lost his limp and gotten promoted.

McCloud was played for a lot more chuckles than *Coogan's Bluff*, but it was still a well-made series. The partnership of Leslie Stevens and Glen Larson handled most of the production while the creators of *Mannix*, Richard Levinson and William Link, helped establish the tone with Stanford Whitmore, who wrote the original story. Upon the opening of

the series on September 16, 1970, McCloud has been officially transferred to New York's Finest, ostensibly to learn the techniques of a metropolitan force. Naturally he winds up teaching the city slickers a thing or two.

The chief city slickers are his partner Sergeant Joe Broadhurst (Terry Carter) and the long-suffering Chief Clifford (J. D. Cannon replacing Mark Richman from the pilot). Outside that basic comedy conflict, the scriptwriters utilized New York very cleverly. McCloud's best moments came when he was riding a horse down Forty-Second Street and when he got involved in a "High Noon" shoot-out in Central Park.

But all that started in 1970. In 1971, the three other *Four-in-One* shows (*Night Gallery, San Francisco International,* and *The Psychiatrist*) had either failed (the latter pair) or had been spun off. And since the Wednesday time slot they had all prepared was for 90 minutes, NBC did not think *McCloud* should handle it alone. So two new 90-minute shows were prepared and joined him as *NBC Mystery Movie* was born. On Friday, September 17, NBC aired *Once Upon a Dead Man*, the teleflick wherein *McMillan and Wife* first appeared.

Leonard Stern created, executive-produced, and directed this two-hour effort that probably drew on *The Thin Man*. *McMillan and Wife* were as much George Burns and Gracie Allen as they were Nick and Nora Charles because Police Commissioner Stewart McMillan's wife Sally was as wacky as Gracie and as prone to finding corpses as Nora (or Mrs. North, for that matter).

What this variation on the theme had over the prior TV *Thin Man* was its cast and the 90 minutes with which to create an effective mystery. Rock Hudson gave

McMillan and Wife *made the picture of domestic tranquility here. Rock Hudson, as Police Commissioner McMillan, chats with Nancy Walker, playing Mildred the maid, while Susan St. James as wife Sally concentrates on breakfast. But it wouldn't be long before someone would stumble upon a corpse, and another episode would be off and running. (NBC)*

his career a shot in the arm as McMillan. Hudson had proven his acting ability in *The Spiral Road* (1962) and *Seconds* (1966), but people still thought of him as Doris Day's screen husband. When he reached middle age, his roles began to dry up, but he remedied the problem by going into TV and catching hold of McMillan.

Dennis Weaver first found success as the limping deputy Chester in Gunsmoke. *After failing to hit the top ten with two light-hearted series (*Kentucky Jones *and* Gentle Ben*), he hit the big time as* McCloud, *the best sixshooter-packing marshal New York had ever seen. (courtesy of United Press International, Inc.)*

Co-star Susan Saint James got an Emmy for *The Name of the Game*, but she got stardom as Sally McMillan. It is not that easy to be kooky without being cloying or completely unbelievable, but Saint James pulled it off. In every episode, it seemed, Sally would uncover a body or something and spend the rest of the show getting kidnapped, attacked, threatened, or else all three while hubby galloped to the rescue with the help of his stolid assistant, Sergeant Charles Enright (John Schuck).

Adding humor at home was Mildred the maid, a role that brightened the star of comedienne Nancy Walker. The mixture was so frothy and watchable that disbelief was suspended for five years. At the end of the 1975 season, the trouble occurred. Walker and Schuck had been so well received that they accepted offers from ABC to star in their own series. Saint James wanted more out of life than finding corpses and being saved by Rock Hudson, so she left, too. The producers did what any red-blooded TV executives would do in the same situation: they promoted the sergeant, replaced the maid, and let Sally's bad luck catch up with her.

McMillan was given a new dumb sergeant named Steve DiMaggio (Richard Gilliland), Mildred's sister, Agatha (Martha Raye), took over the cleaning chores, and Sally was killed in a plane crash. As despondent as poor Stew was over the death of his beautiful young wife, he still found time to go galavanting all over solving crimes in a show known simply as *McMillan* (why not *McMillan Minus Wife?*).

NBC should have known better. Without Sally around to get into trouble, the Commissioner McMillan had no reason to leave his paperwork-strewn desk.

Hudson, who sported a mustache on and off during McMillan and Wife's *run, seems to be congratulating Nancy Walker on her series-created success. Walker, as if knowing that her own two series on ABC would flop, looks none too pleased. (NBC)*

There was a whole police force to delegate cases to. With Saint James gone and no one to take her place, disbelief was no longer suspended and the reworked concept died a deserved death in a year.

Unfortunately, *McMillan* was not alone in its attempt to keep a show going after the concept was dead. NBC tried the same thing—with even worse results—with the third of the three *NBC Wednesday Mystery Movie* series. Two days before *Once Upon a Dead Man* aired, the actual 90-minute series opened with an episode of *Columbo*. But to find the pilot TV movie of *Columbo*, one had to go back three years.

Prescription: Murder (1968) started as a play by Richard Levinson and William Link that had closed before it got to Broadway. Joseph Cotten starred as a psychiatrist who thought he had committed the perfect murder of his wife only to be tripped up by an unassuming, seemingly absentminded police detective. That detective was based on the character of Petrovich, the policeman in Dostoevski's *Crime and Punishment*, and was played on the stage by Thomas Mitchell. Then 73 years old, Mitchell had been called the "most accomplished character actor of the American stage and screen."

Mitchell, best remembered as Scarlett O'Hara's father in *Gone With the Wind* (1939), died shortly after *Prescription: Murder* closed, so Levinson and Link had to look for a new Columbo for the TV version. Since they had in mind an elderly detective, their first choice was Bing Crosby. After the great crooner turned them down, they settled on a younger actor who had impressed them with his rumpled looks and good nature.

So Peter Falk played Lieutenant Columbo opposite Gene Barry as the murder-minded doctor.

Prescription: Murder was shown and was well received. Nothing more was heard from the character until March of 1971 when Falk and Columbo returned in *Ransom for a Dead Man*. Viewers who remembered the film of three years earlier must have done a double take as the same hunched little man (apparently wearing the same wrinkled raincoat) came marching into Leslie Williams' mansion to foil her plan to get away with the murder of her wealthy husband. This was truly *Columbo*'s teleflick pilot—directed by Richard Irving and written by Dean Hargrove from a story by Levinson and Link—and it translated nicely into the debut episode of the triweekly series.

Roland Kibbee and Dean Hargrove were executive producers of the series for Universal, with Levinson and Link as on-line producers and writers. When they say "on-line" it sometimes means "front line," because these people have to hack out the day-to-day survival of the show. Thankfully Levinson and Link really knew the detective genre. The initial *Columbo* episode was "Murder by the Book," an intricate script which had the lesser of two collaborators on a best-selling mystery book series kill the more talented one as he was about to dissolve the partnership. The in-joke was that the pair was based on Fredric Dannay and Manfred Lee—the men who were Ellery Queen—and their character was based on Agatha Christie's Miss Marple.

But no matter how clever the plan, no matter how brilliant the murderer, *Columbo* always outwitted them in the end. He did it two ways: by being a fabulous

Peter Falk dug through his own closet for the rumpled suit and raincoat he deemed suitable for the character of Lt. Philip Columbo, the messy detective with the steel-trap mind. In this episode, guest murderer Robert Conrad urges the cop to get in shape. Columbo, as always, gets his man. (NBC)

detective and by coming on as the police's answer to Bozo the Clown. He almost always wore his rumpled raincoat, chewed on disgusting stogies, drove a heap that should have been junked years ago, and just generally gave the impression that he could not think his way out of a men's room.

As the years and episodes went on, more and more suspects caught on to what Columbo was doing, which required him to use sharper and sharper detective work. A highlight came in an episode with Leonard Nimoy as a doctor out to kill his mentor, played by Will Geer. For a split second Columbo broke character and got mad—frustrated that

he might not be able to prevent Geer's death after Nimoy's murder of a nurse tipped the police off.

Naturally Columbo was able to prevent the second death, and in all the cases over the seven years he saw justice prevail—occasionally catching the same actor playing a different killer on other episodes. Some of Columbo's favorite recurring actors were Robert Culp, Jack Cassidy (playing the agent of another

None of the killers cornered by Columbo could say that the master investigator didn't keep them amused as he tightened the noose around their necks. Here, guest star George Hamilton yuks it up as Falk beats away at his alibi during "A Deadly State of Mind" episode. (NBC)

mystery author played by real mystery author Mickey Spillane), and Patrick McGoohan. Other stars who wanted Columbo to catch them were Robert Vaughn, William Shatner, Dick Van Dyke, Ruth Gordon, and Louis Jourdan.

Columbo spelled stardom for Peter Falk after 20 years of relative success. "You love him (Columbo) because he isn't pretentious and is good at his job," Falk said, explaining the detective's appeal. "He likes to save his best shot for last. Columbo's got a terrific sense of timing." So did Falk. Just when the series was at its height of popularity, Falk started asking for a bigger slice of pie—a slice he deserved, but which the network did not want to give to him.

The show became more popular as Falk became more restless. By 1977 NBC was paying him two million dollars a year, although he would only perform in four episodes a year. By then he was being tapped for good movie roles (*The Cheap Detective, The Brink's Job*), so he was even more reluctant to spend much time as the lieutenant.

"I love Columbo," he said, "but there's only so much you can do with it. I love pork chops, too. It's just that I don't want to eat pork chops every day for the rest of my life. Look, I did the show for a few terrific years. Sure, there were disagreements . . . there had to be—everyone was coming from a different place. Scripts, that was the rub. I said why can't

Falk got his own reward for all his verbal cat-and-mouse games. First, there was the Emmy he won for "Best Performance by an Actor in a Dramatic Series" in 1972. Then, there were the millions of dollars he collected as salary for his Columbo role. (courtesy of United Press International, Inc.)

we make one or two good ones a year? They couldn't live with it."

So *Columbo* was phased out in 1978, the longest running component of any *NBC Mystery Movie*. As with *McMillan*, the network did not know enough to let go. Fred Silverman, the supposed programming *wunderkind*, hit on a "great" idea. Since Columbo was always talking about his wife, why not create a show about her? And why not make her like Sally McMillan, Nora Charles, and Pamela North all rolled into one? Why not? Because it was a stupid, mercenary, rip-off idea.

Actress Kate Mulgrew felt the same way when NBC approached her. "My first reaction was 'Forget it,' " she said. But Fred Silverman argued the case for the show personally, making her give it a second thought. She finally agreed, so *Mrs. Columbo* went into hasty production. It was a conceptual nightmare, with Mulgrew joining a confused crew that had no script, a tight deadline, and a hell of a reputation to live up to.

The first two-hour episode premiered February 26, 1979, with guest-star Robert Culp, just a week after Levinson and Link's Edgar-winning TV movie *Murder by Natural Causes* aired. The following week *Mrs. Columbo* premiered as a series with Donald Pleasance (another *Columbo* murderer) guest-starring. The scripts were inferior, the concept was shaky, and Mrs. Columbo did not have a first name yet. It made sense that people would call Columbo "Lieutenant" in lieu of a surname (which, according to the "Prescription: Murder" play, was Philip), but were they going to call the wife, "Mrs.?"

They finally gave Mrs. Columbo a first name and announced the fact by chang-

ing the show's title to *Kate Columbo*, even though Falk had revealed her name as Rose on a Dean Martin show. Then, when that did not get anyone to watch, they performed a sacrilegious divorce and changed the title to *Kate Loves a Mystery*, all in the space of a few weeks!

Silverman's biggest mistake was going with the idea in the first place, then casting a 23-year-old actress in the role over the Levinson and Link suggestion of Maureen Stapleton, and finally handling the series like a cut-rate lobotomy lesson. Silverman was not through with NBC's mystery lineup yet, as we shall see.

1972

In 1972 Governor George Wallace was shot, a group of "plumbers" were caught trying to plant bugging devices at a Democratic party office at the Watergate complex in Washington, D.C., and 11 Israeli athletes were killed at the Munich Olympics by terrorists. It was nothing new for TV. But as TV technology grew, so would the coverage. Reality would be perfectly packaged and delivered to your home so you could marvel at it over dinner or while the kids did their homework in front of the tube. Television had made reality fantasy.

For the TV detective, this was the year when everyone tried to copy the *NBC Mystery Movie*—even NBC. They moved *Columbo*, *McCloud*, and *McMillan* from Wednesday to Sunday, then added a fourth character to make the episodes monthly. *Hec Ramsey* joined the newly retitled *NBC Sunday Mystery Movie*.

In 1901 Ramsey was a grizzled old ex-gunfighter who decided to settle down on the side of the law in New

Prospect, Oklahoma. To make life more interesting (and the antiviolence groups happy), he decided to forsake the gun as much as he could in favor of all the new-fangled detection equipment being shipped in from the East.

Given the concept, it was surprising to find Jack Webb in the producer's seat, but not surprising at all to find gravel-voiced Richard Boone in the lead. This, like all the other *Mystery Movie* series, was first introduced as a TV movie. The teleflick was entertaining, as was the se-

ries, but the concept was not strong enough to hold on without the violence which helped make all the past Westerns so successful. *Hec Ramsey* was sent to Boot Hill in 1974.

He was replaced at that time by *Amy Prentiss*, who did not have a TV movie pilot but was given her big chance on an *Ironside* episode. In it, a San Francisco chief of detectives died and Amy was assigned to take his place. A lot of male chauvinism was demonstrated before Prentiss was allowed to show her detect-

Could this photo show that Tony Curtis knew psychically that he would gain the TV success he missed as McCoy on Vega$? Whatever the case, Curtis' starring role would last only a few episodes. (NBC)

ing stuff. Besides the murders that filled the show, there was the conflict between the woman and her men, many of whom resented her promotion.

Many viewers resented watching her every fourth week, so she only lasted on the *Sunday Mystery Movie* for about eight episodes. The network replaced that with *McCoy*, a creation from Roland Kibbee and Dean Hargrove, who produced, wrote, and directed the March 1975 pilot teleflick *The Big Ripoff*. That title may have been a private joke between the two men, because *McCoy* was actually a big rip-off to the Oscar-winning movie *The Sting* (1973).

It was also Tony Curtis' bad choice for a second stab at TV series stardom. He played McCoy, a con man who set up elaborate con games on assignment. He would get money back from crooks for his clients, but only after taking a little off the top for his services. It lasted but four episodes.

One might think that NBC would have learned its lesson by now and quit jamming new ideas in with the successful trio, but no. Not only did they give it one last shot, but they mortally wounded the new project by recasting it at the last minute.

Lanigan's Rabbi had the best chance of the four failures to make it. First, it was based on a best-selling series of mysteries by author Harry Kemelman. Secondly, NBC had tested the waters with a TV movie based on the first of these novels, *Friday the Rabbi Slept Late*. This was the original *Lanigan's Rabbi*, directed by Lou Antonio and scripted by Don Mankiewicz and Gordon Cotler. It starred Art Carney as Police Chief Paul Lanigan of Cameron, California. Lanigan had a murder on his hands, a dead girl found

outside Rabbi David Small's synagogue.

Small was a kind, soft-spoken man with an orderly, analytic mind. With the help of his wife, Miriam Small, and Lanigan, the rabbi solved the murder himself. This story was particularly enjoyable because of Carney and his co-star. Stuart Margolin did a great job as Rabbi Small, especially considering that he had played such an obnoxious lout on *Nichols*. Janet Margolin (no relation) played Miriam when the film aired in June 1976.

Come January 1977, Art Carney and Janet Margolin were still in place, but Stuart Margolin was gone. In his stead was Bruce Soloman, who had played a cop on *Mary Hartman, Mary Hartman*. Some say that Margolin was called away from the rabbi series by his old buddy James Garner to work on another show. Others say that NBC thought Margolin was not attractive enough to carry the series. Soloman achieved heart-throb status on Norman Lear's satiric soap opera, but here he delivered an inferior performance.

Perhaps Soloman's acting was not at fault, but *Lanigan's Rabbi* lasted only six episodes. While NBC was jamming substitutions into the Sunday time slot like pennies into a fusebox, it had the Wednesday night time slot to fill—left vacant when they moved *Columbo* and company. Since they had a lot more mystery ideas where *McCoy* came from, they instituted the NBC *Wednesday Mystery Movie*.

Of the three new concepts premiering, two had TV movies to herald them and one had a theatrical film to work from. The theatrical film was *Madigan* (1968), Don Siegel's tough look at a detective whose New York Police Department job was taking over his whole life. Richard Widmark played the lead, continuing a film career that had begun in 1947 with *Kiss of Death*, in which he played a giggling killer.

For a long time Widmark would not do any television at all, except for a guest-star spot on an *I Love Lucy* episode in 1955, but in 1971 he saw the writing on the wall. The good roles were getting fewer and fewer and the telefilms were getting better and better. So he agreed to star in *Vanished*, a Dean Reisner-written political thriller in which he played the President.

In 1972 he agreed to return to the role of Dan Madigan, a detective in the Tenth Precinct. It hardly mattered that the character was killed at the end of the 1968 movie. Since NBC wanted the series and Widmark would take the part, Madigan was resuscitated. That is the magic of television. The magic of the audience is that they killed *Madigan* a second time by not caring if he was alive or dead.

The first TV movie to herald a *Wednesday Mystery Movie* personage was *Banacek: Detour to Nowhere*, aired in March of 1972. This introduced the character and concept of the most successful of the three series. George Peppard played a Polish-American insurance investigator, Thomas Banacek (pronounced Ban-uh-check), who solved "impossible" crimes, usually in competition with insurance agents who wanted to beat him to it so he could not collect his 10 percent reward.

In *Detour to Nowhere* he located an armored car that disappeared off a Texas highway. In the premiere episode of the series, "Let's Hear It for a Living Legend," he solved the disappearance of a football player who vanished before

thousands at a stadium and millions watching on TV. Peppard played the part as casual and capable, while the scripts kept viewers guessing (essentially because of the talents of writers Levinson and Link).

Perhaps Peppard played the Boston-based freelance detective a little too cool, because the show's run was shorter than it should have been, lasting only 18 months.

Even so, it was better than *Cool Million*'s track record. That series started as a TV movie in October of 1972. James Farentino starred as Jefferson Keyes, a man who would have scoffed at Banacek's measly 10 percent. Before Keyes would take on any job, he wanted a million dollars up front. But he was willing to give his clients a money-back guarantee if he did not deliver.

Larry Cohen, who also created *The Invaders*, thought up this one and added some other interesting touches. For instance, Keyes located his office in Lincoln, Nebraska, where phone lines are always open, so he would not miss a call. In addition, he had a special number—303-0100—which only Elena (Adele Mara) could answer. Although he came expensive and had all this detail backing him up, the series only lasted nine months.

And still NBC was not satisfied with the number of detective shows it had on the air. Following the *NBC Wednesday Mystery Movie* was *Search*, another *Name of the Game* knock-off which was based on a TV film called *Probe*. In *Probe*, *Wyatt Earp* graduate Hugh O'Brien played Hugh Lockwood, a secret agent who is electronically connected to a computer system controlled by B. C. Cameron (Burgess Meredith).

Hugh O'Brien shot off more than his mouth on this episode of Search. (ABC)

Supposedly this "bionic" link would help Lockwood with his special assignments.

Leslie Stevens devised this series that he also produced. But to hedge his bets, he brought it to NBC including two other agents who would share the load with Lockwood. He also ran into some problems, the biggest being that the title *Probe* was already owned by a news program. So when the series started in September, it had the less jutting title *Search*.

In that version, Cameron headed The Probe Division of World Securities Corporation with an agent roster that in-

cluded not only Hugh Lockwood, but Christopher R. Grove (Doug McClure) and Nick Bianco (Tony Franciosa) as well. These men carried a miniature spy arsenal on their persons. They had transmitters in their ears, cameras on their rings and tiepins, and implanted monitors under their skin. All this stuff saved them from hiring legmen to check out their leads since the computer did it for them.

That did not mean that the production house did not have to hire actors to play the assistants, however. Every time the scene switched back to Cameron, 10 extra actors were on camera occupying themselves by looking intently at their readouts and pressing buttons. And since the scriptwriters did not have to write long scenes with the detectives researching clues, they scrambled for other ways to waste time.

Search, in short, was pretty much a joke, and not a very good one at that. The plug was pulled after a year.

Two other major networks came up with variations of "Name of the Bold Ones." ABC-TV's version was *The Men*, which aired on Thursday night and featured three rotating series.

Each of the new concepts was given a tryout in March and April. First came Warner Brothers' *The Delphi Bureau*, a whimsical creation of Sam Rolfe. Broadway actor Laurence Luckinbill starred as unconventional, reluctant secret agent Glenn Garth Gregory, the one-man investigative arm of The Delphi Bureau, created ostensibly to do research for the President. Instead, Gregory takes on secret missions armed only with his photographic memory and shaky sense of humor. His one government contact is Sybil Van Loween, a professional party giver in Washington, D.C. In the film she was played by Celeste Holm, but in the short-lived series, Anne Jeffreys took the role.

Whoever played what, *The Delphi Bureau* was worse than *Search* when it went to series. Everything looked very rushed, from the scripts to the production. This was an attribute all three *The Men* shows were to share. The next in line, *Jigsaw*, was about Lieutenant Frank Dain, an investigator for the California Department of Missing Persons, headquartered in Sacramento. James Wainwright, a red-haired, flat-nosed actor

who specialized in tough-guy parts, played the kind, considerate Dain in an attempt to soften his image. If only the scripts had been as tough as he looked.

Finally there was *Assignment: Vienna*, which should have been shelved when its pilot movie *Assignment: Munich* fell apart. Not that the latter was bad. On the contrary, the teleflick written by Eric Bercovici and Jerry Ludwig, with direction by David Lowell Rich, was pretty good. It was about special agent Jake Webster, who used his bar in Munich as a front to do jobs for Major Bernard Caldwell of U.S. Intelligence. The film did not fall apart until after it was over—then the actors who had made it a success all left. Roy Scheider (*Jaws* [1975], *All That Jazz* [1980]) played Webster and Richard Basehart was his government contact. But after the success of *The French Connection* (1971), in which Scheider co-starred with Oscar winner Gene Hackman, he did not want to be Webster in the series. So while the producers were reportedly suing Scheider, they made Robert Conrad Webster and cast Charles Cioffi as Caldwell.

On September 5, 1972, the Munich Olympics were shattered by the attack of terrorists. On September 28, Robert Conrad starred as Webster in *Assignment: Vienna*. It would have been in poor taste to present the series with its original title. As mentioned before, it was not in the best of taste to run it at all. *The Men* marched off the air the following year.

This takes care of the junk the networks foisted on the public under the guise of anthology series. But it does not take care of the junk the British were still sending over. If *The Adventurer* was the best they could dish up, they should have watched reruns of *Secret Agent*, *The Saint*, and *The Avengers* and left it at that.

Catherine Schell and Gene Barry toast their taste in clothes during the short run of
The Adventurer. *(ITC Entertainment, Inc.)*

But now, instead of teaming an American actor with a Britisher, they let the American star on his own. And the American was a well-respected mystery hero (who should have known better).

Gene Barry starred as Gene Bradley in *The Adventurer*, a series of 26 syndicated half hours which looked like they were produced for a dollar and a half. He played what was described as "a multimillionaire businessman who adopts the guise of an international film star" to go on secret missions for the U.S. government. How does one "adopt the guise" of a film star? Put on a Roger Moore mask? Also wasted in this ludicrous effort was Barry Morse playing his

partner, Mr. Parminter, who "adopts a guise" as a film producer.

Slightly better was *The Protectors*, not to be confused with *The Bold Ones* segment of the same name. This was another English show produced by Gerry Anderson, the maker of many Saturday morning puppet shows like *Supercar, Thunderbirds,* and *Captain Scarlet.* Instead of marionettes, this time he had Robert Vaughn, Nyree Dawn Porter, and Tony Anholt as three crime specialists who band together to battle evil in all the European capitals.

It was a colorful effort and consisted of a full 52 half-hour episodes, but Vaughn, for one, was not very happy about doing another series. When asked why he did it, he replied, "Anyone who isn't in TV to become a millionaire is a simpleton at heart." When asked what he liked least about the show he said, "The violence made me sick."

These two were not the only foreign imports of the year. Canada got into the act with *Police Surgeon,* not to be confused with the English show that became *The Avengers.* This was a show that developed from *Dr. Simon Locke,* which was described as the "adventures of a cut-rate Welby." Initially it was supposed to be a mainstream medical show with American actor Sam Groom playing the lead. He was in awe of his senior partner, Locke, played by Jack Albertson. Albertson was so turned off by the cheapness of the production that he nearly tore up his contract when he exited the show to star in *Chico and the Man* (1974).

This left the Canadians with a show but without a co-star. So they made Locke a member of the Emergency Medical Unit of the Toronto Police Department. Groom had nothing else to do, so he stayed in the series. But the same haphazard attitude that afflicted the original format assailed this one.

"I don't know what a police surgeon does," one member of the staff was quoted as saying, "but that's what Sam will be doing." Is it any wonder the program went off after a year?

It was a mystery, however, why *Banyon* went off the air so fast. Initially it seemed the show had everything going for it. It began as a March 1971 film for television and was produced by Richard Alan Simmons and Ed Adamson, who had visions of Sam Spade and Philip Marlowe dancing before their eyes. It was a period private-eye piece, set in Los Angeles in 1937. Miles Banyon was a mediocre peeper who would take on any case for 20 bucks a day. He was played by Robert Forster, a newcomer to TV who had only done some guesting on *N.Y.P.D.* and *Judd for the Defense.* Making life tough for him was Lieutenant Pete McNeil of the L.A.P.D. Darren McGavin did a good job in that role. Lending nostalgia to the film was Joan Blondell as Peggy Revere, the head of a secretarial school located in the same building as Banyon's office (filmed at the atmospheric Bradbury Building in Los Angeles). The plot was standard issue: a dead girl is found in Banyon's office, shot with his gun. The director, Robert Day, gave this worn scenario some life, as did the hard-working cast.

Banyon took his time getting to series, and once he arrived he was being produced by Quinn Martin Productions. Forster and Blondell were still in place but McGavin had gone to make way for Richard Jaeckel in the McNeil part. Everything else was as it had been, up to and including the voice-over narration by Forster. "The case was taking more curves than a ball pitched by Dizzy Dean," and stuff like that. The actor was a little too somber, tight-lipped, dry, and surly to pull off the self-mockery, but he was watchable.

The first network episode was cut from the same plotting cloth as the teleflick. The guy Banyon is supposed to protect gets killed. Viewers had seen it all before and did not want to see it again, no matter how nicely mounted. *Banyon* checked out at the second season.

It looks like Karl Malden is advising Michael Douglas never to leave home without it. Whatever the conversation, the duo made The Streets of San Francisco *a hit. (ABC)*

Quinn Martin may have missed with *Banyon*, but he hit with *The Streets of San Francisco*. The series was preceded by the inevitable TV movie. The characters came from a novel by Carolyn Weston, *Poor, Poor Ophelia*. In the book, Santa Monica detectives Al Krugg—the old pro—and Casey Kellog—the new boy at HQ—take on a sticky case of a murdered girl. In the teleflick their names were changed to Lieutenant Mike Stone and Inspector Steve Keller and they were pushed up the California coast a bit, but their case is still the same.

They solve the case with style, thanks to a good script by Ed Hume and on-location photography. Once the actual hour-long series started the following week, the ingredients were still the same: good scripts, solid direction, nice atmosphere, and all on-location filming. But the best thing about the show and the basis for its success was the chemistry between its two stars: Karl Malden and Michael Douglas.

"We're true partners in every sense of the word," Douglas said. "I'm the young, college-educated student of criminology and Karl's character never went beyond high school, but he learned on the streets. We work together as equals. I respect his experience and he respects my training."

The same was true of the actors as well as the characters. They set up a mutual admiration society that the audience could see and appreciate. "He's cool and professional and I learn a lot from him," said Douglas of Malden. "He's a remarkable young man," said Malden of Douglas. Together they pushed *The Streets of San Francisco* into the top 10.

"We premiered the year after the movie actors came to television," Mal-

den recalled. "Anthony Quinn (*The Man and the City*), Shirley MacLaine (*Shirley's World*), Hank Fonda (*The Smith Family*)—and they all flopped. I was determined that was not going to happen to me. I was pushing, driving it."

Malden was a good driver with Douglas in the passenger seat. The series sped on for four highly rated years before an unforeseen event caused the *Streets* to be blocked before their time. The event was *One Flew over the Cuckoo's Nest* (1975), which Michael Douglas produced, having bought the screen rights from his father, Kirk Douglas. The film went on to reap millions as well as awards, while Michael Douglas went on to produce and star in *The China Syndrome* (1979).

The actor Douglas left to pursue his film career while the character Keller left to pursue a teaching career. Replacing him at Stone's side was Dan Robbins, played by Richard Hatch. Hatch and Malden did not have the same chemistry and before the producers could come up with a new formula, *The Streets of San Francisco* was closed in 1977.

Not only was Quinn Martin represented this year, but Aaron Spelling was back with a TV movie and series which might be called "The Mod Squad in Uniform." It might be called that because the concept he produced in conjunction with Leonard Goldberg concerned three young people intent on curing the world's ills from inside the system. They were *The Rookies*, and also like *The Mod Squad*, they were shepherded by an outwardly gruff but kindly police veteran. In the March teleflick Darren McGavin played Lieutenant Edward Ryker, but in the series Gerald S. O'Laughlin took the part. Unlike *The Mod Squad*, however, the three were all males: Sam Mel-

Gerald S. O'Laughlin turned his clichéd role of Lt. Ryker on The Rookies *into an acting challenge for his co-stars by doing the very best job possible. (ABC)*

Sam Melville went from his role of Danko on The Rookies *to co-star in the movies. (ABC)*

Georg Stanford Brown, another Rookie co-star, enjoyed success as a director as well as an actor. (ABC)

ville as ex-Air Force man Mike Danko, the toughest of the trio; Georg Sanford Brown as black "Linc-alike" Terry Webster, another ghetto graduate; and Michael Ontkean as college graduate William "Willie" Gillis. For this show the femininity was supplied by Kate Jackson, who played Nurse Jill Danko, Mike's wife.

This crew managed to get through two seasons although the cast felt the scripts did not hold as much water as a Bounty paper towel. "What we're doing is not real life," explained Brown. "In real life police work is garbage and a cop is mostly a paperwork factory." Ontkean criticized the show on an acting level. "*Some* acting," he scoffed. "It's not ideal, but it's moving me along."

It moved him right off the set as he left to do movies like *Slap Shot* (1977) and *Voices* (1980). Taking his place was Bruce Fairbairn as new rookie Chris Owens. They made it through two more seasons of cliché-ridden stories that have since become an Aaron Spelling staple. It got to the point that the only thing the rookies could do week after week was save Nurse Jill from either a psycho with a gun or a psycho with a knife.

1973

The year 1973 had some good news and it had some bad news. In earlier chapters, this statement could be qualified by saying either "in real-life" or "on television." In the seventies, however, it was hard to make a distinction. *All* the news was on TV. Anyway, the good news was that American involvement in Vietnam ended. The bad news was that G. Gordon Liddy and company were found guilty of breaking into and attempting to bug the Democratic headquarters. So now television had something else to cover to death: the disintegration of a Presidency.

Within the mystery genre the same standard could apply. The good news was that several excellent and/or long-running series would premiere. The bad news was that several networks were still trying to palm off remakes of "Name of the Bold Ones." NBC was the main perpetrator. In addition to their on-going attempt to get a fourth for Sunday night, they were still trying to get Wednesday right. *Madigan* and *Cool Million* failed, so they dusted off some previously aired television movies and turned them into series.

First came *The Snoop Sisters*, a Leonard Stern written, directed, and executive-produced effort which aired in December of 1972. It was a knowingly cute comedy/mystery about two spinster mystery writers who get involved with murders outside their own fiction.

Charm was supplied in large doses by Mildred Natwick and Helen Hayes as Gwendolyn and Ernesta Snoop, two old biddies who could stumble across bodies with the best of them. The ingredient that really made the film work, however, was Art Carney as Barney, an ex-con hired by the sisters' nephew to serve as their driver and guardian angel. He was a charming, comforting presence who could deal with the ladies with sensitivity and respect.

When the show went to series, Carney was replaced by Lou Antonio, a talented director who usually plays tough-guy roles when acting. He was a few generations younger than the Snoops, and the chemistry that made the film so effective and engaging was destroyed. All that was left were the abundant murders and a few Grey Pantherisms (Helen Hayes leaping into a karate stance has to be seen to be disbelieved).

The next *NBC Wednesday Mystery Movie* was *Tenafly*, a Levinson and Link creation intended to be more realistic than *The Smith Family*. Instead of Henry Fonda and family, there is Harry Tenafly, just a detecting cog in a big corporate investigations machine. He is a black family man who works at Hightower Investigations, Inc., in Los Angeles. James McEachin played him effectively, but the inherent problem was how to make a small-time, nine-to-five private eye stumble upon exciting cases realistically.

The key word is "realistically," since realism was what Levinson and Link were striving for—an answer to all those razzle-dazzle sleuths who were straining production budgets and viewer credibility. They tried to give him an inside man on the police force in Lieutenant Sam Church (David Huddleston), but to do *Tenafly* correctly would mean not having much of anything happen to him at all. In the pilot movie he was already investigating a murder and things could not get much higher than that.

The final new Wednesday addition to the *Mystery Movie* was a man without a teleflick. *Faraday and Company* arrived full blown on October 3, 1973, with famous song-and-dance man Dan Dailey playing Frank Faraday, a disgraced detective who was incarcerated in a Caribbean jail for almost 30 years. He finally manages to get away and comes home to his son, Steve (James Naughton), who has carried on the family business. His first order of business is to find the man who framed him. The second order of business is to get back into the business.

Interest in this show was supposed to be fostered by the generation gap: both between father and son as well as the modern world versus the world Faraday knew before going to jail. Things we take for granted—like television—were strange to him. Imagine how he would feel if he knew that NBC was going to take the *Wednesday Mystery Movie* and make it the *Tuesday Mystery Movie* as of January 4, 1974? And imagine how he would feel if he knew that his show, as well as the other two, would be canceled that September anyway? It would probably make him wish he had stayed in the Caribbean.

After CBS watched *The Men* die and all those *NBC Mystery Movie* attempts fail, one would think they would not touch the format with a 10-foot programmer. But the first thing to learn in TV biz is never put anything past the network executives. For every failure someone else might have, they have a better idea. Like *The New CBS Tuesday Night Movies*, for example. This was a foolproof scheme to succeed where the others had not.

See, they would buy a whole bunch of TV movies to show two times a month, then create a series for a big movie star and create another series based on a hit movie to show during the other two weeks. Perfect, right? Not quite. Their first mistake was ruining the series adapted from the hit movie. The movie was *Shaft* (1971), one of the first and best "blaxploitation" movies made. Its theme song by Isaac Hayes won an Oscar and noted photographer Gordon Parks directed it with style. The story was of John Shaft, essentially a black Mike Hammer. It did so well with white and black audiences alike that *Shaft's Big Score* came out the next year and *Shaft in Africa* premiered the year after that.

Then someone made the horrible mistake of homogenizing the man for TV. Veteran Shaft viewers knew there was going to be trouble as soon as the show started. Someone had taken the funk out of the orchestration and erased the suggestive lyrics of the theme. Richard Roundtree, the actor who had portrayed him in the films, was hired, but that was all. The skin was there but the soul was gone.

Rather than being his own man who did what he liked to whom, Shaft was put at the beck and call of Lieutenant Al Rossi of the New York Police Department, played by Ed Barth. And more often than not, Rossi would sic him onto murders that had nothing to do with the black community or even anything relevant, for that matter. In the film, Shaft let someone he did not like have it across the face with a beer bottle. On the TV show, he poured a drink into Tony Curtis' lap. *Shaft* did not make any new friends and he lost all his old ones.

"Shaft on TV makes Barnaby Jones look like Eldridge Cleaver," said Cecil

This is what television can do to a hip detective like Shaft. Dig the crazy plaid suit. Gee, just like the one Mannix used to wear. (CBS)

Smith of the *Los Angeles Times*. After the fiasco was over and only eight episodes were aired, producer William Woodfield tried to explain. "We (he and co-producer Alan Balter) were very conscious of the movie image and deliberately worked against it. We knew we would get bad reviews, but we thought the American public would accept this man as a friend." What more can be said?

A man the American public did accept as a friend was actor James Stewart. This friendship was based on over 35 years in the movies, playing a wide variety of roles exceptionally well. He was a master comedian in *Destry Rides Again* (1939), *You Can't Take It with You* (1938), and *Harvey* (1950). He was a

master dramatic performer in *It's a Wonderful Life* (1946), *Mr. Smith Goes to Washington* (1939), and *The Flight of the Phoenix* (1965). And he was a master investigator in *Call Northside 777* (1947), *Rear Window* (1954), *Vertigo* (1958), and *Anatomy of a Murder* (1959). But being a friend to the American public and being the star of a TV show are two different things.

He had tried once before with *The Jimmy Stewart Show* in 1971, and he would try again with *Hawkins*. The initial hint of his plans came with the March 1973 film for television *Hawkins on Murder*, which introduced the character Stewart would play as well as the direction the subsequent series would take. Producer/writer David Karp and executive producer Norman Felton were approaching West Virginia lawyer Billy Jim Hawkins like *Columbo*. Stewart's halting speech pattern, which mimics love to exaggerate and which has become part of Stewart's persona, was made to seem like senility was not long off.

Billy Jim would "Um," and "Wall . . . wall," his way through conversations until his clients felt he could not defend a saint in a paternity suit. Of course, he turned out to be the best lawyer this side of Perry Mason and used his brilliant mind and good ol' common sense to win the day. As writers loved to put rumpled Columbo into opulent surroundings, so they loved to put down-home Hawkins in seamy surroundings.

After getting an heiress off for triple murder in the TV movie, the series' debut was "Murder in Movieland" and it had Hawkins tangling with bisexual hustlers, homosexuality, raped teen-agers, and dirty tricks. It's likely that the viewers were not ready for or interested in these subjects. *Hawkins'* case was rested after seven episodes.

Another public friend was Lorne Greene, who, after almost 15 years as Ben Cartwright on *Bonanza*, was regarded as the strong, noble father we all wish we had. It is safe to assume that Greene had his pick of almost any show he would like to do, so it was a shame that *Griff* had to be the one that went to series. Previously, Greene had been on the right track by starring in two exceptional teleflicks—*Destiny of a Spy*, written by Stanford Whitmore and directed by Boris Sagal, and *The Harness*, based on a John Steinbeck story.

Curiously, a movie pilot of *Griff* called *Man on the Outside* was not shown until more than a year *after* the series that was

based on it went off the air! In it, retired Los Angeles Police Captain Wade Griffin's son is shot down before his eyes and he is also witness to his grandson's abduction. He is so incensed by the police force's handling of the case that he sets out to make things right himself.

The series was set after the killing and kidnapping had taken place. The opening episode had Griff take on the son of a dead friend as an associate in his newly opened Wade Griffin Investigations office. When asked by this new man, Mike Murdoch (Ben Murphy), why he had quit the force, Griff replied "personal differences." That is what Greene should have told ABC, producer David Victor and writer/creator Larry Cohen, then gotten the hell out of *Griff*. As it was, *Griff* got the hell out of him in three months.

Every network had its share of bad shows this year, but it appeared as if NBC was shooting for a monopoly on awfulness. In March they released a TV movie, and in September they unveiled a series, about a professional magician who made it his business to go around correcting the evils of the world with prestidigitation. As if that was not enough, this magician lived in his own sumptuously appointed private jet and had a large office in Los Angeles' The House of Magic, a magician's nightclub.

To illustrate just how inept this concept was, no reason was ever given for the magician's motive or the source of his wealth. Whenever someone asked why or how, all the magician's aides would give a verbal shrug. And the magician himself found the whole thing just too traumatic to talk about. Bill Bixby played Anthony Dorian in *The Magician*.

This was a great show to snort at. Much was made over the fact that all the

Bill Bixby did better turning into
The Incredible Hulk *than he did
pulling rabbits out of top hats for
the abortive mystery series,* The
Magician. *(NBC)*

tricks were actually done live and by Bixby with no camera tricks. For all the hoopla, the tricks themselves might as well have been done by the camera for all the effect they had. Opening an umbrella in front of some gunman and then disappearing from behind it is not thrilling. Knowing just how he disappeared from behind it is. But *The Magician* was not talking. And the viewers were not watching. The series disappeared after a season.

Lightning hit NBC twice with *Chase*, both the TV movie and the subsequent series. It was probably the worst thing

Jack Webb ever unleashed. *TV Guide* got it right when they termed it "bottom of the barrell stuff."

Mitchell Ryan starred as Captain Chase Reddick, a cop with motors on his brain. He ran a secret undercover police unit out of Los Angeles that specialized in speed. His underlings were an ace hot rodder named Steve Baker (Michael Richardson), a motorcycle maniac named Fred Sing (Brian Fong), and a helicopter hell-driver named Norm Hamilton (Reid Smith). With the help of Sergeant Sam McGraw (Wayne Maunder), a trainer of police dogs (if you'll believe it), they run down hardened criminals. And when I say "run down," I mean it.

This show might have singlehandedly brought on the oil shortage of the early seventies. It was ludicrous: the team kicked up the dirt every chance it got in a feeble effort to gain ratings. Thankfully *Chase* ran out of gas after a season. The audience probably ran out of patience long before.

It must be comforting to American TV executives to know that, after all the good public relations British television got with *Elizabeth R, The Six Wives of Henry the Eighth* and all the other PBS presentations, the English could make

bad series, too. *My Partner the Ghost* is a case in point. Retitled from *Randall & Hopkirk (Deceased)* for stateside distribution, NBC picked up this curiosity for late-night airing. Mike Pratt played British private eye Jeff Randall, the "My" side of the title. The partner was played by comedy actor Kenneth Cope as a murdered associate named Marty Hopkirk.

He comes back from the dead to help his friend solve crimes in a combination of *Topper* and *Get Smart*. As in the former comedy, only one person can see the ghost, and that is Randall, who also has to explain the weird goings-on to Jean, the ghost's widow (Annette Andre)

It was a different kind of English detective series, all right. It was dumb. (ITC Entertainment, Inc.)

MY PARTNER theGHOST

there's something different about this pair of private eyes ... one of them is DEAD

murdered while on a case, Marty Hopkirk comes back as a GHOST to help his partner catch his killer

a DIFFERENT kind of detective series

and Inspector Large of Scotland Yard (Ivor Dean, basically reenacting his *Saint* role for laughs). NBC ran this for a season before *My Partner the Ghost* disappeared for good.

Quinn Martin proved lightning can strike thrice in one season by getting *Banyon* and *The Streets . . .* on in September 1972, and then getting *Barnaby Jones* on in January of 1973. Unlike the "gimmick eyes" the networks were so partial to, Jones was not blind, lame-brained, or fat—he was old. The concept was a combination of *Griff* and *Faraday*. Prior to the January 28 premiere episode, somewhere in the fictional characters' Twilight Zone, Barnaby Jones, played by Buddy Ebsen, had retired from the private detective business after a long and fruitful career, leaving his clients and office to his son, Hal. When Hal is killed, Barnaby resumes work, even though he is getting on in years.

As a matter of fact, the old and the overweight got together in this two-part opening segment. William Conrad guested as Cannon when Barnaby went on the vengeance trail. But once the elderly detective bagged the murderer, it was not clear what made the show click with viewers. The *Los Angeles Times* said that the series was "an agreeable addition to TV's melodramatic hokum," but they saw no way the series could last.

They were proved wrong the same way most critics were proved wrong with *The Beverly Hillbillies*. The comedy and mystery shared a common star—a man with almost 50 years' experience entertaining people—Buddy Ebsen was not just some old guy off the street. This was the Buddy Ebsen who had worked with Eddie Cantor and Shirley Temple. The same Ebsen who had been funny in

Breakfast at Tiffany's (1961), riveting in *Attack* (1956), and lovable in *Davy Crockett* (1955).

As Barnaby Jones, Ebsen quickly took up residence at the top of the ratings chart again. And with the show there, in the words of a CBS executive, "You could not kill it with a stick!" The same reviewers who had predicted its demise still could not understand how such a low-key series could be such a hit.

Philip Saltzman, the line producer in the sixth season, had his own theory. "Each show has an intriguing puzzle," he said, "and it's pleasant to watch Barnaby unravel it. At eleven o'clock the viewers can switch off the set and go peacefully to bed. We're never nasty."

Barnaby Jones and Buddy Ebsen leisurely wound their way through four seasons, never being nasty themselves, while the nastiest things happened to everybody else on the show. The producers, writers, and directors had the uncomfortable habit of terrorizing their victims before their murders occurred off screen. The program could be counted on to show a woman attacked in her bedroom, a man crowned with a shovel after digging his own grave, and Barnaby's daughter-in-law Betty (Lee Meriwether) getting run off the road.

Having vicious hoods threaten an old man and his female assistant was a little unsettling, so in 1976 the producers added a young cousin to take the brunt of the rough stuff. Mark Shera played Jedidiah Romano Jones, also known as J. R. Even with him around to get slugged, shot at, and chased, the series still incorporated such sights as an autistic child being stalked by a killer.

Meanwhile Barnaby patiently sleuthed. "I just try to make *Barnaby Jones* the best

Tony Musante played a real-life New Jersey vice cop, Dave Toma, for one successful season before he decided TV stardom wasn't for him. (ABC)

work I've done yet," Ebsen said affably. And he wanted to keep up that work, but at the end of his eighth season, the word came that *Barnaby Jones* was cancelled because of an ailment far worse than anything old age could bring: gradually declining ratings.

The reason for *Toma*'s cancellation was almost unheard of. The actor who portrayed the real-life New Jersey cop did not want to be a TV star. *Toma*'s bumpy road to success started when producer/writer Roy Huggins heard of

As a master detective, Barnaby Jones made a good old man, which was the series' gimmick. Paternal, grandfatherly Buddy Ebsen continued a successful, surprising career with this long-running show. (CBS)

the exploits of a Newark undercover vice cop named Dave Toma. Toma was a living legend in his city, a man capable of donning a thousand disguises—and had an arrest record to prove it. The pimps, pushers, and numbers runners held him in awe and treated him with grudging respect. Here was a cop, Huggins discovered, whose exploits outdid those of television detectives!

Writer Ed Hume went East to ride with Toma and then write a two-hour TV pilot incorporating Toma's guises, his junky 1963 Plymouth Valiant, and his happy home life. Hume finished the script with the help of Gerald DiPego, line producer Jo Swerling, Jr., and director Richard T. Heffron casted the role. Initially they were looking for a type similar to Toma himself—a Joseph Campanella or a Ben Gazzara or a Jack Palance. But once they met Tony Musante, star of *The Bird with the Crystal Plumage* (1969) and *The Last Run* (1971), they knew they had their man.

Musante worked hard in the role opposite Susan Strasberg as his wife, Patty, and Simon Oakland as his harried boss, Inspector Spooner. The teleflick was aired in March 1973 and ABC opened a Thursday night spot for it on their September lineup. The plot of the series and the movie was basically the same. Bucking his superiors, Toma dons a wide assortment of disguises to battle what this show called The Organization, another name for that unmentionable underworld operation that began in Sicily. In between infiltrating as a hippie, a junkie, a bus driver, a drunk, a barber, a short-order cook, a priest, and a painter (all of which he did the first few weeks), the show detailed his home life with his wife and two kids, Donna and Jimmy.

The series started slowly but built steam. When it was moved to late Friday night it was doing better. By the end of 1974, it seemed assured of a renewal. Then Tony Musante left. The network had a hit on its hands and no star. Huggins worked fast. He found a terrific actor who had been doing great movie roles since 1959 but had never been given a chance to shine. The guy was willing to do anything for his acting career, so the producer signed Robert Blake to take over *Toma*.

Blake started his film career as Mickey Gubitosi in the *Our Gang* short comedies of the late thirties and early forties. As Bobby Blake he worked in the *Red Ryder* Westerns playing the Indian lad, Little Beaver. That led to many other parts in films like *Humoresque* (1947), in which he played the John Garfield character as a boy, and *The Treasure of the Sierra Madre* (1948). Leaving a hellish home life, he progressed on a self-destructive cycle which included juvenile delinquency, several arrests, and drug addiction.

Pulling himself out of the nosedive, Blake started back up the mountain, reaching a high plateau with his performances in *In Cold Blood* (1967) and *Tell Them Willie Boy Is Here* (1969). But even after these films, he was still known around Hollywood as a "talented unknown." Both Huggins and Blake knew that he was not the type to be a happily married vice officer in Newark. Everything was put on hold while Huggins' partner, Stephen Cannell, did a face lift with Blake's visage in mind.

The proposed *Toma Starring Robert Blake* did not materialize in the fall of 1974 as projected. Instead, Cannell succeeded in doing one of the best plastic surgery jobs in TV detective history, turning what had once been *Toma* into an intrinsically more honest, as well as entertaining, show. Borrowing the name of a small but effective weapon, the new series was called *Baretta*, and it premiered in January 1975.

Toma lived in a nice little house with a beautiful wife. Baretta lived in the run-down cellar of the King Edward Hotel with a cockatoo named Fred. His best human buddy was Billy Truman (Tom Ewell), a former cop and presently the rummy manager and house detective at the hotel. Toma's beat was New Jersey. Baretta worked out of the 53rd Precinct house in Los Angeles. Toma carried a gun, but did not like to use it. On his show, he rarely had to. On *Baretta*, the

Toma's exit led to Baretta's entrance, making star Robert Blake an Emmy winner.
He suffered for his art, however. On the right is Blake as he appeared in the "Red
Ryder" cowboy movies of the fifties. On the left is how he occasionally disguised
himself on Baretta. *He's come a long, long way. (ABC)*

world of pimps, racketeers, prostitutes, rapists, crooked officials, and slum violence was laid out for all to see. Baretta did not like to use his gun either, but he would use anything when he had to, and he had to often. Even his best stool pigeon was a pimp named Rooster (Michael D. Roberts).

In the first season, Baretta tried the patience of Inspector Schiller (Dana Elcar, a bald little man who went on to play The Chief in the *Get Smart* movie, *The Nude Bomb*), but the burlier Edward Grover took over as Lieutenant Hal Brubaker in the fall. Occasionally appearing in the

cast were Chino Williams—reportedly a drunk who Blake rehabilitated—as a cop named Fats and John Ward as Detective Foley.

Blake made *Baretta* work on sheer force of personality. Everything was written for and around him, or else he would rewrite it to his satisfaction. By the second season he had basically taken control of the production—eating, sleeping, and dreaming *Baretta*. The crew was reportedly devoted to the feisty actor and together they presented Blake's fantasy points of view to a watching world.

Blake stressed antiviolence, but

One of Baretta's most popular co-stars was his pet cockatoo, Fred. Here actor Blake shows off what he called "some I-trailion flash" in his cellar apartment. (ABC)

Baretta lived in a violent world of mobsters, nun-rapers, child molesters, and psycho hoods. The show tried to be honest yet still very entertaining. It was as if the leader of the Bowery Boys had grown up to be a super cop. Blake's mangling of the English language lived on after the series' demise in 1978. His "You can take dat to the bank" and "Dat's da name a' dat tune" are still being quoted.

Since *Baretta*, Blake's road has been rocky. He made a TV pilot movie called *Joe Dancer* in 1980, but it was not aired until 1981. In it, Blake played a private

eye that Garfield might have played back in the forties, complete with cynical voice-over narration. Two films he starred in, *Coast to Coast* (1980) and *Second-Hand Hearts* (1981), were badly handled by distributors and critics, so Blake's star is up there, but so far it is not moving.

Walking a similar line to stardom was Telly Savalas. After co-starring in many films, the best being *The Birdman of Alcatraz* (1962), *The Dirty Dozen* (1967), *The Scalphunters* (1968), *On Her Majesty's Secret Service* (1969), and *Kelly's Heroes* (1970), and in all but the last, playing a madman or a villain, Savalas switched over to the side of the angels in one of the best TV movies made.

Abby Mann wrote and executive-produced the hard-hitting, realistic three-hour adaptation of Selwyn Rabb's *Justice in the Back Room*, a novel about the real-life murder of two Manhattan girls and the black man who was framed for the killings. Retitling it *The Marcus-Nelson Murders*, Mann created the character of strong, honest, charismatic New York Police Department Lieutenant Theo Kojak and cast Savalas to play him. It was a match made in television heaven. The actor brought his own sense of machismo to the role and made Kojak indistinguishable from his own persona.

The film proved so popular with critics, the public, and the TV Academy (both Mann and director Joseph Sargent got Emmys), that producer Matthew Rapf worked up a series to premiere in the fall. It was the most anxiously awaited cop show of the year, and *TV Guide* trumpeted its October premiere: "TV has a fat detective, a rumpled detective, a Hawaiian detective, a Polish-American detective, a black detective, a detective in a wheelchair, a detective in a loud sports coat, and now, at long last, television has a bald detective. Let's hear it for Theo Kojak!"

Hear it they did. Savalas got his own Emmy after the first season, and *Kojak* was named the No. 1 cop show in a nationwide survey. "I love it," Savalas reacted to his new-found glory. "My fan club has grown. Once it was just my

"Who loves ya, baby?" Well, the lollipop makers of the world, for one. There was a resurgence of sales for the candy when Kojak started sucking them in order to quit smoking. Telly Savalas made more friends by playing the part with a casual machismo that almost everyone seemed to love. (CBS)

mother and my immediate family. Now it's fifty or sixty million people."

Savalas returned his family's faith by showering them with money and arranging it so that his brother George, who went by the name of Demosthenes, got the supporting role of fat, curly-haired Detective Stavros. Among the other squad room members of Manhattan South were Chief Frank McNeil, a man Kojak had once been partners with (Dan Frazer), Detective Robert Crocker (Kevin Dobson), fall-guy Detective Saperstein (Mark Russell, not to be confused with the political comedian), and Detective Rizzo (Vince Conti).

Although *Kojak* was only filmed on location for one season out of its five-year run, the show was a model of realistic plots and production. Lieutenant Kojak was both a businessman and a humanitarian. He was compassionately tough, brutally sensitive, and cynically understanding. And he proved without a shadow of a doubt that a hero did not have to look like Cary Grant to get the girls or break heads to be tough. Kojak could make lollipops (which he sucked to stop smoking) look like deadly weapons.

Tom Tannenbaum, Universal-TV's vice president, put Kojak's personality into perspective when he was talking about Savalas: "He's a suave, bright guy who always gives you the forbidding feeling that he can get *very* tough."

"The minute they make me a super-cop, I'll quit," Savalas himself added. "And I won't stay one minute after it becomes boring. I revolt against monotony, but I don't loathe TV. If we take it out of the hands of the accountants and put it into the hands of the artists, we'll have a great medium here."

The monotony did not set in until 1978, when *Kojak* left the air with a full head of steam. Savalas' "Who loves you, baby?" joined "Just the facts, ma'am" as a classic quote and the series took up residence on the syndicated stations where it still runs. Savalas went on to star in *Hellinger's Law*, a 1981 teleflick written by Lawrence Vail and Jack Laird and directed by Leo Penn. In it, Savalas plays a defense attorney "whose flamboyant life style and courtroom theatricality mask his profound integrity," according to the press releases.

According to a prospectus written in the early 1970s by a real-life cop, a realistic cop show would be just what TV needed and what TV did not have. "Who else," said the proposal, "sees people when all the masks are dropped—during moments of acute rage, fear, pain, grief, or happiness? The flashing red lights and siren chases are not the thing, but rather the overwhelming fear—or perhaps erotic elation—that the officer feels. The chase says something about the human condition."

Producer David Gerber, executive producer of *Cade's County* as well as *Nanny and the Professor* and *The Ghost and Mrs. Muir*, discovered the proposal after it had been rejected by all the major networks. He was intrigued with the idea of picturing "the total police experience," so he contacted the concept's author, L.A.P.D. Officer Joseph Wambaugh. Wambaugh, as most fiction readers know, was not just a policeman. He was the best-selling author of police novels,

Aiding and abetting in Kojak's arrests were, from the left, Dan Frazer as Chief McNeil, George Savalas (Telly's brother) as Stavros, and Kevin Dobson as Crocker. (CBS)

Telly Savalas' influence reached behind the cameras after awhile. He directed several episodes of the long-running and award-winning show. (Universal Television)

including *The New Centurions* and *The Choirboys*. He went to Gerber ready to extend his influence into television. He went armed with the knowledge that a cop's greatest threat is not physical, but emotional and spiritual.

Convincing the producer of that was another matter. And once convincing everyone, getting them to actually use that realization was another matter still. Once Columbia TV backed it, NBC-TV bought it and Stanley Kallis was chosen as producer, Wambaugh's concept— *Police Story*—went into production with Wambaugh as consultant. For the next four years, the real cop locked psychological horns with nearly every person associated with the show. He visualized it as an anthology series, with no regular cast, which would describe the

essence of being a police officer. If it did not, he told reporters, "I'll want no part of it."

Several times during the hourly show's first rocky season Wambaugh was prepared to quit and write *Police Story* off as a loss, but executive producer Gerber refused to let him say die, even while he was mounting gun-filled shoot-em-up episodes he knew would drive the consultant crazy. Finally Wambaugh issued an enraged decree: *"Gunfire does not replace good writing."* And finally the scriptwriters got the message. Once they started showing the pain as well as the car chases, *Police Story* became popular.

The humanity of the series attracted a cross section of the public. By delineating the problems and pressures on cops and their loved ones, *Police Story*

Joseph Wambaugh, the real-life cop who served as guardian angel for Police Story, *in addition to writing a string of best-selling books and producing a few well-praised films. (NBC)*

touched everyone. Wambaugh's goal was to portray cops not as "boy scouts, eunuchs, or supermen," but as human beings. For four years the show created believable characters in affecting stories. Although no actor was identified as a regular, actors like Pernell Roberts, Chuck Connors, Vic Morrow, Robert Forster, and Ed Asner were spotlighted, while Tony Lo Bianco and Don Meredith portrayed the same characters several times over the years.

In its fifth season, NBC and David Gerber agreed that the series would be better served as an occasional "Special Presentation." "Now, in effect, we will be making movies," the producer announced. "We will be able to tell vital stories in depth and get bigger stars to dramatize these stories."

But while Gerber was doing that, he was industriously spinning off cop series from popular episodes of *Police Story*, often losing the reality of the characters in the process. In a 1974 *Police Story* episode called "The Gamble," for example, Angie Dickinson played Vice Officer Lisa Beaumont with Bert Convy as Sergeant William Crowley.

"Audience reaction was tremendous," Gerber remembered. "And so was mine. We convinced Angie that a series would not get dull because as a vice squad officer she does a different 'cover' characterization in each segment. She's not just playing a fantasy 'super-chick.'"

It is interesting that he said "She's not just," because that means she was, in addition to some other things. *Police Woman* premiered in the fall 1974 with

Ed Asner has a way of playing strong, dependable, and human characters unlike any other TV character actor. His talents were put to good use on Police Story, *where he starred in several episodes before becoming* Lou Grant. *This picture is from the "A Dangerous Age" episode.* (NBC)

Dickinson playing Sergeant Suzanne "Pepper" Anderson of the vice squad with Earl Holliman taking Convy's place as Crowley. Robert Collins created the new series without the consent or contribution of Joseph Wambaugh. "I was never asked to work on the show," the officer/author stated, "and I have no idea what they are doing."

What they were doing was flying in the face of everything Wambaugh had at-tempted to achieve with *Police Story*. On the opening credits alone, there are at least five instances of gunplay or fighting. And in the first season, at least, the writ-ers regularly put Pepper in compromising positions that required deep cleavage here and some naked skin there. The feminist press, which had grown quite large by this time, howled in unison.

Producer Douglas Benton started whipping things in line during the follow-

The opening shot of Police Woman, *in more ways than one. The credit sequence didn't start until actress Angie Dickinson pulled the trigger of her police weapon—then the violent action got underway. (NBC)*

ing three seasons, stressing atmospheric direction and relevant, realistic stories over flesh and fantasy. The feminists soon became as full of praise as they had been derogatory. Inspired by that success, Gerber took another *Police Story* episode, "The Return of Joe Forrester," and spun it off into the 1975 series *Joe Forrester.* Their approach was encapsulated by the publicity releases: " 'The neighborhood's gone downhill enough—give me a chance to stop it!' That's Joe Forrester, laying down the law—to his superi-

ors and on the street. Lloyd Bridges as the kind of cop-on-the-beat who makes a difference!"

On the show, as in the episode that the series was based on, Forrester was an aging uniformed patrolman who was supposed to be kicked over to a desk job, but demanded to remain on the street. Eddie Egan, the cop-turned-actor on whom the book and movie *The French Connection* was based, played Sergeant Bernie Vincent, the man who agreed to let Forrester stay there. People seemed to

Dickinson (left) played Sgt. Pepper and was backed up by a regular male crew which consisted of Charles Dierkop (far left) as Royster, Ed Bernard (far right) as Styles, and Earl Holliman (center) as Sgt. Crowley. Here they interview guest star Lynn Loring during the atmospheric "Flowers of Evil" episode. (NBC)

prefer *Adam-12* to this walking version of the same story, so Joe hung up his night stick after a year.

As each preceding spin-off withered and died, David Gerber always seemed to have another lined up to replace it. The worst of these was the ludicrously titled *David Cassidy—Man Undercover.* It was ludicrous because Cassidy was the name of the actor, a teeny-bopper idol from *The Partridge Family* who was trying to make a comeback. The character was Dan Shay, an undercover officer,

sort of a Mod Squad person. It had a ridiculously short run of two months and its passing hardly caused a ripple in the programming pool.

The final *Police Story* spin-off (so far) was based on one of those "Special Presentations," a four-hour, Ernest

---

Before it was decided to name the series after the lead character, Joe Forrester—played by Lloyd Bridges—was set to be called "The Metro Man." (NBC)

Tidyman-written script based on the Robert Daley book *To Kill a Cop*. The special aired in April of 1978 and told the story of a militant black terrorist squad preparing to eradicate most of New York's Finest at the funeral of a fallen comrade. Joe Don Baker, the star of Phil Karlson's *Walking Tall* (which was also adapted into a 1981 TV series starring Bo Svenson), played Deputy Police Commissioner Earl Eischied (pronounced Eye-shyed) who foiled the plot at the last second.

It took Earl a year to get back on the tube, but only after a title change and a demotion. In the short-lived series, the man had become chief of detectives and the name of the show went from *To Kill a Cop* to *The Force* to simply *Eischied*. Even with a year's grace, Eischied was a rushed affair, having to be postponed twice while they finished up the initial three-hour episode, "Only the Pretty Girls Die." This was a realistic (read: *sadistic*) manhunt of a mass murderer based loosely (and reprehensibly) on the name and fame of Son of Sam, the .44 Caliber Killer.

The *Eischied* production further glorified a real killer with an episode about a nut who kidnapped women from discos so he could tattoo, rape, and kill them. TV detectives had come a long way, but not for this. *Eischied* blessedly left the airwaves in two months. How could Joseph Wambaugh have known back in 1973 that his good intentions would spawn all this?

1974

On August 8, 1974, President Nixon resigned from office . . . and you are there! Television programmers respond with the likes of *Happy Days*, *Little House on the Prairie*, and other shows designed to get us back to a simpler time—anyplace but 1974. There are even some detectives who try to serve as a time machine.

First, there was *The Manhunter*, with Broadway veteran Ken Howard playing a 1930s bounty hunter named Dave Barrett. He was introduced in a February film written by Sam Rolfe in which he went after two murdering bank robbers who bore more than a passing resemblance to Bonnie and Clyde. When it came time for the series, its promotion came on like the program was a reincarnation of *The Untouchables*: "Make way for Ken Howard: 6'6" of brawn, brains, and bulldog determination to see justice done in the Public Enemy days of John Dillinger. Tonight: 'The Ma Gantry Gang.'"

Ma Gantry and her train-robbing boys terrorized the tube the night of September 11, but Dave, armed only with a rifle, a shotgun, and a pistol located in the secret panels of his car, brought them to justice.

The similarity to Eliot Ness was no coincidence. This was another Quinn Martin Production, but a failed one. The big difference between Barrett and Ness was that the Manhunter had the weapons, while the Untouchables could *use* them. Many hearings on TV violence had taken place between the earlier show and *The Manhunter*, so while Barrett was heavily armed, he saved a lot of money on bullets. There is nothing wrong with nonviolence; the point is not to mount violence-based shows and then not deliver. The public will do what they did to *The Manhunter*—ignore it off the air in six months.

Viewers went from the crime-ridden

city to the crime-ridden desert with *Nakia*, a variation on the *Hawk* and *Cade's County* themes. On the Hawk side there was a full-blooded Indian hero. On the Cade side there was the vast expanse of Davis County, New Mexico, the series' locale. Coming from failure with *Banyon*, but success on *Police Story*, Robert Forster played Deputy Nakia Parker, a Navajo who is caught between his people, his heritage, and the white man's law, represented here by Sheriff Sam Jericho (Arthur Kennedy).

Hawk failed. *Cade's County* failed. *Banyon* failed. Even *Dan August*, which also dealt with racial clashes, failed. So who in their right mind scheduled *Nakia*? Whoever it was saw it canceled at the second season.

David Wolper, too, was witness to failure this year. The producer who brought us *The Undersea World of Jacques Cousteau* and *The Making of a President*, and who would bring us *Roots*, also brought us *Get Christie Love!*, one of the worst series about a black policewoman ever witnessed.

The series came to ABC in a roundabout fashion. In January, Laurence Turman and Peter Nelson produced the pilot of the show, based on *The Ledger*, a novel by former policewoman Dorothy

Robert Forster, another **Police Story** *favorite, just couldn't seem to find a successful series format. The 1930s private eye concept,* **Banyon,** *failed; as did* **Nakia,** *where the actor played a modern-day sheriff.* **(ABC)**

Teresa Graves showed spunk, flash, and skin in her leading role of Get Christie Love, but it did not help. The self-consciously produced series was canceled quickly. (ABC)

Uhnak. In the book the heroine was white policewoman Christie Opara (whom Donna Mills played in the 1973 made-for-TV-movie *The Bait*). Here, writer George Kirgo created a hip, flip, sexy, and saucy black detective who calls people "sugah" a lot.

Even though policewoman Olga Ford of the N.Y.P.D. was a consultant, *Get Christie Love!* turned out to be a bad example of racial equality and police procedure. Teresa Graves, who got her start on *Rowan & Martin's Laugh-In*, did her damnedest with the one-dimensional role, but even Ruby Dee would have

been stymied by the dialog. The program was uncomfortable and demoralizing to watch. Christie "eased on down" the cancellation road come the following summer.

Aaron Spelling and Leonard Goldberg joined the failure parade with *Chopper One*, a sort of "The Rookie Whirlybirds." While *The Whirlybirds* was about two charter helicopter fliers, the Spelling-Goldberg production was about California policemen who assist patrol car drivers by dropping a helicopter on bad guys. Jim McMullan and Dirk Benedict were embarrassed as Officers Don Burdick and Gil Foley, since the show was about as good as *Chase* and lasted 13 weeks as a second season replacement.

The high-flying failures continue with *Sierra*, the stirring saga of our nation's park rangers. Park rangers? That's right. Jack Webb came up with this brilliant idea for a show starring Ernest Thompson and James Richardson as rangers Matt Harper and Tim Cassidy of the fictional Sierra National Park. The series was as bad as everything else so far this year, so it too died after 13 weeks. Mr. Webb must have been hurting for "actual police files" to get this on.

Trodding the same path was *Kodiak*, one of two series that tried to steal a little *Kojak* thunder by sticking a "Ko" in front of the title. (The other was *Kolchak: The Night Stalker*, a fine monster show that was based on one of the highest rated teleflicks, *The Night Stalker*. Why the producers and/or the network decided to cheapen it with the "Kolchak" addition is beyond understanding.)

Kodiak's leading character was Cal McKay, an Alaskan state trooper played by Clint Walker. The natives called Cal "Kodiak" because he was big like a Kodiak bear. Walker was considerably animal-like, but by the fourth episode, *Kodiak* froze to death. Although canceled after a month, there were not too many gripes from the crew—the show had been filmed on location in bitterly cold Alaska.

It's **Petrocelli** *for the defense. Barry Newman played the city slicker attorney practicing in the Midwest, while Susan Howard played his wife. (NBC)*

Out on another sort of frontier was *Petrocelli*. The main character had the distinction of being presented in both a theatrical film and a TV movie before going to series. The film was *The Lawyer* (1970), directed by Sidney Furie and based loosely on the real-life Sam Sheppard murder case (a doctor accused of killing his wife).

In March 1974, *Happy Days* producers Thomas L. Milkus and Edward K. Miller took the title character and moved him to San Remo, Arizona, to get away from the hustle and bustle of big-city crime. Instead, he stumbles across small-town murder in the teleflick, *Night Games*.

In both cases, Barry Newman played the attorney, an Italian-American Harvard graduate named Anthony Petrocelli. Joining him out in the boondocks was his wife, Patsy in the TV movie, but Maggie in the series. In both cases she was played by Susan Howard. As soon as the two settled down in their house trailer—where they lived temporarily while Petrocelli built their new home—the lawyer hired a local cowboy as his private investigator. In the film he was Pete Toley; in the series he was called Peter Ritter. Either way, he was an ex-cop played by Albert Salmi.

The internal conflict in *Petrocelli* was meant to be that of a city slicker who gets his country bumpkin clients off the hook. There was supposed to be a clash of styles and the constant mispronunciation of the lawyer's name. (They call him Pet-row-cell-ee. He keeps correcting them to Pe-tro-chell-ee.) It was not much of a concept, but other shows have succeeded on less. What *Petrocelli* had going for it was its engaging cast and fairly unusual locale. They were only good for two seasons. NBC took the lawyer's shingle down in March 1976.

With all these mediocre to very bad series, it might seem unjustified to call the year a high point for the TV detective. However, on the strength of just two shows—the last two of this season—1974 has to be included as one of "the Glory Years." In fact, 1974 might be termed the finest year of the decade because of *Harry O* and *The Rockford Files*, the finest private-eye shows ever.

The face was familiar. David Janssen was back playing another private detective. He started by starring in a February 1974 film called *Smile Jenny, You're Dead*, about a model stalked by a killer who loved her too much. But for one of the few times in television history, the plot was secondary to the character, Harry Orwell, or Harry O as he was called, was everything.

He was an ex-cop, forced to retire when shot in the back. The bullet was lodged too close to his spine to operate, so at any moment, the bullet could move and he would be paralyzed or dead. Upon leaving the force, he moved into a shack on the San Diego beach and started renovating a boat he named "The Answer." To supplement his disability pension, he occasionally took private investigation jobs. But because his car did not work and he did not have the money to get a new one, he took the bus or got a ride wherever he had to go.

It was a quiet, wistful creation by writer Howard Rodman. Producer/director Jerry Thorpe—the executive producer of *The Untouchables*—took the creation even further. Janssen and Thorpe worked to make Harry O into a real human being—a man who grimaced through life because he knew that was all

Harry O *had much on his mind, little in his pocket, and a bullet in his back. David Janssen played the weary private eye with an expertise born of his roles in* **Richard Diamond** *and* **The Fugitive**, *and a debilitating life filled with injuries and illness.* **(ABC)**

there was and he did not want to waste it. Even so, he was hesitant to get involved. He knew himself for what he was—a solitary plodder. He could not move fast because of the bullet in his back, and he did not want to. This was a TV movie and a show that had a reason for a voice-over narration. Orwell/Janssen's tired, cynical yet still vulnerable voice explaining his thoughts gave *Harry O* dimension and texture.

During Harry's first season on ABC, his neighbor was Sue, a vivacious stewardess played by Farrah Fawcett. His police contact was Detective Lieutenant Man-

uel Quinlan, played by Henry Darrow. As the seemingly run-of-the-mill plots unwound, Harry's motivating characteristics did, as well. As time went on it became obvious that Harry wanted to give of himself, but he had learned never to rely on anything or anyone. His car did not work. His body did not work. Sue had a boyfriend as big as a bull. Everything he had done in the past was for nothing. Everyone he touched seemed to get hurt.

Sue was kidnapped by thugs. Harry's girlfriend was killed in his seashore home. The mechanic who was forever working on his car was killed when a bomb meant for Harry went off. And finally, Lieutenant Quinlan was shot down at the end of the first season. Harry had learned the hard way to be a reluctant hero. Unlike most of the other TV detectives, Harry could, and did, lose.

The second year found Orwell in Los Angeles, still working on his boat, still living at the beach, but with a new, more brittle police associate. He was Lieutenant K. C. Trench, a sour-faced, greasy-haired creation of the brilliant actor Anthony Zerbe. It was this team that really set *Harry O* off on the success run. Orwell's weary cynicism juxtaposed beautifully with Trench's growling pessimism. By the end of that season the show was in the top 20.

Then it was canceled. The question was why? The answer came from Anthony Zerbe in 1980 at the Long Wharf Theater in New Haven, Connecticut, where he was starring in *Cyrano de Bergerac*. David Janssen had died earlier in the year at the age of 49. When asked about the demise of the *Harry O* series, Zerbe responded with the story that Fred Silverman had just come over to ABC from CBS to "fix" the third-place network. The first thing he did was to get rid of the shows he had nothing to do with. *Harry O* was one of them.

There is no way of telling if *Harry O* would have continued to add depth to the private-eye character. All that can be said is that it was unjustly killed long before its time. It remains a monument to Janssen's work as an actor and television detective.

The face, again, is familiar. James Garner had returned, this time teamed with Roy Huggins, Stephen Cannell, Jo Swerling, Jr., Juanita Bartlett, and Meta

Rosenberg to give life to Jim Rockford. Based on a story by John Thomas James, the TV movie of *The Rockford Files* aired in March 1974. Rockford had been jailed for five years on a bum rap, then got his private investigator's license to prevent others from having the same thing happen to them. This idea certainly was not new, but the approach to it definitely was.

In addition to the Westerns Garner made that seemed to lead to *Nichols*, Garner had made *Marlowe* (1969) and *They Only Kill Their Masters* (1972), two amiable detective movies strong on morality and reality. These performances paved the way for Jim Rockford. To that skeleton of a character some nice touches were added.

Rockford lived in a trailer on the Malibu beach. He described the trailer as "cheap, tax-deductible, earthquake-proof, and when I get a case out of town, I take it with me." His other mode of transportation was a gold Pontiac Firebird that he drove like Richard Petty. That was the one thing Rockford was really good at—driving. His best friend was his father, Joseph "Rocky" Rockford—played by Robert Donley in the film, but by Noah Beery in the series—who really cared for him.

> Rocky: Two inches to the right and you might be missing that eye!
> Jim: Look at it this way. Two inches to the left and it would have missed me completely!

Rocky was the salt of the earth. The salt of hell was Angel, Rockford's unwelcome buddy who was never out for anybody but Number One. Stuart Margolin made Angel the best-loved weasel of the decade—the man you love to hate and laugh at. The salt of the police station

James Garner as Jim Rockford of The Rockford Files *sits where he was most at home; in a moving vehicle. Not only did he live in a mobile home, but he could drive like nobody's business. He was an exceptional creation who knew his limitations and wasn't afraid to be human. (NBC)*

was Sergeant Dennis Becker, a harried but cooperative cop friend played by balding, broken-nosed Joe Santos.

The Rockford Files premiered as a series on Friday the 13th of September. The initial idea was that Rockford would take on cases the police had closed. That is, when the cops closed their files, he opened "the Rockford files." TV Guide watched the premiere and called it "relatively interesting." Five years later The Village Voice—New York's prestigious,

nearly counterculture newspaper—said, "The Rockford Files is a cult favorite and we can understand why. Buoyancy like Garner's looks deceptively easy, but when you compare him with TV smoothies like Ricardo Montalban, their nonchalance looks like rigor mortis."

Rockford was more than buoyant. He had something no other serious TV detective had. And that was exasperation. No one could do exasperation like Garner could and no one needed it as much as Rockford. Producers Charles Johnson, David Chase, Meta Rosenberg, and Stephen Cannell loved dumping the craziest characters this side of the cuckoo's nest into Rockford's lap. All the zanies of Southern California that the rest of the country just heard about were right there to be seen every week on *The Rockford Files*.

There was one other great ingredient in Rockford's personality. He knew his limitations. When Rockford knew he could beat someone, he let them know it in no uncertain terms. "I'm six inches taller and twenty pounds heavier. You want to change your approach before I decide that I don't like you very much?" On other series, the writers were very careful not to expose their hero's limitations. *Barnaby Jones*'s writers would never create a scene that would require the detective to fight like James T. West. But the *Rockford* writers delighted in creating scenes where Jim was obviously outmatched, and then they went on to detail how Rockford, and only Rockford, would deal with the situation.

Rockford had the cunning of a survivor, not a coward. He was not stupid. He did not see himself as a hero, so he did not do many foolhardy things. He

was just an easy-going guy who was pretty content with himself and the way things were. This made his character so fresh, so new, and so beloved that *The Rockford Files* soon became one of NBC's biggest and most consistent hits. Garner won a Best Actor Emmy in 1977 and Fred Silverman did not cancel the show when he came to NBC from ABC.

In 1980, Garner decided to call it quits. "Rockford did me in," Garner admitted. "You work twelve to fourteen hours a day every day for six years and it kinda gets a little tough. I was in a lot of pain and I didn't know what I was doing it for. I was getting sicker and everyone else was as happy as can be. I didn't think that was right!"

Since Garner's company, Cherokee Productions, made the series, he was in a perfect position to close up shop. They stopped production in the spring of 1980, a perfect time to end. The six seasons of shows were sold to syndication, where each one begins with a different message on Rockford's answering machine and the Rockford theme song by Mike Post will be heard for a long time to come.

Harry O and Jim Rockford will be missed, but they make a fitting close to the glory years of the gimmick eyes.

Jiggle, S.W.A.T., and Future Cops

Television experienced a nervous breakdown. Midway through the seventies it all became much too much for the tube to take. News shows had gone from 15 minutes to a half hour and then expanded to an hour, 90 minutes, and two hours. Eventually one-minute news capsules would be interjected between shows. Did news happen that fast, or did TV make it happen that fast?

Over in fantasy land, programmers finished biting their nails and started chewing away on their fingers. The mortality rate for new shows was getting higher and higher. Was the public getting smarter, or were the shows getting dumber? Did it matter? To help out, a third season was instituted. The fall season lasted until January, when the "second season" started. That lasted until May, when the summer season started. That went until September, when it all started over again. And again. And again . . .

The pressure groups came down hard on Congress, and Congress came down harder and harder on the Federal Communications Commission (FCC), so the latter came down hard on the networks. As a consequence an industry-wide policy called "Family Viewing Time" was implemented, which meant that the first two hours of prime time—7:00 P.M. to 9:00 P.M.—should be suitable for all age groups. Translation: no *excessive* sexual or violent content.

If it were not for words like excessive, TV might not exist. It was up to each network or its constantly changing executives to discover exactly what *excessive* entailed. If the 1975 season is any sample, bring back the good old days!

1975

The Cop and the Kid, a comedy without distinction, premiered December 4, 1975, and ended March 4, 1976. It was about Patrolman Frank Murphy (Charles Durning, an otherwise unimpeachable actor) who gets custody of a ghetto-smart black kid named Lucas (Tierre Turner). Jerry Davis created and executive-produced this half-hour NBC reject which was "not from the police blotter, but the school blotter," as *TV Guide* so aptly put it. It came and went so fast, people hardly knew what they had missed.

This was not a representative detective show, but it illustrates a mid-seventies crisis. Networks went through all the trouble and expense of putting shows on, and then if there was not an immediate positive reaction, they would be yanked before any audience had a chance to take shape. *Mobile One* is another example of this. Not that it was a good show done wrong. On the contrary, it was another bad show produced by Jack Webb that richly deserved to be thrown

off in 10 weeks, but worse shows have remained on the air for at least two seasons and had a chance to get better.

It is possible that viewers were confused by the show. After all, just a week before its series premiere, a pilot film was shown with the title *Mobile Two*. Maybe people thought *Mobile One* was a gas station sitcom or a documentary about motor oil. What both the series and teleflick were, however, was an absurd glorification of a TV reporter's work. Jackie Cooper played Peter Campbell, a roving reporter for KONE-TV in California— Channel One on your dial. He would show up at the scenes of murder and disaster in his mobile unit to stick mi-

Here's a suitably dull scene from the ludicrous TV movie Mobile Two, *which was made into the awful series* Mobile One. *In the teleflick, these investigative TV reporters worked for station KITE. In the series they worked for KONE. In both cases they were played by Mark Wheeler (left) and Jackie Cooper. (ABC)*

crophones and cameras into the faces of anyone who happened to be passing by.

In the premiere episode, Campbell, with the help of his driver and cameraman Doug McKnight (Mark Wheeler), reported on a robbery, invaded the privacy of a movie star, rescued two children from a fire, interrupted a rodeo, and, incidentally, solved a big murder. *Mobile One* was moronic in the first degree and sentenced to cancellation.

Also moronic, and even worse because it was an unabashed rip-off of The *Wild Wild West*, was *Barbary Coast*. Douglas Heyes, a writer and director on such shows as *Laramie*, *Cheyenne*, and *The Outlaws*, wrote and produced the pilot that aired on ABC in May. In it, William Shatner, having recuperated from his three stormy years as Captain Kirk of *Star Trek*, played Jeff Cable, a state agent stationed in the San Francisco of the 1880s. Dennis Cole played casino owner Cash Conover in this TV movie, a reluctant partner in Cable's mission to prevent a national disaster.

William Shatner was chosen to imitate Ross Martin for Barbary Coast—*which was originally titled* Cash and Cable. *The past and future Starship Captain played a a Wild West secret agent who specialized in disguise.* (ABC)

Doug McClure was the other half of The Barbary Coast *team, but his boyish charm couldn't give credence to the weak, derivative scripts. (ABC)*

In the subsequent series which started in September, Doug McClure had the Conover role. Held over from the teleflick was Richard Kiel (known to audiences as Jaws from two James Bond movies) as Moose Moran, the bouncer. Behind a secret panel in the casino wall Cable donned a wide variety of disguises. This was about as good as the series got. The episodes looked cheap and set-bound, the camaraderie between the two stars looked forced and uncomfortable, and Shatner's attempt to be both James T. West and Artemus Gordon was unsatisfactory. *Barbary Coast* disappeared during the second season.

Caribe, another Quinn Martin Produc-

tion and another QM flop, lasted for 18 episodes beginning in February 1975. Produced by Anthony Spinner and created by Charles Peck, Jr., seemingly it was their attempt to make another *Hawaii Five-O*. It had the same sort of special police force in the same sort of tropical paradise, in this case Florida and the Caribbean. It was a pale copy, however, of the tight *Five-O* production. Even if they had copied McGarrett's dialog word for word, it would have been cliché-ridden because Jack Lord said and did it first.

Stacy Keach, a fine actor with excellent performances under his belt, must have signed on as Lieutenant Ben Logan for the money. Carl Franklin as his black partner Sergeant Mark Walters was no Dan-O, but to his credit, he did not try to be. To round out the cast, Robert Mandan, soon to be starring in *Soap*, played Captain Rawlings of Miami. The show made it through almost five months before sinking in August.

But none of these failures can compare to the disaster that was *Khan*. It started with the best of intentions. Writer Chet Gould created a San Francisco detective who lived in Chinatown with his two children, one a college graduate and the other a doctoral student in criminology. Essentially, this was a modern Charlie Chan, and one hoped that the update would be done with wit and affection. Producers Laurence Heath and Joseph Henry started well by casting Khigh Dhiegh (pronounced Ki Dee) in the title role, with Irene Yah-Ling Sun as his daughter and Evan Kim as his son.

Between casting and presentation the whole thing fell apart. Dhiegh was so amazed at the series' treatment that he refused billing. The CBS network was amazed as well. *Khan* started on February 7. It was yanked off the air three weeks later, after only four episodes.

Dhiegh was given much better treatment in the 1974 TV movie *Judge Dee and the Monastery Murders*. Based on the series of books by Robert Van Gulik about the Chinese detective Ti Jen-chieh who lived in the eighth century, the screenplay by Nicholas Meyer (*The Seven Percent Solution, Time After Time*) and direction by Jeremy Kagan was a change from the gun-'n'-grunt norm.

Also apart from the norm was *The Blue Knight*, a 1973 four-hour TV movie which instituted the format of the mini-series. Over four nights, the story of

Bumper Morgan's last days on his beat was shown an hour at a time. William Holden won an Emmy for his performance as the aging patrolman torn by conflicting pressures. E. Jack Neumann adapted Joseph Wambaugh's novel, and Robert Butler got another Emmy for his direction.

NBC and Wambaugh were very proud of this production. But it was CBS who thought it worth extending beyond the mini-series. Lorimar Productions had Albert Ruben do a new script based on *The Blue Knight*'s characters and got J. Lee Thompson to direct it. What they could not get was William Holden, so the role went to George Kennedy. From this 90-minute second version aired in May 1975, they went to series in December 1975 with Kennedy still in the lead.

The Blue Knight was failing, and no one could understand why. Part of the problem may have been the cast. Bumper had an informant named Wimpy (John Steadman), a mongrel dog named Leo who would follow him around, and a lot of arbitrary action. Cute, yes. Realistic, hardly.

To make amends, they brought in Joseph Wambaugh himself to get things right. Wambaugh tried hard, but he did not have enough time. CBS canceled the third version of *The Blue Knight* in 1976.

Meanwhile, the rest of the detectives were lining up and falling down. Writer E. Jack Neumann sought to pacify the Women's Liberationists with *Kate McShane*, a St. Patrick's Day-full of Irish clichés. There was Katie-girl, a lawyer, reportedly the first female TV attorney. It was an ominous distinction since CBS only aired eight of her court cases. Helping her out was her father, an ex-cop with a brogue as thick as the Blarney Stone. Her brother, wonder of wonders, was a Jesuit priest who also happened to be a professor of law.

Sean McClory played the father, Pat (what else?), Charles Haid, a chunky but exceptionally personable actor, played Edward the brother/priest/professor, and Anne Meara, the female half of the comedy team of Stiller and Meara, made her television dramatic debut as Kate. Unfortunately, when she is not saying something funny, Meara's nasal accent is pretty hard to take. The public only took it in this form for a TV movie set in Denver and eight series episodes.

Carroll O'Connor, the star of *All in the Family*, is a busy and talented man. In addition to playing Archie Bunker and doing stage roles, he owns a few restaurants, and in the mid-seventies, he tried his hand with a production company. Out of this company came two TV detectives, both of whom were well conceived but then lobotomized by other forces.

The first series was *Jigsaw John*, based on the exploits of the few special investigators sprinkled throughout the country. Jack Warden played John St. John, called Jigsaw because of his methodical way of piecing together clues. He was introduced in the MGM-backed teleflick *They Only Come Out at Night*, which was seen in April 1975. In the movie, his

Jack Warden (left) played Jigsaw John, a famous police commissioner developed for television by Carroll O'Connor. Charles Ynfante played Detective Tallchief in the pilot teleflick, **They Only Come Out at Night.** *(NBC)*

assistant, an Indian named Tallchief, was played by Charles Ynfante. In the subsequent series the less exotic Alan Feinstein played his associate Sam Donner. They lasted 25 weeks in stories that were nothing to get excited about. No one did, so *Jigsaw John* was sent to the old detective's home for the canceled.

O'Connor's second shot was *Bronk*, which was given the royal treatment when it premiered on CBS in the fall of 1975. Both the concept and the star were interesting. A special detective, Lieutenant Alexander Bronkov, was assigned by the Mayor of Ocean City, California, to seek out corruption within the ranks. Veteran movie heavy Jack Palance played Bronkov. Well aware of Palance's reputation, they loaded up his character with everything but the kitchen sink. He smoked a pipe, was allergic to cats, played a harmonica, drove a 1955 Cadillac, and had a crippled daughter.

Studio conceptualists worked overtime to suggest vulnerability, but judging by the results, they should have outfitted Bronkov with boxing gloves, a machine gun, and a machete and let him get on with it. Bronk was too sensitive to be true. In their attempt to create a human being, all they did was fashion a stick figure with an overdose of idiosyncrasies.

In the first episode or two, Bronk actually went after corrupt policemen within the department, but soon thereafter CBS decided that "not enough viable stories could be found about corruption in high places." So CBS supplied its own ideas as to what was "viable" and Bronk went right down the drain. He lasted until the summer of 1976.

Following close behind were two detectives with very famous literary and film backgrounds. Two detectives who

should have done better on television. First there was Lew Archer, the character many critics feel is the successor to Spade and Marlowe. Novelist Ross MacDonald (a nom de plume of Kenneth Millar) started writing about the noble but insecure knight-in-tarnished-armor in 1949 with *The Moving Target*. That book was made into one of the very best private-eye movies of 1966, *Harper*, with Paul Newman playing the lead.

Although other Archer books were under option for filming, nothing happened until the mid-seventies when the lonely detective had a fitful resurgence. In the meantime, MacDonald's books achieved critical and popular acceptance. His biggest seller to date was *The Underground Man*, so that is what Paramount and producer Howard W. Koch decided to make into a TV movie.

Douglas Heyes wrote a good script that was pretty faithful to the original story, and Paul Wendkos, who had done work on *The Untouchables*, *Tightrope*, *Naked City*, *I Spy*, *Burke's Law*, and *Harry O* and directed the *Hawaii Five-O* pilot, was set to direct. Then they blew the whole works by casting Peter Graves as the dour, quiet, slightly self-pitying private eye. The final result was pretty stiff and terribly average.

The name of Lew Archer attracted enough viewers anyway to get the character on NBC as a second season substitution. *Archer* started the last week of January 1975. The producers tried to remedy their past mistake by hiring Brian Keith, complete with a new wig and face lift, to be the detective. Keith could certainly handle the thespian chores, but he was hardly the visual equivalent of the Archer described in the books. It seemed as if the producers could only go from

one extreme to the other without considering anything in between.

Whatever the reason, *Archer* left the air in March. Ironically, Paul Newman was to return as Lew Harper that same year in *The Drowning Pool,* and even he did not get it as right as the first time, despite a great cast (Joanne Woodward, Anthony Franciosa, Richard Jaeckel) and a good director (Stuart Rosenberg).

Premiering in September was the other famous sleuth, Matt Helm. Only the Matt Helm of the books and the Matt Helm of the movies were two completely different people. When introduced in 1960 by author Donald Hamilton, Helm was a rustic sort who made his way through life as a writer, photographer, fisherman, and hunter. In the first novel, *Death of a Citizen,* he was recruited by a government official known only as Mac to do some secret mission stuff.

In *The Silencers* (1966), the first Helm film, Dean Martin played the title role, and Phil Karlson directed him as an easy-going buffoon out to steal a little box-office thunder from James Bond. In the three subsequent films, the farcical elements got worse and worse until Dean Martin was sleeping through the part—playing Dean Martin renamed Matt Helm. *Murderer's Row* opened in 1966, *The Ambushers* in 1967, and *The Wrecking Crew* in 1968.

Just as the book and film Matt Helm were different, so too was TV's Matt Helm. Executive producer Irving Allen, producer Buzz Kulik, and writer Sam

---

Jack Palance poses in this odd publicity photo for **Bronk—another Carroll O'Connor creation. Odd, because the cop character is supposed to be allergic to cats. (CBS)**

Rolfe tried to make the teleflick Matt a combination of both the book and the film Helm. When he appeared in the TV movie in May, he was played by Tony Franciosa and was now a former spy turned private eye. A supporting role was created in Helm's female lawyer, Claire Kronski, played by Laraine Stephens.

The producers were aiming for what they called "pure escapist fare," and the network's PR read, "Dangerous assignments and beautiful women make up the larger than life world of one of the screen's most flamboyant and exciting detectives." Though it was a nice try, no one was fooled. *Matt Helm* lasted all of three months as a series.

The remaining original series of the year fared better than these botched-up book heroes. Leading the way were two action shows from the prolific production house of Aaron Spelling and Leonard Goldberg, each working on the same success formula: a few young men shooting a lot of people down. The most violent and unrewarding of the two was *S.W.A.T.,* an aptly named show which followed the rounds of a Los Angeles *S*pecial *W*eapons *A*nd *T*actics unit.

Gents like the ones pictured on this show were actually trained by state governments after terrorist organizations and assorted single psychos declared open season. S.W.A.T.ters were, for all intents and purposes, storm troopers. The TV show *S.W.A.T.* made them look like five young men in love with their guns. It premiered in the second season of 1975 with an opening credit sequence that has to go down in history as one of the most violent ever made.

While the *Police Woman* credits showed a variety of violent acts being committed, *S.W.A.T.* was insidious in that

Tony Franciosa starred as TV's Matt Helm. Unfortunately, the producers decided to make the famous literary and film secret agent into a private eye—probably alienating readers and viewers who enjoyed the Matt Helm movie spoofs starring Dean Martin. (ABC)

it showed violence *about* to happen—drawing the viewer into the show to see if the action was to pay off. Each star of the show was introduced by having him climb down a building, jump through a window, etc., and then there'd be a freeze frame with the character pointing his big, black, nasty-looking automatic weapon. There was Rod Perry as Sergeant Deacon Kay, James Coleman as Officer T. J. McCabe, Mark Shera (who went on to *Barnaby Jones*) as Dominic Luca, and Robert Urich as James Street.

Leading the gang was Lieutenant Dan "Hondo" Harrison, played by former *Baron* star Steve Forrest. The brother of Dana Andrews, Forrest had been waiting all his life for this. While making movies like *Phantom of the Rue Morgue* (1954), he dreamed of a TV show that would make him a star. *S.W.A.T.* was it, as far as he was concerned, and he defended the show faithfully as a drama about highly trained men who were offering a needed service to their state and country.

Maybe the real S.W.A.T. teams were, but as these guys were presented, they could not figure their way out of an exit. They appeared to have overactive thyroids, as they blasted through a wall, fell from a skylight, and tunneled their way through the floor in order to riddle a stop sign with bullets. One of their most brilliant maneuvers came in the premiere episode, in which they had to get a girl away from her psycho father who was on the deck of a sightseeing boat. Knowing he had a gun, they decided on a subtle approach.

Their first objective was not to tip off the crazy man that they were after him, so they cleverly told every other person on deck a story that boiled down to this: "Hello, we're police officers. Don't look now, but there's a nut holding his daughter hostage behind you. Get out of here, but act nonchalant." Naturally everyone slithered away from the guy, but looked at him as though he had rabies. What was even more impressive was that the scene was directed that way—having all the extras staring at the man and creeping away.

So the man realizes he has been cornered and pulls out his gun, giving the S.W.A.T. members an excuse to kill him. The whole show was an excuse for gunplay. All the villains, it seemed, were psychos, and all the heroes had to nobly put them out of their misery with at least nine millimeters of firepower.

The same people who had been happily watching shows that complied with the antiviolence doctrines watched

Here they are, the S.W.A.T. team, tensed and ready to go out and shoot anything that moves. From the left, Mark Shera (soon to co-star on Barnaby Jones*), Rod Perry, James Coleman, Robert Urich (who would find pay dirt in* Vega$*), and Steve Forrest. (ABC)*

S.W.A.T. with mouths agape. Then they started screaming. Violence has a place, if the action is used within the context of a well-structured plot, but bullets for bullets' sake is reprehensible and *S.W.A.T.* seemed to be a slap in the face to the nonviolence decrees.

Although doing fairly well in the ratings, *S.W.A.T.* went off the air in its second season. No one came right out and said it, but many assumed it was because the series was so lead-filled. The other Spelling-Goldberg success was also fairly violent, but at least *Starsky and Hutch* was within an initially engaging framework.

Starsky and Hutch were two hip Los Angeles plainclothes detectives created by William Blinn. Dave Starsky was a casual junk-food maven who drove a souped-up Ford, carried an Army .45 automatic, and liked wearing either a bulky sweater and knit cap or a leather jacket. Ken "Hutch" Hutchinson was a more sedate organic health food eater who drove a wreck, practiced yoga, wore baseball jackets, and carried a .357 Magnum. Both wore sneakers.

Together they were two "wild and crazy" guys whose crime-busting methods were maniacal. They treated scum like scum and only used "the book" for reading. Their credo seemed to be never walk when you can run, never run when you can leap, never leap if you can get in a car chase, and never get in a car chase unless you can rough up or shoot the people you are chasing. Undermining their underworld victims was their stool pigeon, a bar-hopping nobody named Huggy Bear.

The show worked because of its young stars. David Soul (Hutch) had gained notice on *Owen Marshall* and *Here Come the Brides* (1968). Paul Michael Glaser (Starsky) had done a pretty bad job as co-star of *Fiddler on the Roof* (1974), but he was better here. Both men were energetic and personable, making their outlandish adventures watchable. These adventures started with an exciting teleflick aired in April, in which they went after some hit men who are also after them.

The series opened with Antonio Fargas playing Huggy and big black Bernie Hamilton playing the gruff Captain Dobey, the team's superior. The violence-filled, action-filled plots were made palatable by the engaging personalities of Soul and Glaser. They both worked hard at their roles and the fans took both men to heart, making them teen idols and giving the show a steady audience.

But as the years dragged on and the scripts became hackneyed, the two men were worn down by the mediocrity. Soul gained weight and grew a mustache. Glaser looked tired. The shows gradually stopped making any sense at all. The series, which had once been sharp and snappy, became a rehash of tired plots.

The series was canceled in mid-1979 and both men went on to better things. Glaser did a fine TV movie, *The Great Houdini,* and a John Huston film, *Phobia* (1981). Soul continued the singing career he had started (he is bigger in Japan than here) and did some exceptional teleflicks on relevant themes.

The producer Glen Larson was well-represented this season by *Switch,* the

Starsky and Hutch, as they appeared in their first, fast-moving season (before repetition and self-satire moved in). Paul Michael Glaser (left) soon lost Starsky's wool cap and found a leather jacket, while David Soul, as Hutch, later grew a mustache. (ABC)

lot (Gregory Sierra, basically taking his role as Julio Fuentes on *Sanford and Son* and making him a cop). There was Sergeant Wojehowicz, the token Pole who worked hard not to be a Polish joke, although he was, a bit. His dream was to finally pass the sergeant's exam, which he had flunked five times (Max Gail). Then there was Sergeant Nick Yemana, the token Oriental who made the worst coffee in the city and usually got all the piddling jobs like filing (Jack Soo).

The initial reaction to this crew was not good. "Too many cliché characters," said one critic. Several critics pointed out that "police work is not funny." At first, it seemed as if they had a point. It took a while for the intrepid actors and producer Danny Arnold to break through the thick skulls of many of the network executives. They wanted the freedom to make the caricatures real, while the network was afraid of the idea. Several times during the bumpy first few months, *Barney Miller* teetered on the edge of the cancellation abyss.

To their credit, there was a solid group of ABC executives who stood by the show. "It's the one 'quality' show we've got," one exec said. "We're not going to let it die." Instead they took the Tuesday night hit *Welcome Back Kotter* and scheduled it before the cop show. That did the trick. *Miller*'s ratings moved up into the top 20 and stayed there, even after *Kotter* faltered and died.

For, while they were scheduled well, they also discovered the secret of their success. They listened to the critics. The reviewers were right; police work is not funny. And the police work is not the thing that is funny on *Barney Miller*— that is often deadly serious—the people are funny. Lines that would fall flat on

other shows are hilarious because it s almost all humor of character. It als makes writing difficult. A big yuk for Fisl would not work for Harris, for example Each character on the show became accepted as an individual, not as part of a group, like say, the Sweathogs on *Kotter*.

Things changed as *Miller* went on and got better. Chano suffered a crisis after killing a bank robber, then actor Sierra left after a season to star in Danny Arnold's *AES Hudson Street*, a failed attempt to be the *Barney Miller* of medical comedies (*M*A*S*H* accomplished that, and like the *M*A*S*H* doctors, the 12th Precinct detectives joke because if they did not, they would go crazy). With Chano gone, Fish got most of the good lines. He was forever griping about his wife and his internal disorders. Arnold brought in two women: Florence Stanley to play Bernice Fish, and Linda Lavin to play policewoman Janet Wentworth.

Wojo and Wentworth had an affair while Mrs. Fish became enamored of some juvenile delinquents. When Lavin left the show to star in *Alice*, June Gable did a few episodes as Detective Battista. Meanwhile these juvenile delinquent orphans kept showing up to bug Fish more and more. Actually, it was all a ploy. Abe Vigoda had been complaining loudly and often that if it were not for Fish, *Barney* might be a bust. He wanted more attention, more credit, and more money. It has even been said that he wanted the show's name changed to *Fish and Barney*, although he would accept *Barney and Fish*.

Danny Arnold responded by allowing Fish to have his own show while still appearing at the 12th Precinct. But to cover his bets, the new character of Detective Arthur Dietrich was introduced, a wildly overeducated dry wit with a deadpan delivery and devastating timing. Steve Landesburg, a stand-up comic who had guested on *Barney* previously as a bogus priest, played him and effectively stole the show from Fish. It must have been very strange for both of them the last few months, because the character of Dietrich was forever raising Fish's ire by having to sit at the older man's desk because he did not have one of his own. The character Fish, nearing retirement age, knew that Dietrich was his replacement while the actor Vigoda also must have known it.

The spin-off show, *Fish*, flopped after a season. It was a domestic sitcom that did not have the sharp writing of *Miller*. The story goes that Vigoda asked to come back as a regular and also asked for a substantial jump in pay. Arnold would have none of it. Fish was written out in a powerful two-part episode in which he refuses to retire, feeling that it is somehow a judgment of his worth as a man. But finally, quietly, he leaves. For good.

His departure meant bigger slices of time for the others, including diminutive Officer Carl Levitt (Ron Carey), who overcompensated for an inferiority complex by being eager to do anything and wearing very loud suits. Another recurring character was inspector Frank Luger, a veteran of the "lawless years," played by the same actor who starred as Barney Ruditsky, James Gregory. (It is said that Captain Miller got his first name from Barney Ruditsky, since Danny Arnold supposedly knew a guy by that name.)

The characters changed over the years. Barney suffered through a trial separation from his wife, who wanted to move out to Connecticut . . . or Sweden. Wojo fell

painfully in and out of love with a hooker, then finally passed his sergeant's exam. Harris finally wrote his best-seller, *Blood on the Badge*. Yemana finally revolted against all the secretarial assignments and demanded his worth be announced, which everyone happily did.

Jack Soo died of cancer in 1979. The other actors stepped out of character on the program televised May 17, 1979, to pay homage to Soo. Afterwards, Yemana was not replaced and the other characters were broadened. Dietrich took part in an antinuclear rally and was arrested. Barney was passed over as inspector for the third time in a row. The next crisis came when Danny Arnold, the guiding force of the series, had to have a multiple bypass heart operation. He left the show before it wound up killing him from overwork.

The first episode after his departure was a disaster. The men of the "old one-two," as Inspector Luger was fond of saying, were made into a homicide unit. What could have been an insightful two-part episode about the ultimate dehumanization of solving murders was turned into an irrational, unbelievable travesty with everyone regressing back to their 1975 caricatures. The episode even had the audacity to maintain that Harris would find it more important to put the make on a beautiful black police photographer than find the nut who chopped people up and put them in plastic bags.

In the earlier seasons, Harris' amorousness probably would have been revealed as a defense mechanism to keep him from thinking about the real murderer and real victims. But not here. The big joke was that Harris finally caught the killer because he had left his wallet in one of the Baggies. Yuk, yuk. The episode laid waste to all the excellent work that had been done for five years before.

At this writing, *Barney Miller* is continuing production. It is hoped that it will return to being an exceptional series of extraordinarily well acted comedy-dramas.

1976

In the bicentennial year the TV detectives were dreadful. Nearly finishing everybody off right away was *Holmes and Yoyo,* an incredibly dimwitted show that seemed to rip off a recent detective teleflick as well as try to re-create the high points of *Get Smart.* Viewing this half-hour comedy about a human detective and his robot partner right after examining *Barney Miller* makes the *Yoyo* show look even worse. It was for this that *McMillan* co-star John Schuck left his Sergeant Enright role to play Gregory Yoyonovich, a super "computerperson" teamed up with a hapless hound dog of a detective, Alexander Holmes (Richard Schull).

This same concept was first put forth that year by *Future Cop,* a May TV film that starred Ernest Borgnine as a Joe Forrester-like cop and Michael Shannon as his metal sidekick, a humanoid android. As written by Anthony Wilson and directed by Jud Taylor, it was not a horrible movie, it was just that the concept had been stolen from authors Ben Bova and Harlan Ellison, who successfully proved it in court.

Those two noted science-fiction writers had collaborated on "Brillo," a short story about a robot cop (metal "fuzz," get it?), and even wrote a script for Para-

mount, who wound up going with Anthony Wilson's highly familiar *Future Cop* instead. After its premiere, ABC tried it as a series which started and stopped in 1977. Then they tried to sell it again as another teleflick called *Cops and Robin* in 1978. At no time was the public buying. But the producers were paying—paying Bova and Ellison for their transgression.

The only thing *Holmes and Yoyo* transgressed on was good taste. The two characters here were closer to Maxwell Smart and Hymie the robot than they were to Brillo. The reason was that producer Leonard Stern, who had worked on *Get Smart,* also produced and created this one. Unfortunately he used basically the same jokes in both. Not only had we heard them all before but there was no Don Adams around to say "Sorry about that, Yoyo." The robot and the series were disconnected at the second season.

Funnier than Holmes and Yoyo was *Most Wanted.* It was supposed to be a drama about an elite task force in Los Angeles assigned to bring in the "most wanted" criminals. Initially the premise and the production seemed promising. Two of the men who had made *The Untouchables* were reunited: producer Quinn Martin and star Robert Stack. Together they made a TV movie pilot with Stack playing Captain Lincoln Evers, the head of the gang. Backing him up were young, handsome Sergeant Charlie Benson (Shelly Novack, doing more work for QM Productions after co-starring in *The FBI*) and young, pretty Leslie Charleson as Dr. Lee Herrick, a psychiatrist. Together they captured a mass murderer of nuns.

Here was an example of an unsettling

trend in TV detective writing. As was the case in *S.W.A.T.*, as is the case in *Most Wanted,* and as will be the case in many of the shows we will examine, murder does not have to have a motive anymore. It can just be done. What with Richard Speck, Albert DeSalvo, Charles Manson, and Son of Sam, the more TV creators saw real-life events, the easier it was for them to write about a killer who murdered just for the hell of it. This kind of villain did not take any thought: just create a mad dog who could be used to titillate the audience before he is eliminated by the hero. Sadly, soon the villain would not be punished because of misguided antiviolence decrees.

Once *Most Wanted* went to series, Jo Ann Harris replaced Leslie Charleson by playing Officer Kate Manners, a beautiful rookie. To follow up the nun killings, the series had to come up with something appropriately steamy, so they settled on white slavery. How they managed to make nun killing and white slavery dull and laughable, heaven knows, but they did it. The character of Link Evers came off like a retarded man who had picked Eliot Ness as his role model, while the other two cops were so unprofessional viewers worried whether they could tie their shoelaces. *Most Wanted* made it to the following summer, when, after 23 episodes, what viewers "most wanted" was not to watch.

Quinn Martin was not finished for the year, however. His *Bert D'Angelo, Superstar* appeared and disappeared earlier in the season. Bert was sort of a reverse *McCloud.* Instead of having a nice guy transferred to tough turf, *Superstar* had a tough, streetwise N.Y.P.D. veteran of 10 years get traded to San Francisco where the punks are not as rotten. Robert ·Pine and Dennis Patrick were fine as

D'Angelo's San Fran superiors, but Martin made a major boo-boo in the casting of Bert.

Paul Sorvino was signed to play D'Angelo, a far cry from the commercials the chunky, lovable actor began his career with. From there, Sorvino co-starred, usually as the lead's best buddy, in *The Panic in Needle Park* (1971), *A Touch of Class* (1973), and *The Gambler* (1974). That is the sort of guy Sorvino looks like. A buddy. A pal. A sweetheart. Not a 10-year veteran of the N.Y.P.D.! *This* was the show Jack Palance should have starred in, which would have given it a chance. As it was, it limped through 14 episodes before dying.

Running alongside *D'Angelo* was *City of Angels,* another mid-season replacement which looked to have a chance in the long run. First, it was produced and created by Stephen Cannell and Roy Huggins for actor Wayne Rogers, who had recently left his *M*A*S*H* role as Trapper John. Audiences discovered that it was a rehash of *Banyon,* however, complete with the office in the Bradbury Building and the sardonic voice-over narration. It was a good rehash, with Rogers portraying whimsy better than Robert Forster, but a rehash nevertheless.

It started well. Cannell wrote a three-hour pilot called *The November Plan* to get the cases of Los Angeles private detective Jake Axminster rolling. Jake/Wayne Rogers started the show by saying that the L.A.P.D. is presently considered one of the least corrupt police forces in the country. "But it wasn't always that way." (The show was set in the 1930s.) Then things got off and rolling on Jake's efforts to foil a mad politician's plot to take over the country. From there things went downhill.

"*Angels* is a classic example of convoluted, disconnected, bad story-telling," said Rogers after its cancellation in August 1976. "I hated the stuff they gave me."

Wayne Rogers was exactly right. *Angels* was a classic example of bad story-telling. Not *City of Angels* but *Charlie's Angels*. Evidently Aaron Spelling and Leonard Goldberg had learned their lesson: with *S.W.A.T.* eliminated and people coming down harder on *Starsky and Hutch* every day, they decided not to concentrate on violence. Instead, they put the spotlight on flesh.

Contrary to popular belief, *Charlie's Angels* was not a sex show: it was a skin and hair show. The contest always seemed to be which star would have the best outfit, the best smile, and the best hairdo.

It all started March 21, 1976, with a pilot film. There the Los Angeles chapter of the Charles Townsend Detective Agency was shown populated with three female agents and a male control. The girls, commonly referred to as "Angels," consisted of Sabrina Duncan (Kate Jackson), a former showgirl turned cop turned private eye; Kelly Grant (Jaclyn Smith, who was reportedly promised special consideration—*read:* more camera time—from co-starring in the Spelling/Goldberg *The Rookies*), the multilingual college girl; and Jill Monroe (Farrah Fawcett-Majors), an athletic ball of fluff displaying pearly whites and flowing mane.

The male boss was John Bosley, played by David Doyle. As initially conceived, he was to be the girls' confidant,

The original Charlie's Angels *before fandom and favoritism moved in. From the left: Kate Jackson, who was supposed to be the star and was considered the "brainy" one, Farrah Fawcett-Majors, who dropped her last name and the show when she was heralded as the "next big thing," and Jaclyn Smith, who stayed steady and serene throughout. (ABC)*

father-figure, and comedy relief, but just like everything else on the show he turned into a human-shaped nothing. Charlie himself was never seen except for an occasional shot of his back or in silhouette. His voice was supplied by John Forsythe, of *Bachelor Father* fame. Ivan Goff and Ben Roberts wrote and produced the TV movie that led to the series that fall.

At first the show was watchable all the way through. The plots held together, there was enough movement to keep one's attention, and the constant parade of costume changes kept girl-watchers on their toes. In other words, there was initially some mystery. If the mystery was

not a whodunit to be solved, then at least it was the mystery of these Angels—what they looked like underneath and who they really were. Kate Jackson added some spice because she was not as well built as the other two.

Then came the media hype of Farrah Fawcett, whose posters sold by the millions. This instant adoration seemed to fool her into thinking that she was a talented actress worthy of better things. She decided to leave the series for movie fame. This sort of maneuver may have turned off her fans, or it may have been that she picked bad movies to appear in. Whatever the cause, the movie stardom did not materialize and she was not a

The second shift for Charlie's Angels. Cheryl Ladd (center) replaced Farrah Fawcett. Then Shelley Hack replaced a departing Kate Jackson. A year later, Hack was dropped and Tanya Roberts was brought in. What no one seemed to notice during this game of musical angels was that the series was failing because of lousy writing—not lack of feminine flesh. (ABC)

talented actress yet. She may be becoming one, but she was not at the time she left *Charlie's Angels.*

Cheryl Ladd was brought in as Jill's sister, Kris Monroe, another Los Angeles-trained policewoman. At that point, the show as a watchable commodity began to falter. *Charlie's Angels* was in the top 10 constantly, so everyone behind the camera seemed to figure that viewers were only watching to see the girls flounce, so why bother? Why bother trying to put together anything but the most rudimentary stories upon which the Angels could jiggle? Things did not improve when Farrah Fawcett returned for three episodes to fulfill her contract in 1978. But when Kate Jackson left after seeing the message on the girls' room wall, the bottom really fell out.

The producers made a big deal of replacing Jackson with model Shelley Hack (of "Charlie" perfume fame) as Tiffany, a San Francisco-trained policewoman, but they did not do anything about the boring scripts. At this point they were putting in about one action scene a half hour, and that "action" usually consisted of one person running or pointing a gun. A mystery show does not have to have violence, but it has to have something besides pretty girls and atrocious dialog. The makers of *Charlie's Angels* did not seem to think so.

Hack was pretty much blamed for the ratings drop which occurred during the 1979–1980 season, and she was fired when production stopped for the year. Another big to-do occurred when Tanya Roberts—a beautiful young actress who had made her living up until then by getting killed in *Tourist Trap* (1979) and the Aaron Spelling-produced *Waikiki* teleflick— was cast as Julie, an ex-model

turned undercover narc agent. Again they went through the trouble of finding a new girl but did nothing about the awful writing, only to be surprised when the ratings did not pick up.

The fifth season premiere of *Charlie's Angels* in 1981 was a three-hour fiasco of boring situations, incredibly stilted dialog, ludicrous plot developments, and general atrophy. It also had one of the best examples of the "no-motive" murders that were assailing the small screen. In the first half of the two-part premiere, Jack Albertson was cast as a man who murders women after taking pictures of them. When he is finally caught—not from detection, mind you, but by purest coincidence—he gives this as his reason for killing: "I had to do it. I don't know. I don't know."

This is what the likes of *Charlie's Angels* has led us to: motiveless, irrational crime spotlighted and glorified by titillation. The series was at its nadir. Female guest stars were on *Charlie's Angels* merely to be terrorized or murdered. Male guest stars were there merely to leer, terrorize, or kill.

Delvecchio was not a terrible show. It was simply a sadly average one. Sad because its star, Judd Hirsch, is anything but an average actor, and the teleflick he starred in before succumbing to the cop series was as exceptional as *Delvecchio* was mediocre. The TV movie was *The Law*, an incisive examination of the modern American legal system that starred Hirsch as driven Jewish lawyer Murray Stone. The show won the Emmy that year for "Outstanding Special, Drama or Comedy," and director John Badham also received a nomination.

For some reason the broadcaster of *The Law*, NBC, could not see it sustain-

ing a full series, so William Sackheim, the producer and co-writer, took Hirsch over to CBS to star in *Delvecchio*. This show was as close to *The Law* as the show's new network wanted to get. Instead of being a driven, intense lawyer, Hirsch played a driven, intense Los Angeles cop with a law degree. Sergeant Dominick Delvecchio, badge number 425, was too busy arresting every felon he could find to take the bar exam—much to the chagrin of his father Tomaso (Mario Gallo), a barber. Delvecchio's intensity also took his partner aback, the well-meaning but lazy Paul Shonski (the wonderful Charles Haid again).

As far as the audience knew, Dominick would not take his bar exam because he was stubborn. As long as one knife-wielding psycho remained on the streets, Delvecchio would track him down. Then, and only then, would he become an attorney. What sank *Delvecchio* more than anything was its self-conscious dialog. *TV Guide* reprinted this:

Lieutenant, they've got my tooky in the squisher. Whaddaya want me to do?

All through the series, the writers thought of such clever words as "tooky" and "diddley-do" to take the place of obscenities. *Delvecchio* made it to the summer by the seat of its tooky before getting canned.

Serpico also endured a roundabout trip to the small screen, getting a little

worse along each step of the way. First there was the real Serpico, a New York City vice cop who reluctantly exposed corruption in the ranks simply so he could continue to be "clean." His fellows marked him as a stool pigeon and ostracized him. Then, Serpico was shot in the face by a drug pusher. The weapon was of low caliber, thankfully, so he survived, only to quit the force and move to Sweden, a defeated man.

Peter Maas wrote a book about Serpico, which Dino De Laurentiis bought for the screen. Sidney Lumet directed a powerful 1973 film called *Serpico*, which starred Al Pacino. The television people did not think that was enough. Robert Collins—a writer/director for *Dan August*, *Police Story*, and *Police Woman*—wrote and directed another version of the Serpico story called *The Deadly Game*, which was broadcast on NBC in April 1976.

In September the series *Serpico* aired starring David Birney, who also did the teleflick part. NBC thought they had a winner on their hands. Many saw Serpico as the first hippie TV detective. He had a beard, smoked a pipe, wore jeans, ate health foods, rode a motorcycle, played the guitar, loved the opera and ballet, and lived in Greenwich Village. Cool. What no one seemed to realize, however, was that Serpico, the man, had been media-saturated. There were the newspaper reports of his actual situation, the book, the movie, and the teleflick. The story had already been told better several times before. There was nothing left to be said, but the series tried to say it until it was cut off at the second season point.

NBC finally got it right in 1976. They finally found a fourth concept that

Judd Hirsch, a lauded stage (Talley's Folly) and screen (Ordinary People) actor, played attorney Murray Stone on the acclaimed mini-series The Law, only to be stuck in the all-too-familiar and unsuccessful cop series Delvecchio. John Beck (background) played the deputy district attorney in The Law. (NBC)

proved to be as successful as *Columbo* and company on the *NBC Sunday Mystery Movie*. Just so that NBC does not take all the credit, let it be known that if it were not for the show's star, *Quincy, M.E.* would have died as dismally as *Hec*, *Amy*, and *McCoy*.

The star was Jack Klugman, who bucked the typecasters by not doing another comedy right after the end of his successful *The Odd Couple* run. He bucked them further by not playing a sloppy gambler in the drama. Instead, he chose to play a fastidious, thorough medical examiner, known only as Quincy, who had left a prosperous private prac-

tice to take up forensic medicine for the L.A.P.D. (An M.E. performs an autopsy on a person who has been murdered or has died without apparent cause.)

Klugman's choice and the show's subject matter was bold, and it seemed to be the wrong move at first. In the series premiere, the humor was downright sick, and it was extremely hard to think of the man the public had come to know as slob Oscar Madison as a crusading doctor who cut up bodies. The cliché characters around Quincy did not inspire confidence either. He has a prissy, pompous superior named Dr. Robert Astin (John S. Ragin) who kept reaming

Who wouldn't trust this face with a hot body? Jack Klugman, noted for his "Oscar Madison" role on the TV Odd Couple, *traded his poker chips for a police lab as the lead in* Quincy. *(NBC)*

him for doing his own investigations outside the police lab; he had an assistant named Sam Fugiyama (Robert Ito) who really did not seem to do anything important; and there was Lieutenant Frank Monahan, L.A.P.D. (Garry Walberg, who played Speed on *The Odd Couple*), who wished Quincy would do his job and let the police do theirs.

Quincy, M.E. turned out to be a success. It gained distinction over the other Sunday mystery movies by being the first to get its own time slot (*McMillan and McCloud* were canceled, leaving *Columbo* alone the following year). NBC moved Klugman's show over to Friday where it really took flight. The actor took Glen Larson's concept and stretched it until it fit neatly over his own personality. Quincy became more than a doctor in the coroner's office, he became a crusader for worthy movements.

Instead of a scalpel, Quincy should have been using a soap box and a bull horn. Klugman was intent on having the series be a platform for truth, justice, and all that jazz. The audience lapped it up. People got a thrill out of waiting for Quincy to explode. The M.E. would stalk through every scene like a cross between Groucho Marx and a raging bull, using his forefinger like a blunt instrument every time he talked. He pointed, cajoled, demanded, begged, pleaded, yelled, and generally had a ripping good time.

At this writing, *Quincy, M.E.* is still in production, with Klugman looking for fresh new ideas, fresh new writers, fresh new movements, and fresh new corpses.

1977

Although other mini-series had been presented (*Rich Man, Poor Man* being the best received), Alex Hailey's epic *Roots*—adapted by William Blinn, the man who gave us *Starsky and Hutch*—cemented the mini-series as a serious, effective, and popular form. Over the years these efforts would cost more than TV films, but their rewards would be greater. It was only the television mini-series that could truly be called an event. Among these events would be *Holocaust, Centennial,* and *Shogun.*

In 1977 the TV detective found weeds rather than roots. Take as an example *The Hardy Boys/Nancy Drew Mysteries.* These characters needed no introduction to most viewers. The Hardy Boys, Joe and Frank, were the teen-age sons of renowned detective Fenton Hardy. Nancy Drew was another teen-age sleuth, the daughter of renowned attorney Carson Drew. These three pubescent peepers have been featured in over a hundred novels that have been best-sellers for most of this century.

All were created by Edward L. Stratemeyer, a prolific writer who produced—or was responsible for—the Tom Swift, Bobbsey Twins, Bomba, the Jungle Boy, and Ken Tracy characters, among others, under many pseudonyms. Since his death in 1930, his publishing empire has been taken over by his daughter Harriet S. Adams, who has also taken on the roles of Drew author Carolyn Keene and Hardy Boy author Franklin W. Dixon.

Compared to the story of their creator, the two-and-a-half-year TV series is of only minor interest. Glen Larson brought the gang to TV after Walt Disney had made a Hardy Boys adventure in the sixties and a series of Nancy Drew movies had been made in the late thirties (starring Bonita Granville). As the producer of *Quincy* and *McCloud* worked them,

This was the frumpiest The Hardy Boys *looked in their entire series run. Parker Stevenson and Shaun Cassidy (left to right) were usually decked out in the best the studio could afford. (ABC)*

they started as alternating one-hour adventures on Sunday night. Parker Stevenson played Frank Hardy, the elder of the siblings, with Shaun Cassidy (David Cassidy's younger brother) as Joe. Edmund Gilbert played their dad. All performed with earnest determination.

Pamela Sue Martin, an ambitious and attractive actress, played Nancy Drew with a flighty assurance that bordered on the obnoxious. William Schallert played her father with experience born of playing Patty Duke's father on *The Patty Duke Show* (1963). All went swimmingly on both shows until Cassidy parlayed his appearances into a singing career much

like his brother's. He soon became a teeny-bopper star, a fact that overshadowed the show itself.

Nancy drew soon found herself playing second fiddle to the boys, until Larson decided they should incorporate the three characters in one plot line every week. The boys and Drew met in Europe and sleuthed together until Ms. Martin decided she did not like that idea very much. She left the show to find greener pastures, only to turn up in teleflicks, a *Playboy* pictorial titled "TV's Nancy Drew Undraped," an exploitation action movie *The Lady in Red* (1979), and the TV series *Dynasty* (1981). Actress/model

The original TV Nancy Drew family featured Pamela Sue Martin (center, seated) as Nancy, William Schallert (center, standing) as Carson Drew, her lawyer father, George O'Hanlon as Ned Nickerson, and Jean Rasey as George Fayne, the teen sleuth's pal. (ABC)

The second TV Nancy Drew, played by Janet Louise Johnson after Martin decided not to play second fiddle to The Hardy Boys. (ABC)

Janet Louise Johnson replaced her for awhile before the Drew character was phased out completely, leaving the boys to fend for themselves.

They fended until 1979, when Cassidy's fans alone could not sustain the series. Also unable to sustain a show was the beauty of model Kim Bassinger. She was featured as the selling point of *Dog and Cat*, a Walter Hill creation which started late in 1977's second season. The idea here was to team up a hardened 14-year vet of the L.A.P.D.'s 42nd Division with a vivacious Southern belle rookie.

The vet was Sergeant Jack Ramsey, played by actor/director Lou Antonio—a man who was behind the camera for some episodes of *Griff, McCloud, Owen Marshall, McMillan and Wife,* and *The Rockford Files.* Bassinger was J. Z. Kane, his new long-haired, full-lipped, curvy partner. At first they grated on each other's nerves, going at each other like "dog and cat." In addition, the phrase is police lingo for intersexual teams, so they became *Dog and Cat* officially.

Both actors liked each other and both did their best with the one-dimensional writing, but the production seemed to have breasts on its mind more than bad men. The series was scratched out of existence after 10 weeks.

Somehow it is comforting to note that 1977 also saw the presentation of the most woebegone lawyers ever to disgrace the tube. Producer Leonard Stern, after attempting to bring back great comedy duos like Abbott and Costello in the unlikely form of *Holmes and Yoyo*, was now trying to re-create the breezy partnerships found in the comedy mysteries of the forties.

Why not try to revive the style of the

Bob Hope films as well as those of the Bowery Boys, and others? The reason not to is that one would probably wind up with something like *Rosetti and Ryan,* and that is to be avoided at all costs. At first, things looked good for the series. NBC aired an Edgar-winning pilot film titled *Men Who Love Women* in May, with a script by Don M. Mankiewicz, Gordon Cotler, and Sam Rolfe.

But the bad news came with the September series based on the TV movie about two free-wheeling, amorous criminal lawyers. The network handed out some publicity fliers which were incredible. The descriptions of the characters are especially heinous and offer solid evidence as to the superficiality of the whole project.

"Frank Ryan (Squire Fridell) is a former cop who studied law in night school. He is shy and fumbles for words, but . . . women tend to mother him and he plays it for what it's worth. Joseph Rosetti (Tony Roberts) is bright, brilliant, and suave; is from an upper-middle-class family and dresses in keeping with his background. An egotist, he considers himself God's gift to women."

How NBC could seriously believe that anyone, even the most ardent male chauvinist, would take to these buffoons is beyond comprehension. Not only were the pair flippant, insipid, and morally vacuous but the producers had them always winning in court against a female assistant district attorney played by Jane Elliot. In addition, all the judges were actually pictured as taking a severe dislike to the pair—an emotion shared with much of the viewing public. *Rosetti and Ryan* argued only seven cases before the court of cancellation disbarred them for contempt of public.

The legal half of Rosetti and Ryan was played by Tony Roberts, who was better served by his movie and Broadway roles. (NBC)

Regular commercial fixture Squire Fridell played the detecting half of the stridently whimsical pair of Rosetti and Ryan. (NBC)

Fairing far better was *CHiPs,* which premiered a week before the lawyer show and stayed on the air long after. What the show had going for it was authenticity, an engaging cast, and lots of action.

The realism came easy since it was created by Rick Rosner, a former reserve deputy sheriff for Los Angeles. He conceived of two motorcycle cops in the Starsky and Hutch mold. There was blond, affable, serious, and studious Jonathan Baker and macho, darkly handsome, muscular, eccentric, and mischievous Francis "Ponch" Poncherello. Together they worked for the California *Hi*ghway *P*atrol—hence, their nickname CHiPs.

The actors were Larry Wilcox, a gangling cowboy, chopper enthusiast, and ambitious thespian, and Erik Estrada, a hearty, hefty, ambitious Latino actor. They worked well together, Wilcox' shy grin contrasting well with Estrada's dazzling smile.

The action on the show was akin to watching one of those auto-thrill shows they have at state fairs. At least once a half hour some spectacular car, van, cycle, or truck stunt would occur to dazzle viewers and give the CHiPs something else to do. The action got so dangerous that the actors who used to do some of the minor stunts themselves were not allowed to after the first season.

That decision came after a shocking accident during which Estrada was almost killed. He spent several weeks in the hospital because of it, while actor Robert Pine, playing Sergeant Joe Getraer, took his place on the chopper at Baker's side. After recuperating, Estrada was back, but his troubles were not over.

After a secret marriage, he had a far more public divorce.

CHiPs just rolled on, going through two female co-stars in the process. Brianne Leary played Officer Cindy Cahill, a patrol car "Chippie," for one season, then blonde Randi Oates arrived in 1979 as Officer Bonnie Clark to take the redheaded Irishwoman's place. At this writing all the CHiPs and Chippies are still riding high on NBC's list of popular shows.

Much lower on the scales would have to be CBS's short-lived *The Andros Targets.* With Watergate in full flower and *All the President's Men* (1976) a best-selling book and a hit movie, in 1977 TV producers rediscovered the attraction of the investigative reporter. Mike Andros was one of the first of a new breed. Working out of *The New York Forum* newspaper, Andros picked the subject he thought needed exposing and made it one of "The Andros Targets."

He hit more than he missed, what with diet doctors prescribing drugs, police cover-ups, and mob infiltration. The show still did not have what it took to last from the second season through the summer. James Sutorius played Andros with eagerness, but this sort of part would have been better suited to an older, crustier type like Brian Keith (it would have been perfect for blunt, outspoken Jack Klugman). But since Woodward and Bernstein, the reporters who blew open Watergate, were young, An-

Heartthrob Erik Estrada, who suffered great physical and emotional setbacks during his tenure as "Ponch" on CHiPs. (From the MGM television series CHiPS © 1977 Metro-Goldwyn-Mayer Inc.)

dros was young too. CBS did not give him the chance to get any older.

An older, crustier reporter did succeed in Andros' wake, however. It was an astonishing success story. Who would believe that a beloved comedy character who spent seven years on a hilarious half-hour sitcom could make the transition to another state, another job, and a full hour's drama? Whatever the odds, Lou Grant did it, although the series did not look promising at the start.

Lou Grant was Mary Richards' boss at the WJM-TV newsroom on *The Mary Tyler Moore Show*. He began as a cantankerous coot (Lou: You know what? You've got spunk! Mary: [flattered] Well . . . Lou: I *hate* spunk!), but soon turned into a lovable softie—a noble, dedicated, loyal teddy bear who still knew how to growl. On the last episode, everyone in the newsroom was fired except for the hapless egocentric idiot anchorman Ted Baxter (Ted Knight).

Fifty years old, jobless, divorced, Lou moved from Minnesota to Los Angeles. There he found the city desk job on the *City Tribune* open. As the *Lou Grant* show started, Lou got the job and was immediately surrounded by clichés. The paper's managing editor was a spineless, apathetic dupe named Charlie Hume. The publisher, Mrs. Margaret Pynchon, was a tyrannical, opinionated daughter of the late owner. Art Donovan, the assistant city editor, was a prissy clotheshorse

Larry Wilcox portrays Jon Baker — the other half of the original CHiPS team. (From the MGM television series CHiPS © 1977 Metro-Goldwyn-Mayer Inc.)

who was upset because he had not been promoted to Lou's position. There were two hotshot reporters—Joe Rossi, a Dustin Hoffman/Carl Bernstein type (Hoffman played real-life reporter Bernstein in *All the President's Men*), and Carla Mardigian, a sharp-faced, eager girl reporter. Finally there was a staff reporter named only Animal, with the name and appearance of the wild-eyed drummer on *The Muppet Show*.

Things did not look good. Grant was the captain of a clichéd ship that seemed to be sinking fast. The thing that buoyed them up was that all the actors were professional and terrific, and the men who created the concept were willing to work to get it right. Allan Burns, James Brooks, and Gene Reynolds worked with the cast until their characterizations became real, and they did it with only one casualty.

Rebecca Balding, who played Mardigian, left the show to co-star in *Soap* and the horror film *Silent Scream* (1980). She was replaced by Linda Kelsey who played Billie Newman. Kelsey was brought over from *M*A*S*H* by Reynolds, having worked with him there playing a nurse. Charlie Hume became a professional, understanding boss through the efforts of actor Mason Adams, one of the most recognized voices in TV. Nancy Marchand made the haughty Mrs. Pynchon an earthy, loyal friend. Art Donovan was toned down and opened up by actor Jack Bannon. Robert Walden still resembled Hoffman/Bernstein, but at least he was realistic. Even Animal, played by Darryl Anderson, was made three-dimensional by the writers, producers, and directors.

In its second season, Lou Grant became one of the most popular, effective, entertaining, and informative shows on the air. The crew deserves a lot of credit, but the lion's share of credit should rest on the shoulders of Ed Asner, the man who is Lou Grant. Asner began his career late, in the sixties, when he was already in his 30s, and his first featured roles were as cops and cons in movies like *The Satan Bug* (1965) and *Gunn* (1967). It was on TV, with the *Mary Tyler Moore Show*, *Rich Man, Poor Man*, and *Roots*, that he proved to be a commanding actor, winning three Emmies in the process. *Lou Grant* spotlights his versatility in handling both comedy and drama. He is an exceptional performer and his series is a shining example of what can be done with this genre. *Lou Grant* is the TV detective at its best. Weaponless save for brains and conviction, the now renamed *Los Angeles Tribune* staff investigates and solves relevant, fascinating mysteries every week.

Long may they continue.

1978

The year 1978 should not be termed a banner year for anything, let alone television detectives. It was the year of the Son of Sam killings and the Jonestown massacre.

In the face of such irrationality, almost everything else palls. The response of the networks was well intended, but absurd in the long run. ABC decreed that there would be no more than "three acts of aggression per show." CBS announced that no character whom the audience has met can get killed, and villains may not directly threaten any leading character.

These moves were not only ludicrous but actually made the situation worse. You can count on the fact that if ABC will only allow three aggressive acts, then

three they will get; day in, day out, every single week. CBS was worse. If the murder victims are not people we know, they are strangers—people we do not care about; just like all those murder victims in the news. The line between fantasy and reality was all but broken.

The producers tried to work within these rapidly changing guidelines while a few did their best to ignore them. The latter group came up with a bunch of uninspiring concepts this year, the worst being *Sam*, the first series not about a policeman, not about a policewoman, not even about a police robot, but about a police *dog*. No one can forget Lassie or Rin Tin Tin, but who can remember Sam? Who would want to?

For the record, *Sam* premiered on ABC in March and was canceled three episodes later. The dog who played Sam was not given billing, but Mark Harmon played patrolman Mike Breen, his officer and master, while Len Wayland played crusty Captain Clagett, Breen's superior—a man who did not trust dogs to be as good as, say, *Jimmie Hughes, Rookie Cop* and probably did not like kids, either.

In that case, he would not have liked *Richie Brockelman, Private Eye*, a character who was introduced on *The Rockford Files*, given a teleflick, given a series, canceled, showed up on *Rockford* again, then given another series. Richie was a pretty busy boy. As played by Dennis Dugan, he was personable enough to be visible, but too bland to really be noticed. The things he supposedly had going for him were his youthful verve and his belief in the private eyes of old. The TV movie, *The Missing 24 Hours*, was written and produced by Stephen Cannell and Steven Bochco, which pretty much guaranteed an interesting mystery, but no one could foresee Brockelman's rejection by the masses.

The film did all right, but the series died in a month. So, the Brockelman character reappeared in a two-hour *Rockford Files* in which Richie and Jim team up to swindle the swindlers of Richie's dad. After that, NBC tried scheduling the series again in August 1978, but it did not even get to September this time. Richie was grounded for good.

Brockelman's youthful enthusiasm was shared by Eddie Capra. Only Eddie was not bland—he was obnoxious! Eddie's framework was *The Eddie Capra Mysteries*, a format recycled by NBC after the demise of the 1975 *Ellery Queen* show. The show started with a murder and ended with a solution, with Eddie poking around in between.

Instead of being a gentleman detective, Eddie was an unconventional attorney who wanted to solve his cases before they came to trial because he did not want to wear a tie in the courtroom. He worked at the prestigious Los Angeles law firm of Devlin, Linkman and O'Brien, naturally ruffling the feathers of his bosses—but not as much as those of the viewers. Eddie, played by Vincent Baggetta, tried desperately to be cool, but he left the viewers cold. *The Eddie Capra Mysteries* were buried in 1979. Without honors.

Capra was not the only unconventional attorney on the air. Over on CBS actor Ron Leibman created, wrote, and starred in *Kaz*, a series that tried hard to be liked. Just how much people liked it depended on their tolerance of Leibman's painful honesty and conviction. Kaz not only wore his heart on his sleeve,

he wore his stomach, brain, spleen, and intestines there, too.

Kaz is Martin Kazinski, a driven young ex-con who got his law degree while in prison. He is fond of saying things like "Don't ever quit . . . that's the trick," and lives above a club called the Starting Gate where he occasionally plays drums with the band. He gets a job with the Los Angeles firm of Bennett, Rheinhart, and Alquist because Samuel Bennett (Patrick O'Neal) believes he would make a good lawyer—with a little control.

Control was something Kaz rarely utilized. He was so optimistic and idealistic about justice that you wished he would just slow down and get a little realistic from time to time. The series only lasted a few months, but Leibman was as full of conviction as Kaz that the series would work, so CBS gave it another chance in the summer of 1979. It did not work then either, and Kaz took down his shingle in 1980.

Even with *Kaz*'s bad record, at least it was a better show than *Sword of Justice*. According to the plot, Kaz should have bumped into playboy Jack Cole in the slammer, because this son of a dead industrialist had been framed for embezzlement and locked away for three years (which is three years less than Kaz was behind bars and two years less than Rockford). When he emerges, he is supposedly full of new talents, like lock picking, phone tapping, and wall climbing. He brings to justice those who had done him wrong and then decides to devote his life—and his dad's money—to being an unpaid, unthanked avenger.

By the looks of this show, he was unthanked because as an avenger he made a pretty good playboy. Anyone tuning in expecting to see thrilling tales reminiscent of Zorro, the Scarlet Pimpernel, the Shadow, the Avenger or even Buck Rogers were sorely disappointed by the lackluster writing, boring action, and dull direction. The cast was adequate—Dack Rambo was Jack Cole—but he could not breathe life into dead scripts. There was far more excitement on *Bowling for Dollars* than *Sword of Justice*. And by the way, he did not have a sword. He just seemed to have the same rope and grappling hook T.H.E. Cat used.

If any viewer considered running away from all this dross, they would have David McKay to deal with. McKay was a college psychiatrist who served as the one-man enforcement arm of *Operation: Runaway*. This NBC summer show had Robert Reed in the lead. Week after week he went after poor, misunderstood teens who ran from family and personal problems they just could not face. It was a well-intentioned series meant to mirror the real runaway problem that has been increasing of late, but it was not exemplary and it did not continue beyond the summer.

What did continue beyond the sum-

Now what are these girls selling? Certainly not women's liberation. The only things The American Girls seemed to liberate were their bras. Debra Clinger (left) and Priscilla Barnes played investigative reporters who often exposed more than corruption. (CBS)

mer and would make almost anyone run away was *The American Girls*, an astonishingly brainless series which made *Charlie's Angels* look like *Uncle Vanya*.

"Take two gorgeous young women," CBS's publicity notes suggested, "blend in a background of primetime TV, add the entire United States, stir in one deluxe van filled with every type of communication equipment, mix well, and then simmer in action, danger, and personal involvement. The result is: *The American Girls*."

No, the result was . . . unmentionable. And instant hysteria. Here, beautiful brunette Debra Clinger (fitting name) and beautiful blonde Priscilla Barnes expect the public to believe that they are hotshot researchers for *The American Report*, a TV news magazine fashioned after *Sixty Minutes* that actually looked more like *The Fearless Fosdick Puppet Show*.

The premiere episode was scheduled to be about a teen-age prostitution ring that auctioned girls off to the highest bidder. It included such terrific material as the American Girls wondering if they should film some beach footage and then deciding, "The bikinis alone ought to be worth ten share points." Here were some ladies with their heads in the wrong place. Not to mention the writers and producers. Upon seeing the episode in question during pre-season screening, the outrage was so loud that CBS hastily substituted another episode.

When the premiere episode finally aired, excited viewers found that even that morally reprehensible script was dull. If a show is going to be morally reprehensible, it may as well be exciting, too. *The American Girls* was none of the latter and a lot of the former. It was rejected from the airwaves in two months

no matter how many blouses, buttons, nighties, or bikinis were undone.

The only success of the season came from the Aaron Spelling warehouse. As usual, he had the ingredients that worked. Take a strong, handsome, charismatic hero, blend in a dazzling locale, add a dumb but funny assistant and throw in as much female skin as possible, and you have got it.

The hero was Dan Tanna, a flashy but nice guy played by Robert Urich, who had starred in *S.W.A.T.*, the *Bewitched* spin-off *Tabitha*, and co-starred in *Soap* as the tennis teacher who got killed during the first season. The dazzling locale was Las Vegas, where Tanna had his office in the Desert Inn Casino-Hotel. The dumb assistant was called Binzer and played by moon-eyed Bart Braverman. The female skin was all over the place and the show was called *Vega$*.

As with many series, it started off with a pilot movie. There Tanna's Vietnam background is established, as well as that of his two vet buddies—the big Indian Harlon Twoleaf, played by Will Sampson, and the little Costigan, played by Chuck Vennera. In addition, there was the owner of the Desert Inn, Bernie Roth, played by Tony Curtis—who finally latched onto a winner by not trying to be the star. Dan's inner-office assistants were two chorus girls: smart, efficient Beatrice (Phyllis Davis), and giggly, seemingly retarded Angie (Judy Landers).

In the TV movie, Greg Morris of *Mission: Impossible* fame was also on hand as a disagreeable cop named George Nelson. Tanna's friend on the force was a gnomish policewoman named Bella Archer who was played by Naomi Stevens. When *Vega$* went to series, Morris was gone and Archer remained. After a

The 1970s private eye, Aaron Spelling style. For this producer, a lively combination of action, beefcake, and cheesecake was the recipe for success in Vega$. From the left: Tony Curtis as casino owner Roth, Judy Landers as Angie, Phyllis Davis (who was going to be the show's "dumb blonde" until Landers appeared, but stayed on as Bea, the ex-chorus girl turned secretary), and Robert Urich as private eye Dan Tanna. (ABC)

couple of seasons, both the Archer and Angie roles were phased out and Greg Morris was back in. After a while Curtis appeared less and less although he, Sampson, and Vennera have had recurring episodes once or twice a year.

Vega$ now runs on the stock cases that fill many detective hours on TV, but they are given extra octane by the cast led by Urich. At least with him around there is some beefcake in addition to the cheesecake, and his character has conviction and displays righteous anger from time to time. Mostly, though, he displays the .44 Magnum which he keeps in the glove compartment of his renovated 1957

Thunderbird convertible (complete with in-car phone). Binzer has gotten a little smarter, Beatrice's hair went from blond to brown to blond again, but good, reliable Dan Tanna can still be counted on to wear his jeans and tan leather vest while beating the worst Vega$ has to offer.

1979

Things were looking up when America mediated in a peace treaty between Israel and Egypt, then the country's morale dropped when the Three Mile Island Nuclear Power Plant in Pennsylvania nearly blew a reactor, which would have taken about five miles of the surrounding cities with it as well as unleashing a cloud of radioactive particles.

NBC had its own version of Three Mile Island in 1979 when the highly touted Fred Silverman arrived to take the network out of third place and into the limelight. He did it in such a way that it looked as though he were actually a double agent for ABC. One of his several contributions to the detective scene was Whodunit, a game show in which the contest was murder. Given the state of the world, this was a particularly objectionable idea, but that did not stop Ed McMahon from hosting the half hour and Jack Klugman from guesting as the murder victim.

Each week there would be three contestants and three professional panelists (people like attorney F. Lee Bailey), who would try to figure out who the murderer was in a dramatic scenario played out by guest stars. Watching as the game show clichés of prizes and a wildly applauding audience respond to a reenactment of death was slightly chilling. Murder

games were nothing new; there was one back in the late forties at the beginning of network television. But a lot of killings had passed between then and now. Television and the people of the world were no longer so innocent as to accept Whodunit as harmless fun. It went off within the year.

Coming up next on Silverman's schedule was The Misadventures of Sheriff Lobo, a spinoff of the trucking adventure B.J. and the Bear. B.J. was a series that could be directly tied in with the success of such redneck, good-ol'-boy car crash and fistfight movies as Smokey and the Bandit (1978) and Every Which Way but Loose (1979). B.J. was pretty much a conscious rip-off of both those films since it involved a trucker with a monkey as a friend. Sheriff Lobo was a character on B.J., a varmint of a con man who was based on the Smokey character played by Jackie Gleason in the film. He was played on B.J. by Claude Akins, who, curiously, starred in the 1974 trucking drama Movin' On.

In terms of Lobo, however, I think Johnny Carson said it best when he quipped, "It takes brains to spin off a series from a success, but it takes real guts to spin off a show from a flop." B.J. and the Bear was not doing well in the rating department when Lobo became a series, and neither burned up the Nielsens in the eighties. One gets the impression that they stayed on for as long as they did because at least they showed a profit, unlike most of Silverman's late-seventies' creations. Lobo had Akins up to his old money-making schemes and illegal maneuvers with the help of his astonishingly stupid deputy Perkins (Mills Watson) and his naive deputy Hawkins (Brian Kerwin).

The bumbling, self-conscious slapstick of the series continued through 1980 and into 1981, when the trio was transferred to Atlanta from Orly County and the title was shortened from *The Misadventures of Sheriff Lobo* to simply *Lobo*. It was still a minor, weak farce with very little to be proud of.

A new Robert Conrad show, *The Duke*, premiered as a TV movie in April 1979. In it, he starred as a professional boxer who becomes a private eye after his manager, Benny, is murdered and the ring box office is robbed. It was a decently atmospheric affair, with Conrad finally playing the feisty pugalist he always seemed to be. The show went to summer series with Elvis Presley's former bodyguard, Red West, playing an antagonistic policeman and Larry Manetti playing the Duke's friend, Cadillac.

Then Fred Silverman stepped in. He was willing, the story goes, to renew *The Duke* in the fall, but he had a "much better" series he wanted Conrad to star in. Conrad was initially reluctant, but Silverman won the actor over. The "much better" series was *A Man Called Sloane* and it premiered September 22. This was a shoddy rehash of *The Man from U.N.C.L.E.* in which Conrad tried to relive his glory days as James T. West in the personage of Thomas Remington Sloane, a secret agent for UNIT.

Helping out the man from UNIT was Torque, a black giant with a metal hand, and a EFI 3000 computer with a sexy female voice called Effie. These sort of gimmicks were no longer outlandish, but here they seemed especially unnecessary and stupid. The plots, as thin as they were, were held together by lots of female flesh in bathing suits, nightgowns, running shorts, and slit skirts.

A Man Called Sloane was canceled shortly after the turn of the decade. Several non-Silverman shows on CBS shared the same fate. There was *Big Shamus, Little Shamus*, a nice idea about an Atlantic City, New Jersey, house detective trying to keep things in control after gambling is legalized there and keep an eye on his 13-year-old son as well.

Arnie Sutter was the big shamus' name, played by the wonderful, husky Brian Dennehy. The little shamus was Max, played by Doug McKeon. George Wyner played the hotel's new chief of security, a scowling, annoying man named Korman. Even though it was a nice idea, nice ideas often finish last on TV. *Big Shamus, Little Shamus* certainly did. The episodes televised could be counted on the fingers of one hand.

Premiering that same evening of September 22 as the father-son shamuses was *Paris*, which seemed predestined to be a hit. It had to be, if basso-profundo black actor James Earl Jones was starring, didn't it? After all, the man won a Tony Award for his performance on Broadway in *The Great White Hope*, and he was heard all over the world as the voice of Darth Vader in *Star Wars*. Every job he did seemed to be heartfelt and riveting, so why should *Paris* be any different?

Because television is not Broadway or the movies, that is why. Once you have a great script for the stage or screen, you do it, period. In TV, you need the same great script every week, only it has to be different each time. And you only have seven days to produce it. *Paris* tried. It tried to be a warm, realistic, relevant, exciting show about Woody Paris, a detective captain and criminology professor with a beautiful wife named Barbara (Lee Chamberlin). But it did not succeed. The stories were hackneyed, and the tough but tender cop had been done before and better by Telly Savalas, of all people. CBS and Jones kept pushing, but to no avail. Midway through 1980 was the last time people saw *Paris* in the springtime. ABC-TV had better luck than the other two networks. Fifty percent of its detective shows succeeded. Since they only did two, that was no great shakes. Their failure was with *Detective School*, which started as *Detective School, One Flight Up*. Under either title it was a flaccid affair, led dutifully by James Gregory playing teacher Nick Hannigan, an ex-private eye forced to run an investigator's school to remain solvent. He had one good-looking student (Randolph Mantooth), one pretty student (Jo Ann Harris), and an assortment of rejects from general casting which included a wizened old man with the name Robert Redford and LaWanda Page, who played Aunt Esther on *Sanford and Son* and was doing the same characterization here.

We are talking cringe-worthy awfulness here and the sooner we get to the ABC success, the better. Nick and Nora Charles are alive and well and living on *Hart to Hart*. This ABC series premiered on the same night as CBS's two bombs and walked away with the ratings honors. It starred ex-*It Takes a Thief*, ex-*Switch* star Robert Wagner as multimillionaire industrialist Jonathan Hart, and ex-*Girl from U.N.C.L.E.* Stephanie Powers as his wife Jennifer. Their valet-assistant is Max, played by bulldog-faced, frog-voiced Lionel Stander who delights in telling viewers every week at the outset that the Harts' hobby is . . . murder.

These two come from a long, depend-able line of TV corpse-spotters who could find a body perfectly from five miles off. Every week either a friend, an associate, or an acquaintance is bound to croak or be accused of killing someone else. If not that, then Jennifer will be mistaken for someone else, kidnapped out of jealousy, or attacked out of envy. Anyway you look at it, it gives the Harts something to do.

It also keeps writer/creator/producer Tom Mankiewicz off the street. After writing some of the most farcical James Bond movies and helping director Richard Donner through *Superman* (1978), the man conceived this and slipped it on the air. It is fluff, but well-produced fluff with two engaging leads. *Hart to Hart* continues successfully as of this writing.

This volume has examined the TV detectives on the commercial networks only. Yet the Public Broadcasting Service (PBS) has aired some of the best detective programs. With three shows—*Masterpiece Theater, The Rivals of Sherlock Holmes,* and *Mystery*—PBS has outshone almost all the network shows put together.

Over the years *Masterpiece Theater* has presented a variety of mystery-oriented fare. In 1974 they presented *Conan Doyle*, dealing with the man who created Sherlock Holmes. In 1976 they presented '*The Moonstone*, an engagingly somber mystery based on the first English detective novel ever written, by Wilkie Collins. However, in 1972, they introduced their most famous and popular mystery character, Lord Peter Wimsey. Dorothy L. Sayers created the character in 1923 in the novel *Whose Body?* Born Peter Death Bredon Wimsey in 1890, he was educated at Eton and Oxford before serving in the First World War. After he claimed his title, he moved to 110 Piccadilly, London. From then on he became the leading amateur detective in all England. Aided by his faithful servant, Bunter—an associate from the war—Lord Peter went on to a dazzling career which concerned itself with twentieth century morals as much as murder.

The first Wimsey serial adaptation *Masterpiece Theater* presented was *Clouds of Witness*, based on the second Wimsey novel of the same name. In four episodes, viewers were treated to Lord Peter's investigation of his own sister, whose fiancé had been murdered. The stakes became higher when his brother was accused of the murder and put on trial. Triumphantly, Peter invaded the courtroom with the evidence that exonerated both his kin. As a fitting end, Inspector Charles Parker of Scotland Yard fell for Wimsey's sister and she was married after all.

The next time Lord Peter appeared was in 1973 when he invaded a posh meeting place to solve the *The Unpleasantness at the Bellona Club*. The "unpleasantness" was the death of a 90-year-old man at the club. Wimsey handled it in four episodes with his customary panache, and viewers were in for a marvelous time. Based on the 1928 Sayers novel, it only left the public hungry for more.

That appetite was fed by *Murder Must Advertise*, a 1974 presentation based on a 1933 novel of death in the advertising business. Wimsey went undercover in that one to battle a killer who used a slingshot as the murder weapon. There was more Wimsey the following year when Lord Peter went on a holiday in

Norfolk only to stumble over the mystery of a dead man bound with bell-ringer's ropes in someone else's grave. Coming closer to death than he had ever been, Wimsey solved *The Nine Tailors* (which, in bell-ringer's lingo, means the toll for a dead man).

Finally, in 1977, *Five Red Herrings* was aired. A "red herring" is a false suspect or clue, so in this adventure of an artist's colony with six members, five had to look guilty while the sixth was the actual murderer of an artist.

Throughout all the dramatizations Ian Carmichael, a British actor known for his comedy work, played Lord Peter smashingly, considering that most Wimsey lovers envisioned their man as either Leslie Howard or Peter O'Toole. Some of the critics called Carmichael "splendid," "lovely," and "inspired," while the *England Daily Express* went so far as to say "Lord Peter might have been created for Ian Carmichael."

All these PBS presentations were American premieres of BBC productions that were originally shown in England. Although the British can do mysteries as badly as Americans, as we have seen earlier, they can also make spectacularly superior efforts that dwarf our own. For years, mystery connoisseurs were wishing for a whole slew of British sleuths to invade these shores. In 1980, their prayers were answered by *Mystery*.

Quite simply, PBS rebroadcast series already televised in England to American audiences. The British have a TV industry

---

Ian Carmichael used his acting skills to make the role of Lord Peter Wimsey his own, although lovers of author Dorothy L. Sayers' character visualized Leslie Howard or Peter O'Toole in the part. (BBC, courtesy WNET)

The finest legal mind and grandest barrister ever to appear on television: Rumpole of the Bailey. Leo McKern embodied the part, while Peggy Thorpe-Bates played his wife, Hilda, whom he referred to as "She Who Must Be Obeyed." It was a delightful series done to a turn and telecast on the Mystery series. (PBS)

that essentially is made up of as many mini-series as series, which gives their producers far more leeway. These mini-series are presented at any time of the year and can run anywhere from 4 to 13 weeks. The *Mystery* folks have tried to collect the best possible characters and stories for their discriminating audience. In its first season on the air, hosted by Gene Shalit, *Mystery* presented "The Racing Game" based on the novels of Dick Francis, who specializes in mayhem with racehorses; "Sergeant Cribb," based on the novels by Peter Lovesey concerning a Victorian era cop; and "Rumpole of the Bailey," based on the stories by former lawyer John Mortimer.

Of the three, Rumpole—that over-weight, sloppy, cantankerous, boistrous, and thoroughly lovable barrister who called his wife "She Who Must Be Obeyed"—made the biggest splash. He is a delightful creation played by Leo McKern. If anyone is unfamiliar with either Rumpole or McKern, just remember the chubby, bald villain in the Beatles' movie *Help!* (1965) or the man who played Cromwell in the Academy Award-winning *A Man for All Seasons* (1966) and you will know what Rumpole looks like and get an idea of McKern's acting ability.

As if to reward viewers for rallying around *Mystery*, the PBS series called *Great Performances* aired a six-part adaptation of John Le Carré's espionage novel *Tinker, Tailor, Soldier, Spy,* starring Sir Alec Guinness as the wondrous George Smiley. As directed by John Irvin, *Tinker, Tailor* . . . was a claustrophobic, involving, and entertaining work of such exceptionally high quality that it gave the medium that had borne *The Man from U.N.C.L.E.* new meaning and new standards.

These were all such exceptional shows that it is a pleasure to draw the chapter, the decade, and this television era to a close.

Afterword on the Eighties

In the new decade a lot has already happened. The President of the United States is Ronald Reagan—a man who starred in the first Project 120 effort, *The Killers*, as a killer. And in Hollywood, an actors' and musicians' strike delayed the new season's shows by several months. The 1981–1982 season is being threatened by a writers' and directors' strike.

The reason: money. Money from the burgeoning world of videotape players and videodisk machines. Money from cable TV stations. When it is becoming increasingly more expensive to go to neighborhood movie theaters, it is a comfort to watch uncut, uninterrupted films in one's own living room without worrying what might drop down on you from the balcony.

And with cable comes new possibilities. Comp-U-Card Corporation, a shopping service, is introducing its own "shopping channel" under the auspices of its first president, John Fullmer. With "The Shopping Channel" you can buy any brand, any product, at the best price without even leaving home. The goods are delivered to your door without charge.

Television is entering a new era. It promises to bring challenging advances that will change the way we live, work, and relax. The television detective genre is slowly responding, as a whole new breed of writer, producer, director, and executive seeks to cater to the public's changing directions and needs. With the strong competition of the home entertainment centers, the networks no longer are as quick to settle on the mediocre or mundane. While there are still some pedestrian mystery series making their way onto the air, they do not seem to last long, while the quality shows are given a better chance of survival.

The future of your television . . . today! CBS has introduced EXTRA-VISION, a new advance in media communication. Utilizing a pocket-calculator-like device, the viewer can call up the weather, sports, traffic conditions, emergency phone numbers, news, and even close-captioning on their favorite TV series. This computer-based advance is only the tip of the TV iceberg. The future holds many more wonders.
(CBS)

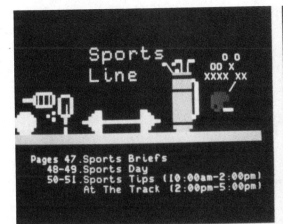

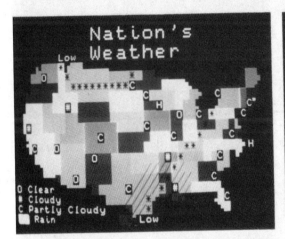

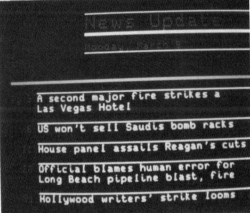

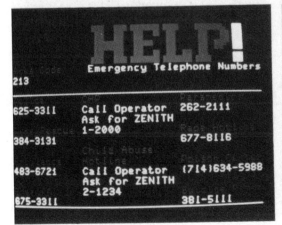

One of the worst side effects of this media change is the programming chaos, which is getting worse. New shows are scheduled and are canceled with a speed that is alarming. These programs appear and disappear at almost any time of year. The television "season"—from September to September—has been blurred almost to the point of nonrecognition. So the shows examined in this chapter will not be organized by year, but by network.

ABC

An astonishingly inauspicious show to start with is *B.A.D. Cats*, someone's very bad idea of a good idea. It seemed to adhere to the formula that if *The Mod Squad* succeeded because it had two guys and a girl, and *The Dukes of Hazzard* worked because it had two guys and a girl smashing up cars, then a cop show about two guys and a girl smashing up police cars would be a hit. The concept gave a new meaning to the word derivative, and the scripts were the sort of awful rehashes of *Starsky and Hutch* a jaded viewer might expect.

The situation was all the more laughable because the producers were not really plagiarizing anyone else so much as reheating some of their own stale material. The team of Aaron Spelling and Leonard Goldberg mounted *B.A.D. Cats*, which stood for *Burglary Auto Detail*. As such, it gave the hip Cats an excuse to come on like a latter-day *Chase*—incorporating at least one car crash every half hour. This bore premiered January 4, 1980, and was canceled February 8, just six episodes later.

Given the show's awfulness, the viewers could not cry "foul play," but that is just what viewers saw when the television version of the successful comedy suspense movie *Foul Play* (1978) premiered in 1981. The film starred Chevy Chase as a cop protecting addlebrained Goldie Hawn as a librarian who knew too much about a plot to assassinate the Pope. The TV series had Deborah Raffin—a popular, fresh-faced model making the transition to full-time actress—as a television star in love with a hip cop played by Barry Botswick.

The movie also featured Burgess Meredith as a landlord conversant in karate. In the video version, real-life real estate tycoons Greg and John Rice were cast as the landlords. Their most notable feature was that they were a pair of twin midgets. Much of the show's whimsy was at the expense of their height. Otherwise *Foul Play* on TV was pretty much business as usual. Raffin and Botswick are an engaging pair of performers—she was great in the taut teleflick *Mind over Murder* (1979), while he shone in *The Rocky Horror Picture Show* (1975) and *Movie Movie* (1978)—but the plots were anything but engaging. This series, too, lasted about a month.

After that, there was not much for the producers to do but say "nobody's perfect." And that is just what Arne Sultan, Chris Hayward, Edward Montague, and Norman Barash did say when their concept—*Hart in San Francisco*—was abruptly pulled from the September 1979 schedule after eight episodes were filmed but not shown.

The first problem was the title. ABC already had a successful series starring Robert Wagner and Stephanie Powers called *Hart to Hart*. Three Harts on one network was one Hart too many. So ABC decided to leave its third Hart in San

Francisco while the producers came up with a new title. No one was completely happy with it, but what was finally decided upon was *Nobody's Perfect*.

The second problem was the show itself. Conceived as a half-hour comedy, it did not seem certain whether it wanted to be another *McCloud* or a derivation of the "Inspector Clouseau" films starring Peter Sellers. It concerned a Scotland Yard inspector named Roger Hart transferred to a Frisco detective squad. Initially the character was presented as an absentminded bungler and he is treated that way by his superiors. But as time went on, it became clear that Hart was merely clumsy. He habitually broke things, but always got his man through sheer ability.

Ron Moody played Hart with a flair borne of the English music hall stage, while Cassie Yates played his American partner, Jennifer Dempsey—a role originally created for a man. Both actors' talents were wasted in the simplistic, strident comedy which failed to be funny. The postponed series was finally aired in mid-1980, then disappeared for good.

Stone was another fast-playing, short-lived series of a higher script quality. It attempted to do *Police Story* one better by spotlighting a Los Angeles detective who also happened to be a best-selling novelist. Dennis Weaver traded in his pearl-handled six-gun for a snub-nosed revolver in the leading role. Vic Morrow supplied supporting talent as Stone's police force friend, but the concept was essentially unworkable. The new wrinkles created by a cop character saddled with a son, a typewriter, and publisher's deadlines were hardly noteworthy. Joseph Wambaugh, the man *Stone* was obviously modeled on, might have wanted to sue, but the public did not give him the chance. *Stone* sank very quickly.

The best ABC had to offer in the early eighties was *Tenspeed and Brownshoe*, a greatly appreciated, well-received effort that just could not hold onto its audience. Stephen Cannell created this and served as its guardian angel. It was an obvious labor of love hamstrung by the network dictums of the time.

Jeff Goldblum and Ben Vereen starred as an unlikely, mismatched pair of private eyes who barely survived their various cases week to week. Goldblum was Lionel Whitney, a milquetoast type who lived vicariously through hard-boiled detective novels about "Mark Savage, Private Eye." An in-joke on the show was that Stephen Cannell's name was on the front cover of these books with his picture on the back as author.

Vereen played E. L. Turner, a slick active con man who lived on the edge of his "stings." Whitney was so conservative he got the nickname Brownshoe, while Turner was so fast, versatile, and adaptable that he got the name Tenspeed. In the three-hour TV movie pilot the two men meet and open their own investigative agency as partners.

The series was produced ably and had large doses of wit and action. Its major problem was that the network did not run it on any one day or at any one time for very long. And all the stories were approached in the same basic way: gullible, naive Brownshoe would attack each case with a chivalrous gusto that usually led to pathos, while Tenspeed's crooked past would usually catch up with him. Both men were constantly degraded by their limitations until they succeeded through coincidence and perseverance.

Further structural problems were

created by a network decree that forbade villains to die at the heroes' hands. These decrees change so quickly that *Tenspeed and Brownshoe* might not have been hamstrung by the order, but the program's villains never got punished. The heroes would get the drop on them only after they had threatened, and sometimes killed, other characters, and they would meekly raise their hands and disappear. The punishment hardly fit the crime.

Finally, the leading characters just were not realistic. They were attractive, capable, and interesting, but one could hardly believe that Whitney was that childish and unknowing or Turner that light-hearted. Whatever the reason, the series died in a matter of months.

NBC

This network was trying; it really was. When *Sheriff Lobo* brought howls of derision from critics—not to mention barely passable ratings—NBC changed its genre somewhat. Its detective contributions were interesting at the very least, and exceptional at best.

The least was *Walking Tall*, an attempt to translate the hard-hitting 1973 movie into television terms. The big stumbling block here was that Sheriff Buford Pusser, the real-life cop on whom the movie and series were based, had died earlier in the decade and the public was not sure whether he was a noble hero or a corrupt, conniving villain.

The original movie was followed by two sequels, both starring Bo Svenson, the muscle-bound Swede who also played the Pusser role on TV. His trademark was to talk brutally and carry a big stick—a hunk of tree he used to trash casinos, brothels, and cars. The series

also played up his rather calculated disregard of police rules and regulations. It would not be surprising to find out that the producers figured America was ready for a hero who went after villains no matter what, but TV's *Walking Tall* did not fill the bill. As pictured, Pusser was an unreasoning mad bull, not an intrepid hero. The show was canceled quickly.

Also interesting was Robert Blake's limited series, *Joe Dancer*. Serving as executive producer and creator as well as star, the ex-*Baretta* lead created a Los Angeles private eye who was supposed to be part John Garfield, part Dick Powell, and part Humphrey Bogart. As he stood, Dancer was all Robert Blake— and that was just the problem. The *Dancer* two-hour episode fluctuated between casual brutality, forced humor, and self-conscious pathos. Either Blake was trying a little bit of everything or someone could not decide what *Joe Dancer* was all about. In the final analysis, the character came off as slightly incompetent and pitiable.

Nero Wolfe was anything but incompetent. NBC introduced this classic mystery character to television in 1981 to the delight of detective fans everywhere. As created by author Rex Stout in many novels and stories, Wolfe was the illegitimate progeny of Sherlock Holmes himself. Wolfe, though, takes after Sherlock's brother, Mycroft, in being grossly overweight, fastidious, very set in his patterns, and devilishly brilliant.

Living in a New York brownstone on West 35th Street, Wolfe weighs one-seventh of a ton and lives only for the food prepared by his four-star cook, Fritz Brenner, and the beautiful orchids tended by Theodore Horstmann on his rooftop greenhouse. To pay for all his luxuries he takes investigative cases found by his full-time assistant, Archie Goodwin. Goodwin also serves as Wolfe's legs and ears, doing all the information gathering while Nero stays in the brownstone and analyzes.

Wolfe first made it to the small screen in 1972 when producer/writer/director Frank Gilroy adapted the 1965 novel *The Doorbell Rang* into a TV movie starring Thayer David as Wolfe and Tom Mason as Archie. It, like the Charlie Chan tele-flick, ran into some network problems and it was not until much later that the film was actually aired. By that time Thayer David had died, so a continuing series was out of the question.

Almost 10 years later producers Ivan Goff and Ben Roberts entered the picture and succeeded where Gilroy had failed—they got a go-ahead to do six episodes in a *Wolfe* series. Utilizing much the same plush, well-appointed sets as the teleflick, the men recast, and the new *Nero Wolfe* was on the air. William Conrad now starred as the great detective, sporting a natty beard and possessing one of the best throaty rumbles available for TV. Lee Horsley, a newcomer to the TV scene, played Archie and fit Goodwin's literary description, although the actor sounds just like Wayne Rogers.

The supporting cast was outstanding, with George Voskovec as the cook, Robert Coote as the orchid tender, and Allan Miller as Wolfe's police contact and friendly nemesis, Inspector Cramer of the N.Y.P.D. One of the series' best running jokes was Cramer's habit of rising from Wolfe's red-leather office chair without using his hands; an act which infuriates Wolfe because he cannot do the same because of his girth. The entire

show was put together with class and style as well as the Wolfian touches that added great flair.

But the best NBC show of the new decade thus far is undoubtedly *Hill Street Blues*, a show that manages to be original and derivative at the same time. It is probably safe to say that without the success of *Barney Miller* and *Lou Grant*, this hour-long comedy-drama from the MTM Production Company would never have appeared. It is written and produced with the same humanistic style as the *Grant* show (and by some of the same people) and concerns a beleaguered police station and its occupants, just like the *Miller* show.

There are overtones of other shows as well in the casting, especially in the case of a gung-ho, S.W.A.T.-like cop who is highly reminiscent of *M*A*S*H*'s Frank Burns character. Otherwise, *Hill Street Blues* is almost right on the mark. Although familiar, the characters are wonderfully delineated by the actors. Most notable is Daniel Travanti as Captain Frank Furillo (the Barney Miller of the Hill Street Station); Michael Conrad as Sergeant Esterhaus, the bearlike desk man who has a soft spot in his heart for high school girls; Bruce Weitz as Belker, the undercover cop who borrows the look of the "Animal" character from *Lou Grant* and the manner of the "Animal" character on *The Muppet Show* (he is best known for occasionally biting a suspect); and Charles Haid as Renko, a beefy patrolman who has to regain his self-esteem after being shot.

The realistic detailing on the show is extensive and exhaustive, while each episode is an exercise in logistics that can be stunning. The sheer number of actors involved in each hour is large, and the camera movement is always fluid and terrific. Here is a thoughtful, important show that also delivers in the entertainment department.

CBS

Hagen was the first cop show of the eighties for this network, and it was the first to go as well. Chad Everett starred as a modern-day bounty hunter who teams up with a lawyer, Arthur Hill, to bring the villains to justice. It was an uninspiring premise in every way and did not seem to tickle anyone's fancy. Although it was well publicized and shown in varying time slots, it was off the air after four weeks.

The network's next genre attempt was a bit classier but just as unsuccessful. It took a well-reviewed French film called *Dear Detective* (1980) and turned it into a series starring Brenda Vaccaro. It was about a big city detective who falls in love with a college professor but does not let it get in the way of her job. Unfortunately, the French seem to have a better talent at this sort of light comedic adventure than American TV does. *Dear Detective* played out a few episodes before it got a "Dear John" letter from the network and disappeared.

Come the start of the 1980–1981 season, things did not seem much better. Set for Saturday televising was *Freebie and the Bean*, based on director Richard Rush's (*The Stunt Man*) violent 1974 black farce starring James Caan as a mooching detective who drove like a maniac and was not above taking some favors from local shopkeepers. Alan Arkin co-starred as his hysterical Puerto Rican partner, "the Bean." Hector Elizondo got the TV role of the Bean,

with Tom Mason as Freebie. This was the same Tom Mason who played Archie Goodwin in the *Nero Wolfe* TV movie, and he would have been better off sticking with Wolfe. The NBC series lasted 12 episodes, while *Freebie and the Bean* was promptly eliminated.

Hanging on for a bit longer was *Enos*, another series that depended more on car crashes than anything else. It was a direct spin-off from *The Dukes of Hazzard*, with Sonny Shroyer as Deputy Enos Strate of Hazzard County doing a *McCloud* by getting transferred to a special Los Angeles Metro Squad. His new partner was a hip black dude named Turk, played by Samuel E. Wright. Together they demolished more autos than the entire history of the Indy 500. Enos was the bumbler Roger Hart turned out not to be, but because he was a good guy, everything wound up right in the end. The only people who suffered were Enos' superiors and the viewers. John Dehner played Lieutenant Groggi, whose slow burns matched those of critics.

Finally, there is *Magnum P.I.*, the only clear-cut CBS success of the new decade in this genre and the best hope for the future of the television detective. The idea for Thomas Magnum, private eye, started as a heap of clichés specifically tailored to fill the hole *Hawaii Five-O* left. Glen Larson conceived of a macho guy in the Dan Tanna mold who would live on the Hawaiian estate of a best-selling author who would always be ab-

---

The private eye, 1980s style. Producers Glen Larson and Donald Bellisario teamed with actor Tom Selleck to turn Magnum, P.I. *from a pile of clichés into a vital, warm, human hero. They succeeded admirably.* (CBS)

sent. The manse's other occupant would be a stuffy, proper British major-domo named Higgins.

Once actor Tom Selleck was cast as the lead, things began to change. Selleck was a ridiculously handsome man whose great looks hid a warm, sensitive human being who believed in certain things. One of the things he believed in was that Magnum could be more than a big cliché. To facilitate that belief, producer/writer Donald Bellisario was brought in to give the series a face lift. Together with Larson and Selleck (and with the grudging blessings of the studio and network), they turned *Magnum P.I.* around.

The show is wonderously entertaining: a tight, involving, exciting detective fantasy that is valid and realistic within its own context. It has action—gritty and unflinching; it has humor—honest and unforced; it has humanity; and it has—most importantly—mystery. Magnum does not stumble across solutions by accident like *Charlie's Angels* did. He detects, investigates, and analyzes. He goes after people who kill for a reason—not the sort of motiveless madness that has

afflicted TV and reality recently—and discovers the truth by working at it.

Magnum P.I. must not be the last of the heroes who believe in something. Hopefully he will lead the way to a resurgence of television detectives who do more than mirror our frailties and shortcomings, who show us what we should be and what we could become by believing in ourselves.

If we are to counter the rising real violence in our world, we must look to ourselves and not TV. Parents must lead with a surer hand and we must all see to it that the line between fantasy and reality is not broken.

Everyone has to be a hero if civilization is to continue. But whichever direction society continues in, the television detective will continue with it. He serves a purpose. Releasing frustrations, creating fantasies, and entertaining millions with classic battles between good and evil.

As long as humans remain human, these battles will continue. And as long as they do, it is comforting to know that TV heroes will continue to fight. And win.

Index

Hundreds of hard-boiled detectives, suave spies, noble knights, detecting attorneys, intrepid cops, and insistent journalists have entered your lives via television. This book is Richard Meyers' salute to those fearless sleuths who have been part of regular programming since television aired its first entertainment show.

The vast realm of the television detective spans more than 30 years and includes an honor roll of over three hundred fictional private eyes, secret agents, adventurers, mercenaries, and just plain busybodies all working to solve a crime or correct an injustice. In this illuminating history of the detective genre, Meyers comprehensively examines each of America's television mystery series.

You will learn about the men and women who have assumed the roles of these daring investigators. You will delve into the fascinating history of such outstanding hits as *Dragnet, The Untouchables, Perry Mason, The Avengers, Columbo*, and many others — as well as such unsuccessful, but interesting, shows as *The Rogues,* 1975's *Ellery Queen* and *N.Y.P.D.* You will re-experience many of the humorous moments and unforgettable lines of these dramas. For instance, the lively combination of 130 photographs, many of them rare.

The TV Detectives is a complete documentary of the mystery genre with intriguing, controversial critiques of the shows and characters. It studies the detective drama in an informative manner and examines the serious effect that television, and this more volatile genre within that medium, has had on the nation. Chapters are also replete with humor — interesting details and trivia concerning the series and stars.

That the intrigue of mystery is here to stay is evidenced by the incredible number of detective shows continually produced since the inception of television. For fans of these absorbing dramas and for everyone who loves television, this easy-to-read and enjoyable work is a must. No other book has so thoroughly captured the evolution of and excitement inherent in television drama.